Imaginary Worlds and Real Ethics in Japanese Fiction

Imaginary Worlds and Real Ethics in Japanese Fiction

Case Studies in Novel Reflexivity

Christopher Weinberger

BLOOMSBURY ACADEMIC
NEW YORK • LONDON • OXFORD • NEW DELHI • SYDNEY

BLOOMSBURY ACADEMIC
Bloomsbury Publishing Inc, 1359 Broadway, New York, NY 10018, USA
Bloomsbury Publishing Plc, 50 Bedford Square, London, WC1B 3DP, UK
Bloomsbury Publishing Ireland, 29 Earlsfort Terrace, Dublin 2, D02 AY28, Ireland

BLOOMSBURY, BLOOMSBURY ACADEMIC and the Diana logo are
trademarks of Bloomsbury Publishing Plc

First published in the United States of America 2024
This paperback edition published 2025

Copyright © Christopher Weinberger, 2024

For legal purposes the Acknowledgments on pp. viii–ix constitute an
extension of this copyright page.

Cover design by Eleanor Rose
Cover images (clockwise from top left): 'Leg of the horse', manuscript
by Akutagawa Ryunosuke, 1925 AD, Edo-Tokyo Museum, Sumida, Tokyo, Japan.
Photo 2016 © History and Art Collection / Alamy; Mori Ōgai report © Archive PL / Alamy;
Portrait of Mori Ōgai (1862–1922) © Chronicle of World History / Alamy;
Akutagawa Ryunosuke, (1892–1927), Photo, 1920s © INTERFOTO / Alamy

All rights reserved. No part of this publication may be: i) reproduced or transmitted in any form, electronic or mechanical, including photocopying, recording or by means of any information storage or retrieval system without prior permission in writing from the publishers; or ii) used or reproduced in any way for the training, development or operation of artificial intelligence (AI) technologies, including generative AI technologies. The rights holders expressly reserve this publication from the text and data mining exception as per Article 4(3) of the Digital Single Market Directive (EU) 2019/790.

Bloomsbury Publishing Inc does not have any control over, or responsibility for, any third-party websites referred to or in this book. All internet addresses given in this book were correct at the time of going to press. The author and publisher regret any inconvenience caused if addresses have changed or sites have ceased to exist, but can accept no responsibility for any such changes.

Library of Congress Cataloging-in-Publication Data

Names: Weinberger, Christopher, author.
Title: Imaginary worlds and real ethics in Japanese fiction: case studies
in novel reflexivity / Christopher Weinberger.
Description: New York: Bloomsbury Academic, 2024. |
Includes bibliographical references and index. |
Summary: "Discovers innovative methods for coming to terms with urgent questions about the ethics and value of the novel in the work of some of Japan's most famous and influential modern writers, Mori Ogai and Akutagawa Ryunosuke"– Provided by publisher.
Identifiers: LCCN 2023031382 (print) | LCCN 2023031383 (ebook) |
ISBN 9798765105382 (hardback) | ISBN 9798765105399 (paperback) |
ISBN 9798765105412 (epub) | ISBN 9798765105405 (pdf) | ISBN 9798765105429
Subjects: LCSH: Ethics in literature. | Japanese fiction–Meiji period,
1868-1912–History and criticism. | Japanese fiction–Taishō period,
1912-1926–History and criticism. | LCGFT: Literary criticism.
Classification: LCC PL747.63.E8 W45 2024 (print) | LCC PL747.63.E8
(ebook) | DDC 895.63/09–dc23/eng/20231010
LC record available at https://lccn.loc.gov/2023031382
LC ebook record available at https://lccn.loc.gov/2023031383

ISBN:	HB:	979-8-7651-0538-2
	PB:	979-8-7651-0539-9
	ePDF:	979-8-7651-0540-5
	eBook:	979-8-7651-0541-2

Typeset by Integra Software Services Pvt. Ltd.

For product safety related questions contact productsafety@bloomsbury.com.

To find out more about our authors and books visit www.bloomsbury.com
and sign up for our newsletters.

For Hanako

Contents

Acknowledgments	viii
Note on Translation	x
Introduction	1
1 Critical Contexts: Modern Japanese Theories of the Novel	19
2 A Framed Narrator: Ironic Perspective in *The Dancing Girl*	33
3 Who Is Ōgai Gyoshi?: Authorial Desire and Ethical Self-Reflection in the Aughts	53
4 Triangulating an Ethos: Ethical Criticism, Novel Alterity, and Mori Ōgai's "Stereoscopic Vision"	71
5 Akutagawa's Affective Ethics	93
6 The "Real" Tears of Fictional Readers: Akutagawa's "Green Onions"	113
7 A Novel Theory of Literary Affect	133
8 Haunting Failures: The Transmission of Alterity in Akutagawa's Late Writing	149
9 Imaginary Worlds and Real Ethics: The Case of Murakami Haruki	169
Notes	192
Bibliography	215
Index	225

Acknowledgments

I am deeply grateful to so many who have provided insight, direction, and inspiration for this book. It owes everything to work first undertaken in graduate programs at UC Berkeley. The electricity in the air during discussions of the novel with Dorothy Hale first sparked my interest in ethical criticism. It was thrilling to follow in the wake of her pursuit of novel ethics and to witness her impossibly lucid orchestration of so many complex viewpoints on questions of the art of the novel. There to rescue me from my own excited flailing was Alan Tansman, whose keen eye for buried insight and whose insistence on cutting down to the essentials shaved—unbelievably, I know—more words from this book than have been printed here. In seminars and conversations that joined theory, criticism, biography, and fiction, Alan caught us all up in the brilliant, problematic, and pioneering intellectual projects of modern Japanese writers. Dori and Alan were incredibly supportive, encouraging, kind, patient, and stalwart in their roles as intellectual leaders, mentors, and friends. I cannot ever thank them enough.

Also at Berkeley I was fortunate enough to work closely with Charles Altieri, whose passionate, inspired reinvention of the language of literary analysis still awes me. And it is thanks to Dan O'Neill's thoughtful explorations of emerging ideas about literary art and value in the Meiji and Taishō periods that I discovered so many of the creative theories that inform this book. I count myself lucky as well to have had so many rich conversations about narrative with Ellen Peel, whose keen work on the constructed body and unnatural narration helped shape my own inquiries into the unusual narrative practices of the authors studied here. In more indirect but no less crucial ways, conversations about comparatism, theory, and literary value with Dane Johnson and Shirin Khanmohamadi during the early years of my work on this project—and the support of all of my colleagues at the Department of Humanities and Comparative World Literature throughout the years—have been invaluable both personally and professionally.

I thank those who have been readers and offered feedback on earlier versions of these pages, including many listed above as well as Rebekah Linh Collins, whose sharp sensibilities, encouraging questions, and friendship helped bring what might have been disparate projects into a cohesive whole. I also owe a debt of gratitude to the late Kamei Hideo, with whom I spent so many memorable mornings watching snow fall outside the window of the Otaru Literary Museum as we discussed early Japanese literary theory and he patiently corrected my misunderstandings.

My deepest gratitude goes out to my wife Hanako and our teenager Sebastian. Our conversations over the years about what we care about, how we come to understand one another, how love comes into our lives, and what roles aesthetic experience might play in shaping us are at the core of this work and my own heart. I admire so much their tremendous creativity, the blend of humor and seriousness they bring to intellectual inquiry, their unflinching pursuits of philosophical and historical questions about human values and conduct, and their joyful enthusiasm for sharing experiences of beauty, inventiveness, silliness, and artfulness with others. I also thank them for their patience, support, and occasional literal prodding to finish this book.

Note on Translation

To make this book as accessible as possible to non-Japanese readers, I offer transliterations of Japanese terms in roman text rather than the original characters. Japanese terms that appear in English-language dictionaries are rendered without macrons. When I use Japanese terms in the primary text, they are rendered with macrons in italics. Quoted Japanese text appears with macrons but not in italics. English definitions are provided in parentheses following the first appearance of Japanese terms in cases where their meaning has not already been explained. The family name is written first when Japanese names are given in full. For writers who adopted pen names, I follow convention by referring to them by their pseudonyms rather than by their family names, even when they retain their family names (e.g., Shōyō instead of Tsubouchi). Occasionally, when the syntax of a sentence calls for it, I will use English instead of Japanese in the primary text even when the specific Japanese terms are highly relevant and appear elsewhere in the primary text. In those rare cases, I provide the Japanese term in parentheses.

Introduction

Mori Ōgai's (1868–1922) *The Dancing Girl* (*Maihime*; 1889) opens with its narrator afloat on a homeward-bound ship docked in a foreign port, poised on the brink of writing the memoir we have just begun to read. The position resonates with that of Japanese literati near the end of the nineteenth century, caught up in global crosscurrents of literary and cultural exchange as they stood on the verge of bringing to Japan a new tradition of modern *shōsetsu*, or novels.[1] The most perspicacious pioneers and later masters of the *shōsetsu* reflected on their situation on the periphery of foreign cultural forms and value systems, poised between a venerated Japanese literary history and the uncertain promise of a new cosmopolitan modernity. They approached the foreign realist novel from the vantage of a prose tradition characterized by relatively fluid understandings of narrators as storytellers whose positions vis-à-vis the fictional worlds they created were rarely if ever a definitive concern. No fixed conventions for manufacturing realism had taken root in Japanese prose fiction; these modern writers were therefore in a position to recognize and evaluate the conventions undergirding Russian and European realist novels.[2] Their outsider status, along with the pressure they felt to demonstrate the value of prose fiction to a culture whose literati had disparaged the form for centuries, led these writers to theorize an ethics of the novel form through creative analysis and experimentation.

Most Meiji (1868–1912) writers distinguished the novel from other literary forms on the bases of the pathos generated by its realistic portrayals of human beings and situations. Some also lauded its singular capacity to represent contemporary life and conscious experience through individual points of view in what would come to be considered forms of "interiority."[3] For writers like Tsubouchi Shōyō (1859–1935), Mori Ōgai, and Akutagawa Ryūnosuke (1892–1927), however, it may have been the capacity of the novel to generate a compelling *ethos*—an implied value system constituted by the sensibilities informing a sustained narrative point of view—that most distinguished the genre from other literary forms.

Modern Japanese writers were outsiders to most of the codified value systems that composed the *telos* of foreign novels, such as the promise of domesticity and social assimilation figured by marriage as an endpoint of the bildungsroman form. As such, they became acutely conscious of the ways that novels could, through the language and perspective established by their narration, invoke value systems never made explicit but assumed to be shared by readers. These writers mistrusted the tendency of Western novels to normalize the sensibilities of narrators and to authorize their points of view by virtue of the implicit homology between the progression of novelistic narration toward a validating conclusion and the development of the "character" of the narrator. Other Japanese writers sought to harness this normative rhetorical force by working within essentially realist forms to produce a novel ethos that invoked modern Japanese, rather than foreign, sensibilities. Such efforts gave rise to the *shizenshugi* (naturalist) and later *watakushi-shōsetsu* (I-novel) forms, wherein authors applied contemporaneous realist techniques to representations of Japanese life. However, in this book I will focus on writers who made a reflexive turn, who staged scenes of reading and writing or experimented with language and point of view to call attention to the manipulative potential of novel narration. These writers critiqued and explored the ethical responsibilities entailed by the production of novel ethos even as they pioneered the novel form.

The reflexivity employed by the writers I examine disrupts the transparency with which novel language and narrative perspective establish windows onto fictional worlds. Such disruption often precludes the kinds of consistency and closure often viewed as measures of novel success. A character's tragedy or dénouement loses much of its emotional appeal when cast in a narrative frame that continually reminds readers that the character, and indeed the whole story, is mere fabrication. It may be unsurprising, then, that we find in both contemporaneous and subsequent scholarship frequent charges of desultoriness and dilettantism leveled against such works for their failure to produce compellingly realist atmospheres. Critics suggest that the genre of the novel and its conventions were too new or foreign for modern Japanese writers to comprehend adequately, let alone master. On such views, modern Japanese writers could not slough off the "storytelling" mode of traditional *monogatari*, and so they failed to produce the immersive verisimilar worlds so often taken as the hallmark of the foreign novel.[4] Masao Miyoshi, for example, argues that modern Japanese authors faced difficulties in working out a "plain discursive style" that would draw readers into represented worlds. Consequently, their *shōsetsu* wound up sounding "artificial," full of "affectation," and more like a "translation style" than the fluid prose of Western counterparts.[5]

More contemporary surveys of Japanese history tend to recognize individual accomplishments but are still prone to situate such work within the broadly sketched landscape of a fledgling novel tradition not yet come into its own. In the introduction to a collected volume on modern Japanese literature, Frank Jacob follows seminal Japanese literary scholar Donald Keene in noting that "One might argue that Japan's long isolation … had a negative influence on a possible exchange of ideas with foreign sources and therefore crippled Japan's literary potential due to a lack of intellectual exchange."[6] The implication is that the earliest novelists of Japan did not yet fully grasp the depth and complexity of Western literature sufficiently to produce a "good psychological novel," since "these changes took more time to manifest than industrialization."[7] Against such critical tendencies, I suggest that these apparent failings, at least in the hands of the writers I examine, function purposefully and effectively as critiques and reshapings of novel ethos.

My goal in this book is to examine the ethical reflexivity at work in modern Japanese critical and literary theories and practices of writing prose fiction. The authors studied here have largely been excluded from global conversations about the ethics of the novel. Moreover, conversations about their oeuvres in Japanese scholarship almost universally neglect to impute any positive ethical value to the forms of self-consciousness that characterize so much of their writing. By diving deeply into the work of such authors, this book puts into evidence the usefulness of the concept of an ethics of self-consciousness for reframing our assumptions, and particularly our mimetic biases, regarding how novels engage ethics. It traces and links radical transformations in their practices over time, revealing the vitality and versatility of the concept for dealing with very different kinds of novels (and conceptions of ethics). Furthermore, by presenting in-depth examinations of their work as case studies, this book tries to model a critical methodology that focuses on articulating the self-theorizations at work in reflexive novels.

In this book I take up *shōsetsu* that either explicitly discuss their own theories of novel value, directly reflect on the effects of reading novels by staging scenes of reading and their consequences, or otherwise employ reflexive strategies to call attention to novel rhetoric and its effects on readers. I compare the kinds of self-theorization undertaken by such texts to claims about the *shōsetsu* form in contemporaneous Japanese scholarship to elucidate some of the aims and effects of their narrative choices. Finally, I consider what such practices and theories offer scholarship of Japanese literature, comparative and world literature, and theories of the novel today.

This project has special relevance for the contemporary moment. Approaching *shōsetsu* as models for (rather than mere objects of) ethical criticism can help address a major methodological concern in our efforts to come to terms with the aftereffects of colonialisms and globalization. We face problems of positioning whenever we presume the right to speak about texts outside, or even inside, the borders of what Edward Said has called our critical "affiliations," our situation within national, ideological, and linguistic fields of power.[8] Scholarship today works hard to avoid misreading or appropriating texts by reading them through extrinsic critical lenses, but such efforts come with their own problems and risks.

In her introduction to *"Contact Zones": Rewriting Genre Across the East-West Border*, Elena Spandri recommends that prior to performing critical operations on foreign texts, scholars should work to expand "contact zones," conceptual spaces wherein negotiation and mutual adaptation replace colonial assimilation as modes of engaging different systems of literary and cultural value.[9] However, such zones have proven notoriously hard to establish in practice. Reviewing several decades of efforts to work out approaches to world literature, scholars including David Damrosch and Jing Tsu even find a danger in the project itself. They warn that in trying to establish a framework for talking about other literatures, we risk arrogating the right to shape the terms of global conversation about literature. Any claims we might make about literary value, however well-intended, make implicit assumptions and privilege certain terms or aspects of literary form and function over others.[10] Thomas Claviez makes a similar case: if we compare literature, he opines, we necessarily assume some measure of value as a common denominator, and hence bias our results.[11] However, as Aaron Gerow warns in *Visions of Japanese Modernity*, we face the opposite danger of Orientalizing in the well-intended gesture of refusing to deploy Western reading practices on Japanese texts, as though the alterity and strangeness of these works renders them incomprehensible to foreign standards of interpretation.[12] We also face the possibility of being overwhelmed by alterity; David Palumbo-Liu, in *The Deliverance of Others*, notes that "too much otherness" can confound and "recede into unintelligibility" just as too little otherness can facilitate assimilation and appropriation.[13]

One of the most well-established means of responding to such opposing dangers (presuming too much similarity or difference) has been to frame literary studies within larger sociocultural narratives, so that conclusions may be contextualized or verified through extrinsic (sociological, historical, political) disciplinary findings. This is what scholars like Prasenjit Duara, Harry Harootunian, and Alan Tansman do so well. The invocation of alternative disciplinary methods mitigates some of the subjective bias endemic to cross-cultural literary analysis. I suggest, however, that novel criticism might also address problems of cross-cultural positioning from within the purview of literary studies by focusing on acts of self-reading performed by fiction. Because the modern Japanese writers that I examine produce reflexive, immanent critiques of the novel form, we can trace the terms on which they frame their self-theorizations with substantially less risk of imposing extrinsic values than we face in analyses of more typical realist prose fiction. By attending to the discussions of novel value and the self-reflexive staging of narrative acts articulated within such *shōsetsu*, we can uncover intrinsically developed terms of critique and ethical judgment that we can then apply to that text and put into to dialogue with other texts and theories of literary value.

As I shall argue, most influential theories of novel ethics today, even those suspicious of the motives and ethical consequences of mimetic strategies in novels, continue to take realist fiction as their principal exemplars. The reigning assumption seems to be that novel realism relays the particularity of real-life experience with a special intensity that gives literature a unique role to play in ethics.[14] Modern Japanese writers who turn to reflexivity, however, suggest that we might begin from very different premises to imagine other kinds of ethical work that novels can perform.

Metafictional novels have never been held as paradigmatic for ethical theories in literature or philosophy, in part because they vex the premise that novels can mirror real life and therefore complicate the notion that represented ethics can translate coherently into real-world principles of conduct. Yet metafictional novels often undertake the same essential functions as *scholarship* on literary ethics: they direct attention to the consequences of performing acts of reading or writing in certain ways; they emphasize the way novelistic narration can manipulate reader's judgment; they consider carefully the difference between real and imagined others; they warn us of the potentially self-serving nature of our emotional responses to such others; and they invite us to reflect on the desires and motivations underwriting our habits of reading and responding to fiction. Moreover, the twenty-first century has seen the rise of novels that use metafictional devices for the express purpose of wrestling with ethical questions, in sharp contrast to the image of "narcissistic narration" that scholarship on metafiction, developed in response to postmodern iterations of the genre, has perpetuated. Contemporary authors such as Ian McEwan, J.M. Coetzee, Alejandro Zambra, Zadie Smith, and, as we shall see, Murakami Haruki all employ metafictional rhetoric in response to ethical quandaries we face in the present day. By discovering a lineage of ethically reflexive novel narration in modern Japanese literary history, and by drawing out the kinds of values those writers themselves ascribed to their efforts, we might reframe our understanding of this current phenomenon.

This book takes up precursors to "metafiction" in the Japanese tradition to examine how their reflections on novel ethics can recast discussions in ethical criticism today. In this effort, I build on the work of Japanese scholars such as Kamei Hideo, Dennis Washburn, and John Treat, who have examined ways certain modern Japanese writers engage ethics through formal experimentation, as opposed to mimesis itself. None of these scholars spends much time on novel reflexivity, let alone the relation between reflexive narrative form and ethical concerns. My work mobilizes their scholarship to rewrite common critical narratives of Japanese literary history and to identify for the first time a lineage of modern writers who experiment with reflexive turns for ethical ends.

This project takes important cues from the comparative work of scholars like David Palumbo-Liu and Shameem Black, who each in their own way argue that twenty-first-century novels have begun to "call attention to their own representational dilemmas, inviting readers to question assumptions about identity and imaginative projection that underlie calcified forms of discursive domination."[15] I find, however, that we see this phenomenon over a century earlier, at one of many novel beginnings in the global history of the form. The very different ways that questions about "identity and imaginative projection" take shape in the modern Japanese tradition might productively inform current debates on novel empathy and ethics writ large.

Each chapter in this book examines theories of novel ethics in Japanese *shōsetsu* relevant for contemporary concerns in global scholarship on novel ethics. For example, I draw on Ōgai's "stereoscopic" narration to point out strong connections between what appear in contemporary Anglo-European scholarship as antithetical positions: theories that emphasize the value of empathy and identification, and those interested in the ways that novels can represent or condition readers to experience alterity as unknowable. I also show how Akutagawa Ryūnosuke's explorations of literary affect and narrative perspective resolve certain tensions between affective and cognitive models of literary ethics.

My goal is to argue that aesthetic experimentation in canonical novels by major Japanese authors was partly driven by an understanding of the deep interrelation of ethics and literary form. Attention to the ethical effects of self-consciousness in their work will allow us to discover affinities among writers not often linked and frequently understood as oppositional in sensibility, style, and philosophy. Such a focus will also reveal how subsequent developments in the genre, especially twenty-first-century returns to metafiction and magical realism, may have at their core ethical impulses whose origins within and across various traditions we might productively trace.

But what does it mean for something to have an "ethical impulse"? How, indeed, is one to define "ethics," especially in cross-cultural and transhistorical contexts? I work from the broad and loose (though theoretically sophisticated) sense that Geoffrey Harpham espoused when he glossed the term "ethics" as both a question, "how should one live?," and as a "perplexity" we face in conduct and understanding. Ethics, for Harpham, requires us to examine and compare value structures, ideological systems, and frameworks for apprehending experience—the constructs whereby we understand and orient ourselves in relation to others. I find it particularly helpful to borrow Harpham's contrast of ethics as a generalized inquiry with *morality*, which he suggests addresses the more situated question "What should I do?" Morality, for Harpham, concerns the principles or sets of rules one must follow within any given value system or worldview in order to measure up to its dictates. For the most part the authors in this study refuse to moralize and even decry moralization; however, the question of morality arises in many of their works and the term will occasionally be used to designate the concerns of characters and narrators.

Of course, conceptions of ethics differ widely from discipline to discipline and tradition to tradition. I bring to this project a personal interest in the conceptual and representational systems through which novels represent, promote, and value forms of interpersonal interaction in given social, political, and ideological contexts. I cannot avoid approaching these texts in terms of my own sense of ethics, the field of study of right conduct, as consisting primarily in how we comport ourselves, interact, and engage in representational acts with maximal respect for and minimal violence to the autonomy and rights to self-determination of others. I am therefore drawn to authors who express interest in similar dynamics—particularly questions about how we respond to representations or experiences of differences in points of view and value systems, and whether engagement with literary representation might have a unique role to play therein.

However, I refrain as much as possible from "applying" any particular theory to the works I examine and even from committing to a particular definition of ethics in advance of analysis.[16] Instead, I attempt to trace how these authors themselves imagined the field of ethical inquiry as it could take shape in and through novel representation. Ethics takes on different qualities in the hands of each author, and often appears in different light from work to work. Accordingly, I try to shift my own focus as well as the terms of analysis in each chapter to accommodate their differing perspectives.

In short, I do not mean to "perform" ethical criticism here. That is, I do not try to ascertain certain principles of conduct that may be extrapolated from modern Japanese writing and valued from the vantages of any given ethical tradition or school of thought. No particular theory of literary ethics serves as a lens through which I attempt to discern values informing modern Japanese texts. Rather, I try to identify some of the contributions that these modern writers imagined novels could make to ethics, as they are articulated through practices of self-reflexive narration. I then discuss how their manner of reflecting on those contributions from within *shōsetsu* might prove instructive for contemporary theories of novel ethics.

If I borrow the terminology of particular ethical theories that inform my own views, as when I draw on the work of Judith Butler and Martha Nussbaum to discuss Ōgai's approach to the representation of alterity, it is in hopes that these terms will be transformed or figured into very different conceptual questions that we might ask about novel ethics than those with which I set out. My goal, in other words, is to put contemporary theories of novel ethics into productive and mobile dialogue with the self-theorizations performed by the writers I examine, and to show how these Japanese theorizations of novel ethics may contribute to or refigure discussions of ethics in contemporary Anglo-European scholarship, rather than simply be clarified by them.

To keep the dangers of cross-cultural appropriation and the confusion that can arise when we discuss theories of the novel in contexts wherein it has been defined and regarded on different terms, I would like to call attention to one of my own contestable linguistic choices. When I refer to conventions of novels in a broad sense, when I speak of certain foreign texts to which Japanese writers were responding, or, perhaps most questionably, when I refer to claims that Japanese writers made about the genre writ large or with foreign forms or influence in mind, I use the term "novel." When I refer to assertions made about the genre as it emerged historically and has since been discussed within the Japanese tradition, or when I speak of modern efforts to distinguish Japanese prose fiction from that of other traditions, I leave untranslated the Japanese term *shōsetsu*. I hope to leverage the very awkwardness of my vacillation between these terms, and the feeling of arbitrariness that some of these choices may occasion, to keep in focus the differences and potential dissonances in the comparative genre claims made by these writers and by myself. This, after all, is one of the main points of my endeavor: to imagine how we might follow these writers in creating a "zone of contact" between Japanese and foreign novels and theories of the novel without subordinating either to an extrinsic framework of judgment.

Some form of mediation must be provisionally adopted for the sake of coherence and expedience; some terms must be chosen. The key is to prevent the terms of mediation from becoming invisible grounds of judgment. I attempt, therefore, to adopt the same method of dealing with my own inevitable appropriations as the writers I examine did with theirs. That is, I reflect on the problems of positioning implied by my own critical choices and point of view, even while committing myself to the provisional value of certain analyses or judgments. The crucial question for my project, and more importantly for these authors, is not what lessons about life given novels may teach us but rather by what methods and to what ends do these novels invite readers to come to value or respond to otherness?

Case Studies

By incorporating reflexivity (obvious formal experimentation, staged scenes of reading, direct address of readers, commentary on the fictitious qualities of a story, discussions of the consequences of acts of writing, etc.) to foster awareness of the complicities and responsibilities that acts of narrative representation entail, the Japanese writers examined here developed what I call an "ethics of self-consciousness." They point, with varying degrees of conspicuousness, to the way that their own writing situates narrators and readers in ethically fraught positions analogous (or otherwise related) to those dramatized by the stories they tell. Reflexivity serves for them a means of exposing the transformative (and potentially manipulative) potential of novel narration and thereby mitigating complicity in the dynamic operations of discursive power whose ethical consequences they explore.

This was by no means a phenomenon limited to experimental writers; even some of the most popular and mainstream authors occasionally drew on reflexive techniques to explore the ethics of the narrative positioning that *shōsetsu* could undertake. For example, in popular gothic stylist Izumi Kyōka's *The Holy Man of Mt. Kōya* (*Kōya Hijiri*; 1900), the parallelism between frame tale and embedded story calls attention to the way that both text and readers may become complicit in the dangerous forms of desire and the temptation to distort for one's own ends. Because the *shōsetsu* makes such a tidy architectural illustration of the kinds of ethical positioning some modern Japanese writers were working out through reflexive narrative turns, I will linger a moment on its accomplishment before continuing to provide an overview of the more in-depth case studies this book will provide.

The Holy Man of Mt. Kōya relates a tale told by a well-respected priest regarding his youthful encounter with an apparently supernatural temptress. The priest's story begins for us in the middle of its telling, at a point when his youthful self, on a religious pilgrimage, was trying to situate himself in an unfamiliar landscape through reference to a map he had just unfolded. Only a few lines into this narrative, however, we are interrupted by the priest's audience, the narrator of the frame tale who met the priest on a train earlier that day. The narrator's boredom on the journey and his expression of disappointment with a train-station lunch led to a conversation with the priest. Anticipating a lonely, dissatisfying night by himself, the traveler asked if the priest would stay with him. The priest invited him to an inn that has closed its doors to all but intimately acquainted guests due to a family tragedy—the loss of their daughter. On their way, the pair was assailed by hotel solicitors seeking their business. Finally, they arrived at the warm hearth of the inn. The traveler disliked going to sleep early and so asked the priest to keep him company. The result is the tale we hear, and which resumes once this context has been conveyed.

In the embedded tale, the young priest arrives at a rest stop where he is taunted by a peddler for his hesitancy to drink water that might be contaminated—as a holy man, is he not supposed to be beyond such worldly concerns with life or death? Later, he learns that the peddler has taken a dangerous wrong path and resolves to follow and assist him, in part because abandoning the other man to his fate would not sit right, given their unpleasant interaction. On the way the priest finds evidence of flooding and hears of a tragedy that had befallen the area years earlier. He encounters snakes obstructing his path, each one larger and more monstrous than the last, and confesses to a particular phobia about them. Still later he is passing under a massive tree when leeches begin to rain down on him, nearly killing him. Finally, he arrives, bloodied and exhausted, at a lonely home in the middle of the natural environs.

A beautiful woman then answers the door and invites the priest to stay and bathe in the healing waters of the nearby river, provided he promise not to share any news of goings on in the capital (once again contributing to the fairy-tale like quality of the tale, recalling here the famous supernatural *yuki-onna*'s prohibition against mentioning an encounter with her in the classic folktale "Yuki-onna" [snow woman]).[17] The route to the river is short but treacherous. Once they arrive, the woman strips herself of her kimono and bathes him, removing the garments he had not ever removed even in front of fellow priests and massaging him clean. The scene painted is one of nearly irresistible temptation. Either the water or her body proves strangely healing to the priest, whose blood begins boiling with desire and embarrassment. Interrupting them occasionally are several wild creatures who seem familiar with the woman; she shoos them away by admonishing them not to bother her guest.

Upon their return, they encounter an old man leading a horse away for sale. The horse reacts wildly at the sight of the priest and is only soothed when the woman once again removes her clothing and suggestively presses herself against the creature. The woman then asks if the priest happened to meet anyone on the way up, and his remark about the peddler seems to settle something between the woman and the old man. Later that night, the priest has trouble sleeping as the house is assailed from all sides by creatures, and the woman complains about it.

Occasionally, and especially when the tale becomes lurid, the priest interrupts his speech to address the traveler, brightening the fire or remarking on the absence of the other guest who should have been arriving but did not—a peddler himself. The priest concludes the tale by confessing that the next morning after departing his youthful self he had been on the verge of returning to the woman to take her up on the implicit offer for him to stay there with her. Just then, however, he ran into the old man who told him the following.

It was rumored that the woman had magical gifts of healing. When a tragic flood occurred many years earlier, she was among the only three spared. Now, the old man reveals, she makes her living by luring travelers and transforming their lustful selves into animals that reflect their depraved nature. She then sells or otherwise employs them. The peddler, for example, had become the horse of the previous evening. The old man then vanishes into the distance, and our narrator tells us that the next morning, after telling his own tale, the priest did the same.

As this select summary emphasizes, the telling of tales is as prominent a subject of the *shōsetsu* as the other remarkable events of the priest's journey. Moreover, a striking echo effect between the nested narratives develops over the course of their telling—one partially hidden by the manner of nesting that somewhat obscures chronology. Most obviously, both frame tale and embedded story prove interested in travel, spaces, companionship, desire, restraint, physicality, intimacy, and the power of speech, among other things. Yet it also turns out that the embedded story of the young priest echoes rather too uncannily the experiences of the traveling narrator. Both begin in the middle of journeys with dissatisfying experiences at rest stations; both involve a decision to make a detour for the sake of an encountered other; the narrator fends off parasitic hotel solicitors and the young priest, leeches; both arrive weary at uncommon accommodations that were the sites of past tragedies; in both cases—indeed, almost at the same time in the telling, as the story and narrative frame both arrive at their crucial centers—there are rattling noises at night and mention of a peddler who should be but is not there; there is the sudden flare-up of light in a telling moment in both frame and tale; and, crucially, both narrators meet strangers who tell them tales that reframe their recent experiences on the previous day. One wonders if the priest, who laughed openly at the traveler's disappointment with his lunch and reminded him of this thwarted desire for comfort, is not converting the stuff of their time together into a rather playful admonishment in the tale he tells.

The Holy Man of Mt. Kōya concludes with a cautionary tale. However, occurring as it does within this oddly doubled narrative structure, the caution may have less to do with the morality of restraint and priestly devotion to ideals of conduct than it does with the reception of tales. First, let us consider the story shared by the old man within the embedded tale of the priest. It speaks through the embedded tale to the present traveler and to readers—a point emphasized when the traveler interrupts the priest's tale to blurt out exactly the question that the young priest had voiced and which the older priest was about to relate: "[What was] the woman?"[18] In response, the old man (along with the priest voicing him) presents us with a classical folktale interpretation about her monstrous nature, justifying readers' likely interpretation of the signs encountered along the way and conveyed as much by the telling as the tale. Yet what have we seen from the woman but kindness, grace, and generosity—besides, perhaps, too much of her physical form and her sensuousness? Should we take the old man's tale at face value? Or should we consider it as it comes to us, refracted through a story that has religiously converted experienced reality into fictional autobiography?

When we map out and align the chronologies of frame and embedded tales, we discover something strange: the telling of the priest's tale occurs in the parallel narrative "moment" analogous to the young priest's healing (but also perhaps dangerous) encounter with the woman. The traveler thus finds himself in the position of the young priest, in danger of seduction by a figure who appears graceful and worthy of admiration. Despite their ostensibly contrastive moral positions, the storytelling priest and the woman turn out to occupy structurally similar positions. Both possess resonant "powers" to transform reality. We have already seen internal (doubly embedded) evidence of such transformation: the tale of the old man transfigured what appeared to be the hospitality of the woman into the tempting ministrations of a monster.

The priest's tale, which ultimately proves a story about storytelling, just like the narrator's, holds up for the traveler a mirror of his desires, attachments, frustrations, and expectations that his encounters with others will provide self-satisfaction. Inasmuch, it harbors the potential to foster an ethical self-consciousness on the part of the listener. Yet at the same time it poses a danger, the threat of seduction alluded to by the priest when he suggests brightening the room due to the suggestive nature of the tale and their secluded occupancy of a darkened room. And yet, the *shōsetsu* also seems to suggest that immersive experience of such danger has value; it is, after all, the harrowing experiences of his youthful self that led the priest to become a renowned and respected figure. I am not here interested in resolving any ambiguities about the morality attributed to desires or physical intimacy, though those are topics worthy of extensive exploration even more than what they have received. Rather, what fascinates me about the text is how thoroughly the reflexivity of its concerns with storytelling prove embedded in questions about the ethics of conduct by virtue of the resonance of the nested tales—how the stories reframe and confer meaning on experience by virtue of their manner of telling even more than the content of what they share. The mise-en-abyme quality of the structure of *The Holy Man of Mt. Kōya* leaves us pondering the dangers of our own ensnarement in the seductive powers of the *shōsetsu* itself, powers exerted by its formal orchestration of its narrative layering as much as any seductions exuded by the language and subject matter. Ultimately, in both frame and embedded stories, we find a strange balance struck between acknowledging the value of recognizing and confessing complicity in desire, on the one hand, and a call to pursue immersive entanglement with the lives of others through the reception and retelling of their tales, on the other.

Kyōka is far from the only modern Japanese writer who threads into more mainstream fiction (rather than more experimental prose) an essentially reflexive awareness of the relationship between literary form and ethics. I will not linger on these in depth here, but even in stylistically contrastive work by the consummate realist writer Shiga Naoya, such as his short stories "The Paper Door" (*Shōji*; 1911) or "The Shop Boy's God" (*Kozō no Kamisama*;1920), one finds ironic self-conscious twists that implicate detached narrators and readers in the ethically problematic decisions and attitudes of represented subjects, precisely because of the manner in which the lives of others are turned into the stuff of gratifying stories. In those texts, for example, opening and closing paragraphs subtly remind readers that Shiga's ostensibly detached narrators share the same habits of interpretation and same privileged points of view that lead characters whom they discuss to treat others in misguided ways.[19] The manner of representation, and therefore the perspective of readers who encounter the story through the point of view of the narrator, proves implicated in the kinds of ethical missteps that the stories portray. This kind of framing attention to the ethics at work in the narrative construction of perspective invites readers to reflect on the ethics of reading even while providing what appears to be a straightforwardly realist tale.

An "ethics of self-consciousness" may turn out to inform the writing of many of Japan's most famous modern authors. In this book, however, I focus on some of the most visible ways that reflexivity emerged as a salient feature of the narrative form in more obviously experimental and self-referential *shōsetsu*. This will reveal the clearest ties between formal innovation, ethics, and self-consciousness as they became interwoven in modern Japanese forms of the genre.

Considering reflexivity as an ethical rather than merely aesthetic or rhetorical mode will allow us to revise common critical assumptions about the trajectories of the careers of major writers and the schools of writing with which they have become associated. I have chosen two such writers never considered to have enduring interests in novel ethics and whose work has rarely if ever been theorized as having much of anything in common. Discovering the strong and startling continuities linking their contrastive work precisely on ethical grounds will demonstrate the utility for literary studies, and especially for theories of the development of the *shōsetsu* form, of the concept of an ethics of self-consciousness as well as its surprisingly foundational role in early Japanese novel history.

Retrospective critical historiographies, written with the rise of fascism in the 1930s as the known inevitable end, often accuse modern Japanese fiction of subordinating ethics to aesthetics. Scholars such as Alan Tansman (in *The Aesthetics of Japanese Fascism*) find that much canonical modern Japanese literature sought an aesthetic sublimity whose totalizing force and demands for unity and integration too readily lent their work to cooption by rapidly consolidating nationalist powers.[20] Yet we may find that even the figures most interested in the aesthetics of novels, among whom one must include Mori Ōgai and Akutagawa Ryūnosuke (1892–1927), turn out to have been engaged in ethical projects all along—projects whose abstraction and abstruseness made their writing vulnerable to appropriation and misrepresentation. Indeed, I will argue that certain works subsequently criticized for elitism, self-absorption, and failing to represent anything outside of the *bundan* (literary world) in fact engage ethics substantially by grappling with the power dynamics at work in the regimes of recognition whereby the very notions of subjectivity and self-other relations are composed and affirmed in novel representation and beyond.

The central figures for my project, Ōgai and Akutagawa, are two of the most prominent modern Japanese authors. Both had tremendous impact on literary history: one pioneered and the other masterfully restyled the novel form in Japan. In scholarship, each has come to stand for a distinct movement and epoch in the early history of the *shōsetsu*. Ōgai drew on Western sources to usher in an age of romantic and realist *shōsetsu* before ultimately turning to historical fiction; Akutagawa turned to classical Japanese literary sources that he reframed in pastiches of psychological realism and sardonic lyricism. Criticism has generally taken them as sharply at odds if not diametrically opposed in their visions of the goals, form, and function of the novel. Indeed, one of the only things that a century of scholarship has consistently asserted as a point of commonality between them has been a mutual failure to acknowledge the ethical responsibilities of literature. Both authors face charges of aestheticism, detachment from social and political issues, essentialism, and elitism. For these very reasons they make ideal test cases for the utility of the concept of an "ethics of self-consciousness" in (a) helping us to recognize the formal innovations of key modern Japanese writers, (b) recovering and articulating innovative contributions that modern *shōsetsu* might make to theories of novel ethics, and (c) highlighting formal connections between writers that critical orthodoxy has overlooked. This case-study approach underscores how deeply an ethics of self-consciousness informs the modern Japanese novel. If it proves fundamental not just to one or two texts but rather to lifelong projects by major authors not principally recognized for their contributions to ethics, then we have strong reasons to trace its workings in *shōsetsu* by other modern authors (such as Natsume Sōseki or Yokomitsu Riichi) whose reflexivity and ethics have been celebrated but not recognized as related phenomena.

Over the course of their individual careers, and as a general historical trend, the works of Ōgai and Akutagawa do not simply evince disillusionment with fiction or become less coherent, as many have concluded. They do, however, become more deliberately self-referential, increasingly calling attention to problems with their own formal structures and positioning of readers. Through experimentation with reflexive narration, I argue, both writers endeavored to create multivalent narrative perspectives that distance readers from the internalized social and ideological standards whose ethics the modern novel, in their views, could effectively critique. The apparent shifts away from pure fiction (to historical and quasi-autobiographical fiction, respectively) at the end of their careers do not merely signify crises of faith in literary representation. Rather, these transformations are consistent extensions and even culminations of career-long explorations of novel ethics and literary self-consciousness.

To provide requisite literary and critical context for this argument, my first chapter begins with an overview of modern Japanese theories of novel value. Thinkers like Tsubouchi Shōyō (1859–1935), Futabatei Shimei (1864–1909), and Mori Ōgai himself famously argued that the novel, interpolated as *shōsetsu*, should be valued for its aesthetics and not its moral qualities. However, I show that their visions of novel aesthetics prove underwritten by what are ultimately ethical values attached to forms of self-consciousness that they theorize the novel to generate. This chapter concludes with brief outlines of the roles that such ethical self-consciousness plays in the prose fiction of Ōgai and Akutagawa over the course of their careers, providing a more conceptual and theoretical overview of what the ensuing chapters will examine in detail through analysis of their literary work.

In the second chapter, I trace in Ōgai's early and middle critical and creative work an ethics of self-consciousness that he later articulates as a "stereoscopic" vision of the novel. This chapter demonstrates how Ōgai's writing systematically calls attention to dissonances between the detached ethos of his narration and the involving pathos of his sentimental plots. It concludes with analysis of his *shōsetsu The Dancing Girl*, a novella-length work that tells the story of an individual trying to work out his values vis-à-vis personal and political commitments. Kamei Hideo credits this *shōsetsu* with marking the emergence of "the modern subject" in Japan—that is, the individual figured as a consistent, interior, and self-aware "point of view" whose psychological struggles to define himself [sic] against a bewildering backdrop of cosmopolitanism, social and political change, and competing ideological forces constitute the narrative of his developing identity.[21] Yet the text has met with considerable criticism on ethical grounds. My research offers some correctives to this trend in scholarship by arguing that Ōgai explores but also critiques from within the power of novel narration to shape ethical judgment.

The third chapter begins with a brief examination of Ōgai's essay "Who Is Ōgai Gyoshi" (*Ōgai Gyoshi to wa dare zo*; 1900). Both its methodology and its argument—that writers must engage in continual acts of self-overcoming—signal the shift toward more overt self-consciousness that is to come in the author's subsequent prose fiction. The rest of this chapter takes up the narrative structure of the *shōsetsu Vita Sexualis* (1909), a work that frames self-conscious narration by one Ōgai-like narrator with that of another. Whereas *The Dancing Girl* engages in self-critique through subtle discrepancies between authorial and narrative point of view, this text dramatically foregrounds literally doubled authorial voices in a story about solipsism and narcissism, marking a new milestone in the development of a "stereoscopic" method of novel narration.

The fourth chapter brings my study of Ōgai to conclusion by focusing on his last work of "pure" fiction, *The Wild Goose* (*Gan*; 1911). The stereoscopic vision at work here (explicitly named such by the narrator) exposes the way that desire and a will to power condition even the most ostensibly objective moments of narrative description both within the story told and as part of the form of novel narration. This approach, I argue, can help us synthesize the highly contrastive theories of novel value by Russian formalist Mikhail Bakhtin (1895–1975) and French philosopher and literary theorist René Girard (1923–2015) at the same that it pioneers new methods of rendering the relationship between novel perspective and ethics.

With the fifth chapter I turn to the work of Akutagawa Ryūnosuke. I examine his early work to discover the very different ways that he, like Ōgai, pits ethos against pathos in stories that involve ethical crises. Unlike Ōgai, however, Akutagawa ascribes ethical value to the felt experience of the aesthetics of the novel form rather than to any edifying intentions of the author or conscious realization imparted to readers. His early *shōsetsu* "Rashōmon" (1915) shuttles readers between states of immersion and reflection that leave them with an unresolvable tension between affective experience and understanding, or what they have come to care about and what they believe about the values they have been asked to adopt.

In the sixth chapter I trace the ethical impulses behind the strong reflexive turns of Akutagawa's later writing. Through openly metafictional texts like the 1919 "Green Onions" (*Negi*), he undoes the premise that novel ethics takes hold through the verisimilar representation of real-life situations. This brief but complex work suggests that novels may harbor an awesome power to shape reality insofar as they condition both the cognitive and the affective modes of receptivity through which we imagine our relationships and really engage others.

The power of ethical self-creation this insight provides, insofar as it enables authors to reform the very bases of human relationships, comes at substantial cost, however. The seventh and eighth chapters explore this cost, beginning with a discussion of the history of Akutagawa criticism and some of the reasons that he has been cast as an aesthete whose breakdown in mental health, combined with supposed ethical failings in his writing, led to a final literary downfall. The eighth chapter then focuses on his final *shōsetsu*, *A Fool's Life* (*Aru ahō no isshō*; 1927) and *Cogwheels* (*Haguruma*; 1927), to explore how perception of the essentially fictional qualities of real-life identities and relationships leads protagonists and narrators to despair. That Akutagawa did not succeed in securing a grounded social or ethical identity through his writing should not prevent us from appreciating the value of his insight into the role of self-consciousness and affective experience in shaping novel ethics.

This book concludes with a turn to the present wherein I examine work by the globally popular author Murakami Haruki to exemplify a new iteration of reflexive ethics in the contemporary Japanese novel. The ninth and final chapter not only connects Murakami to his modern Japanese precursors but also serves as example of the explanatory power that ethics of self-consciousness offers for contemporary turns to metafiction and theories of novel ethics more generally. Following Akutagawa, but through a quite different method, Murakami makes a reflexive turn that calls into question the distinction between the real and the fictional that so often serves as a basis for ethical criticism. In the end, I argue, Murakami asks readers to consider the extent to which our involvement in fictional worlds may enmesh us in responsibilities that must be undertaken and regarded for their immanent effects and values, despite an apparent disconnect from reality and outright refusal of any clear-cut, take-home ethical imperative.

1

Critical Contexts: Modern Japanese Theories of the Novel

Critical Contrasts: Ōgai and Akutagawa

No scholar has ever claimed that Akutagawa Ryūnosuke (1892–1927) took up the mantle of Mori Ōgai's (1868–1922) literary ethics, for good reason. Few think of either writer as deeply concerned with the ethics of literature—indeed, both took explicit stances against criticism that held novels up to particular moral standards. Moreover, their temperaments, styles, typical themes, and publicized theories of the novel appear so paradigmatically contrastive that they have been taken as representative of distinct periods and movements within Japanese literary modernity. Akutagawa in fact publicly distinguished himself from his predecessor with respectful but severe judgments of the lack of *shiteki seishin* (poetic spirit) and literariness in the elder writer's work.[1]

Ōgai promoted a rational, scientific approach to aesthetics and literature. He wrote in precisely and elegantly constructed, often formal and detached prose. If he dealt with ethics he seemed to do so principally through his choice of subject matter, presenting characters dealing (often poorly) with questions of obligation, nation, or polity. He has been read as more or less transparently engaging in a project of national identity formation that had less to do with interpersonal ethics and more to do with public roles and responsibilities. Akutagawa, on the other hand, explored affective states of hope and despair in lonely and often unlovely individuals through prose at turns passionate, ironic, lyrical, wry, entrancing, jeering, and unsettling. He both mocked and called for sympathy on behalf of psychologically flawed protagonists who experienced menacing sensations of alterity—an unknown and perhaps unknowable presence, or *nani mono ka* (something) beyond the self that frayed their nerves. He eschewed the kinds of intellectual understandings that Ōgai thought effective *shōsetsu* could occasion and actively distrusted the notion of politically defined national identity.[2]

Despite such substantive differences in the visions, styles, subjects, and effects of their writing, as well as in the personalities, worldviews, and social positions of the authors, the trajectories of their careers as novelists share deep but little-noticed affinities. Ōgai and Akutagawa both experimented continuously with unusual narrative perspectives in increasingly jarring ways to confront readers directly with problematic relationships between novel pathos, the feelings evoked on behalf of represented beings or situations, and ethos, the values and sensibilities reflected in and cultivated by narrative perspective or the character of the narrator. Each employed self-mocking parody and produced, through self-reference and experimental stylization, a metaliterary self-consciousness with respect to the capacity of literature to shape identities and values. Each proclaimed himself primarily interested in aesthetics and denounced novel ethics early in his career, only to soften that stance later. Each author made his identity the overt topic of discussion in both fiction and non-fiction. That is, each created multiple autobiographical personas and had those personas discuss their ethical failures as both human beings and writers. Throughout their careers, each author returned consistently to such postures of reflexive self-representation, revising both the qualities they ascribed to their authorial personas and the manners of writing whereby they created them (one major argument of this book is that these two evolving phenomena—the ethical qualities ascribed to their authorial personas and the forms of writing that composed them—prove inextricably related). Each writer gradually changed his prose style over time only to make a sudden and dramatic break from previous methods and genres of writing late in his career. Furthermore, each has been cast in subsequent scholarship as having become disillusioned with modern literary approaches to the relationship between life and art. Indeed, this still stands as the predominant explanation for the major "breaks" in both of their careers: they are said to have lost faith in the novel and therefore to have "abandoned" prose fiction in their final writings. Ōgai eventually turned to historical fiction, and Akutagawa to fragmented, quasi-autobiographical works that played upon the conventions of the *I-novel*.[3]

Ōgai's "abandonment" of fiction has been understood as the result of a lifelong pursuit of truth and objectivity in writing. Dennis Washburn suggests that the author could not rid himself of an essentially Confucian sense that fiction amounted to no more than "lies."[4] By contrast, Akutagawa's turn to quasi-autobiographical writing has been understood as the end of a desperate search for salvation in art. Makoto Ueda sums up critical consensus by explaining the move as precipitated by a breakdown in mental health and the realization that artistic representation could not confer coherence on the harsh absurdities of daily life.[5] These different accounts share one core similarity: both assume that transformations in writing style and genres of choice stem from failures to ground the representations of their *shōsetsu* sufficiently in social reality.

Contrary to scholarly orthodoxy, I argue that ethical concerns with novel representation impelled dramatic experimentation and changes in their writing styles. Each author developed his own version of what we might now consider a kind of social formalism—an understanding that the novel exerts ethical force not only through its themes and dramatizations but also, and perhaps principally, through the sensibilities embodied and transmitted by narrative perspective, language, and orchestration of the stories told.[6] Over the course of their individual careers, Ōgai and Akutagawa did not simply become disillusioned with novel fiction or less capable of writing effectively. Rather, each experimented more boldly with metaliterary devices to create dissonances between novel pathos and ethos, discomfiting readers and thereby requiring reflection not on the ethics of some fictional version of real life but on the act of reading fiction. This pattern only becomes visible, however, once we recognize the underlying connection between reflexivity and ethics in early Meiji theorization of novel value.

The apparent shifts away from pure fiction at the end of these writers' careers prove to be consistent extensions and culminations of generational explorations of what I call an "ethics of self-consciousness" that develops, albeit subtly, in some of the most effective and influential early Japanese theories of the novel. By this term, whose nuances we shall soon explore in more depth, I mean to describe a reflexive turn through which writers attempted to reveal the ethical implications of the very literary conventions they employed. For Ōgai, an ethical end of the novel was to produce in readers states of contemplative reflection on the ethical force exerted by literary and social or national conventions and demands. Akutagawa emphasized instead the ethically transformative potential of the intense affect that could be produced by literary aesthetics. Despite their very different visions of the ways that novels could occasion ethical experience, however, both sought to produce their desired effects through self-conscious turns that laid bare the artifice of novel representation.

This chapter aims to provide critical context for the workings of ethical self-consciousness in their *shōsetsu*. I focus for the sake of expediency on two key aspects of this context: the way that ethical concerns turn out to underwrite some of the most famous and influential Meiji (1868–1912) efforts to define the value of the novel on aesthetic terms, and the way that reflexivity (instances of self-reference) and self-consciousness (states of self-reflection enacted, represented, or provoked by reflexive devices) were invoked to explain how ethical effects might take hold in literature. It turns out that novels were theorized on terms very similar to those used to defend the value of literary criticism. Both were thought to provide illuminating perspectives on the complex objects (social reality and novels, respectively) that they examined through oscillation between immersive exploration and detached, sagacious reflection. I conclude by noting how Ōgai and Akutagawa push off from early Meiji theorization regarding the critical and ethical functions of novels to experiment with narrative ethics in the *shōsetsu* form. Against such background we will discover the effects and implications of the self-critical reflexivity that informs and transforms their writing over the course of their careers.

Ethics, Aesthetics, and Self-Consciousness in Mid-Meiji Theories of the Novel

When the 26-year-old doctor and dabbler in literary arts Mori Ōgai returned to Japan in September of 1888, after roughly four years of medical research in Germany, he came back to a literary scene substantially transformed from the one he had left. He had travelled as part of a broad program of *fukoku kyōhei* (national strengthening) and *bunmei kaika* (enlightenment) through the exploration of foreign cultures, technologies, and ideas ushered in by the opening of Japan's borders in the Meiji Restoration in 1868. He came back eager to bring to Japan the analytic rigor and potential for cultural critique and improvement that he discovered in the fields of medicine, philosophy, and literature. And he found an intellectual and literary climate ripe with potential for transformation.

During Ōgai's absence, articles on how Japanese writers should respond to the sudden influx of European literature began to proliferate in numerous new journals such as the *Review Society* (*Hanseikai zasshi*) (first published in 1887 and then renamed *Central Review* [*Chūōkōron*] in 1899, after which it became one of Japan's most popular publications) and *Japanese Women's Education Journal* (*Nihon no jogaku zasshi*) (published 1887–9). The state of literature had become a topic of considerable public debate among intellectuals, many of whom were borrowing new philosophical and critical vocabularies from

European traditions that Ōgai had just studied intensively. Even the form and grammar of the very language of literary writing had changed drastically, with more and more literary texts appearing not in *kobun* (classical Japanese) or *kanbun* (the Japanese way of writing in Chinese), but rather in combined forms of Japanese more closely approximating everyday speech. The transformations in literary language were part of a larger movement that had begun before Ōgai's departure and would come to be known as the *genbun'itchi* movement, a broad term for the coalescence of several political, ideological, intellectual, and social movements aimed in large part at bringing together written and spoken Japanese.[7] This movement had picked up considerable momentum during Ōgai's years abroad.

An almost equally dramatic change occurred in the status of prose fiction itself. As Japanese literary scholar Yanagida Izumi points out in his seminal 1965 study *Ideas of Literature in Early Meij* (*Meiji shoki no bungaku shisō*), literary prose had reached a low ebb, especially in critical estimation, by the start of the Meiji period (1868–1912). Yanagida attributes this state to both an absence of outstanding writers at the time and the fact that the court, clergy, and educated samurai had, in the previous century, come to view prose fiction as suitable only for entertainment. They contrasted vulgar and common prose with the refinement of *kanshi* (Chinese poetry) and the aesthetic beauty of *Nō* drama, which required far more technical learning and virtuosity.[8] Yet as modern Japanese writers and thinkers began to process the weighty tradition of Western literature made available by the opening of Japan's borders with the Meiji Restoration, they began to question entrenched views on the value and seriousness of prose fiction.

Two revolutionary *shōsetsu* published between Ōgai's departure and his return accelerated this critical transformation: Tsubouchi Shōyō's *The Temperament of Today's Students* (*Tōsei shosei katagi*; 1885) and his friend Futabatei Shimei's (1864–1909) *Floating Clouds* (*Ukigumo*; 1887–9). The latter achieved wide popularity and incited many critical debates for its relatively "modernized" version of *genbun'itchi* language and its experimental narrative perspective. As Kamei Hideo observes in his book *Transformations of Sensibility* (*Kansei no henkaku*; 1983), the narration of Futabatei's serialized *shōsetsu* undergoes a dramatic shift in point-of-view.[9] It begins with a narrator speaking as a "storyteller" akin to those found in preexisting Japanese prose forms, especially *yomihon* (entertaining "reading books" of fiction that drew heavily on Chinese and classical Japanese precedents) or *kokkeibon* (books of humor), wherein authorial comments and judgments freely color the story told. Gradually, however, the narrative perspective shifts into that of what Kamei calls a "non-person narrator," an invisible subjective presence that focalizes around the point of view of the protagonist. This produces something like the free indirect style of narrative in vogue in Europe at the time, but one whose point of view remains more firmly embedded in the diegetic world of the text. For Kamei, the true innovation of Futabatei's work lies in the formal transformation whereby the character of the narrator becomes absorbed by the narrated world itself, adopting its values as well as its language in the process, so that it becomes a kind of invisible resident. The novel, in Kamei's view, tells the story of the *narrative transformation* in perspective that it embodies. This idea of the early Japanese *shōsetsu* as producing recursive awareness of its own formal production of point of view is not just Kamei's retrospective interpretation; some of the most influential Meiji theories of the *shōsetsu* imputed to the novel genre a formal reflexivity as the chief ground of its literary value.

Shōyō's *The Temperament of Today's Students*, and other late-nineteenth-century narrative experiments in "Westernizing" prose fiction, owed much to the theory of the novel put forth in the author's groundbreaking 1885 treatise *The Treatise of the Novel* (*Shōsetsu shinzui*). In that essay, Shōyō deplores the current state of Japanese prose fiction and challenges Japanese literati to surpass their European counterparts by writing according to foreign artistic standards. He defines several genres of prose fiction and interpolates rules and methods for writing artistic novels that he hopes will take hold in Japan. Throughout all parts of the essay, however, Shōyō focuses on advancing the argument that the novel should be treated as a work of art rather than a venue for entertainment or moral instruction. As such, he concludes, it should be judged by purely aesthetic standards, which he endeavors to elucidate.

"The Essence of the Novel" famously heralded substantial transformations in Japanese thought about the novel as a genre. It also created a niche for writing about the form and function of prose fiction, and so marks a beginning in the history of modern Japanese literary criticism as well. Late Edo period (1603–1867) and early Meiji literary criticism of prose fiction tended to work in evaluative or prescriptive registers, often leveling impressionistic judgments about the nature and quality of texts when not measuring them against given religious or cultural worldviews. As Japanese literary scholar Tanizawa Eiichi contends in his 1964 study on *The Concept of Modern Japanese Literary History* (*Kindai Nihon bungakushi no kōsō*), criticism at the time continued to condemn or praise prose fiction based on the degree to which its plots accorded with prevailing moral sensibilities first, and aesthetic sensibilities second.[10]

The moral sensibilities which served as the grounds of praise or critique through the early Meiji period were embodied by the idea of *kanzenchōaku*, the principle that good ought to be rewarded and evil punished. Although, as Tanizawa notes, most Meiji writers no longer believed in the moral standards of *kanzenchōaku*, it subsisted as a principle in criticism because no better system for valuing prose had developed.[11] In "The Essence of the Novel" Shōyō explicitly positions himself against the lingering influence of this value system. He offers his own aesthetic theory to replace its moralizing one, and thereby inaugurates a disciplinary tradition of critical writing aimed at theorizing the value of literature principally on aesthetic grounds.

The acrobatics of Shōyō's stance against moral valuations of the novel in this essay reveal the complex and, in the end, mutually dependent relationship of ethical and aesthetic principles in his theory of the genre. Shōyō contends that in traditional Japanese "didactic" fiction, characters and story serve only as means to a moral end, and therefore fail to achieve the vividness and lifelike quality of their counterparts in aesthetically accomplished European literature. The "true artistic novel," he opines, should present as accurately and faithfully as possible the author's experience of the real world (as refined by his imagination):

> The essence at the heart of the novel is *ninjō* (human feelings; also "empathy") situated in the *seitai* (social world). A novel must skillfully spin the thread of an original idea into a tapestry of human feelings, revealing their obscure, mysterious origins and their hidden connections (*inga*; also "fate" and "causal relations") to the world, through beautiful evocations that draw out what might otherwise remain undiscovered.[12]

The resonance of novel representation with the reader's experience of human connections in the world serves for Shōyō as an index of its aesthetic accomplishment. By suggesting that the novel should be judged by its mimetic capacity rather than its illustration of prescribed moral principles, Shōyō shifts the focus of Japanese prose criticism from the predominantly religious domain of morality to more abstract and philosophical terms of "truth" and "reality," the definition and apprehension of which become central to literary discussion in the decades that follow. However, for all of his insistence to the contrary, Shōyō's theory of the novel proves as firmly rooted in ethics, if not morality, as the principle of *kanzenchōaku* he critiques.

To explain this claim I would like first to clarify a distinction I am drawing between ethics and morals. Geoffrey Harpham defines *ethics* as the field of inquiry concerned with the question "how should one live," and within which different value structures, ideological systems, and frameworks for apprehending experience may be considered comparatively. He suggests that we distinguish ethics from *morality* by conceiving the latter as the particular set of rules one must follow within any given value system or worldview. With this distinction in mind, I argue Shōyō makes a compelling case for approaching the novel on ethical rather than moral terms, even though criticism, failing to distinguish between ethics and morality, has generally viewed him as privileging aesthetics over ethics.

When it comes to defending the "benefits" of the artistic novel, Shōyō argues that it "stimulates finer feelings" and "ennobles character" (*hitogokoro wo kandō shite, an ni kikaku wo kōshō ni nashi, kyōka wo hiho suru*), modeling real human behavior in a way that the "discerning reader," who "usually learns from someone else's example" can grasp.[13] He claims that the novel makes its readers better people, more sensitive to the problems that arise in the world they experience. Novels prepare readers to understand others better by grasping the complex ways that social contexts shape sensibilities and judgments. Unlike didactic fiction, novels for Shōyō tell morally ambiguous stories. Yet this makes them all the more ethically valuable for Shōyō, because they mirror the kinds of moral perplexity that one faces in the real world and thereby allow readers to become more sensitive and practiced at navigating it. The aesthetic values that Shōyō advances, especially his emphasis on discernment and refinement in the mimetic representation of social experience, harbors an essentially ethical vision of the novel. *Shōsetsu* simulate the complexity of real social environments (as opposed to the often-reductive simplicity of morality tales lauded under the principle of *kanzenchōaku*) ultimately for the sake of ennobling the character of readers.[14] Thus, even in his attempt to make aesthetics rather than morality the proper sphere of critical discussion, he grounds his arguments for aesthetic values in ethical concerns about the conduct of social relations.

Shōyō remains fundamentally committed to the ethical value of the novel. He does of course break significantly from the tradition of applying the principle of *kanzenchōaku* by refusing to situate the responsibility for novel ethics in the intentions of the author or in the stories told in prose fiction. According to Shōyō, the author need not and indeed should not make any kind of readily apparent moral statement through his story. The ethics of Shōyō's artistic novel emerges, rather, from the interpretive and affective activity solicited by the accomplishment of a prismatic realism, rather than through any effort to "teach" a moral lesson. When she reads a truly "artistic" novel, the perspicacious reader gains insight into the complexity of real human relations that the author has helped make visible. The reader can therefore make better decisions based on her "finer feelings" and "cultivated sensibilities."

In other words, Shōyō argues that a morally ambiguous story takes on real ethical value for discerning readers who can untangle its complex cues because it mirrors the kinds of difficult dilemmas they face in the real world.[15] Here Shōyō does not do away with ethics as a critical standard but rather relocates ethical effects from the content of the story to the experience of its artistic representation. A moral need no longer manifest itself in the dramatized events of the story, plainly displayed at the center of the tale. Novel value need not depend on the edifying intentions of the author. Rather, ethical effects take hold through aestheticized experience of social reality and, as we shall presently see, through second-order reflection on the value of that experience by readers.

According to Shōyō, the novel achieves its key effects by bringing about introspective reflection on one's positioning within a larger social framework. "The novel reveals what is hidden, brings into clarity the indistinct, and encloses immeasurable human feelings within the covers of a book, thereby naturally stimulating to introspection the reader that encounters them" (*dokusha wo shite shizen ni hansei seshimuru mono nari*).[16] Crucially, the artistic novel ennobles readers by moving them into states of self-consciousness, *introspective reflection* on the values of the emotions solicited by reading, and not merely through vicarious participation in unfolding stories.

There remains in this vision an important but unarticulated role for the critic to play. On Shōyō's view, artistic novels lead readers to reflect upon their own experiences and values. It seems to require the critic, however, to explain for discerning readers the ethical and social value of reflection on their experience of novel representations. That is, good novels transmit with edifying clarity the ambivalences and uncertainties of real-life ethical positioning, and good criticism brings into clearer view the social value of the reflective postures produced by reading. Shōyō implies that the critic not only articulates but in some sense catalyzes the ethical effects set into motion by novel experience by suggesting the proper attitudes and understanding required to align novel experience with extra-textual value systems, and so to convert aesthetic experience into ethics.

Shōyō's visions of both the *shōsetsu* and Japanese criticism ascribe ethical value to the forms of self-conscious reflection occasioned by aesthetic experience. In fact, the two genres for him both undertake strikingly homologous and even overlapping functions. Shōyō's realist novel engages readers in ethical (self-)reflection on social reality. Criticism, in parallel fashion, engages its readers in reflection on the novel representation and measures it against external value systems. Criticism for Shōyō must therefore not only reveal the ethical implications of novel representation but also elucidate the standards of value and the processes of interpretation or response that novel revelations make available.

In sum, the successful artistic novel engages readers in a self-conscious and ethically productive introspection that has to do with the feelings and judgments they bring to real or imagined interpersonal encounters. Criticism, on the other hand, works through a further self-conscious turn to reflect on the value of the novel's invitations to make certain judgments or feel certain emotions. Its goal in doing so is to apprehend the literary, ideological, social, and political frameworks through which novels foster ethically charged sensibilities and reflect on the novel's responsibilities and effectiveness in engaging them.

In the process of putting forward his vision of the novel, then, Shōyō ascribes a more-than-analogous function to literary criticism. Both creative and critical writers must reflect and reveal aspects of the (real and fictional) worlds they explore. Both "define what is indistinct" about our experience of those worlds, and both imbue with significance the worlds they uncover for the benefit of their readers. Even the tone and perspective that Shōyō himself adopts in "The Essence of the Novel," which postwar critic Yoshida Seiichi characterizes as "an effort to make critical argument a more objective enterprise,"[17] resonates with what Shōyō describes in that text as the appropriate stance of the *novelist*:

> If a novelist wants to explore the depths of human nature and paint society as it is, then he must write as if describing a chess game he is watching other people play. Should he, as an onlooker, offer even the smallest piece of advice, the game becomes his instead of the players'! It is only when he resists the temptations to change those things he thinks he could improve on and confines himself to the facts that his work can be called a novel.[18]

The success of both the novelist and the critic for Shōyō turns out to depend on their adopting the same perspectival mode. Each must step back from an embedded, subjective point of view to describe his object from a more detached vantage, one that allows him to observe and render perceptible the dynamics of engagement in which the other "players" participate. The implication here is that the straightforward presentation of subjective opinion would destroy the detached purchase needed for the artistic effects of a successful novel. By the same token, the critic must likewise appeal to objective, rational standards rather than personal experience, taste, or expertise, the profession of which would destroy his objective neutrality and "make the game his own." In short, both kinds of writers must recognize and divest from their own potential complicities in the aesthetically and ethically fraught dynamics that they seek to represent, so as to reflect on them from a vantage that can better frame their implications for readers. The ethically motivated "stepping-back" valued here becomes a central dynamic of the ethics of self-consciousness adopted by later Meiji writers.

Although the particulars of Shōyō's argument about novel value would come under much scrutiny and incite numerous debates in subsequent years, his recasting of the relation of novels and criticism exerted a lasting influence on literary and scholarly writing. The implicit analogy he sets up linking the functions of these genres becomes an explicit theory in subsequent attempts to define both genres. Indeed, his justification for the *novel*—that it refines and ennobles the reader, and that in turn an "improved" novel would better the nation as a whole by proving that Japan was not culturally inferior to the West— also underpins arguments for the value of his own and others' *criticism*. Shōyō himself writes:

> If the novel really possesses such possibilities as these, then, would it not be seriously remiss of us not to overhaul and improve our crude Japanese novels, to make them flawless, better than those in the West, to produce a great art form fit to be called the flower of our nation? To do it, we must work out a plan for writing the perfect novel by first understanding the reasons for past successes and failures .... Without a campaign of this nature, the Oriental novel will probably always remain at the level of the old romance, with no chance to develop.[19]

He envisions critical work as the "plans" for a "campaign" to produce a Japanese art form superior to those of the West. If the novel has the power to improve the individual reader, then it seems the critic has the power to organize and direct this power for the good of the nation. Novelists may be commanders in this campaign, but critics are the generals.

Nationalist arguments for the value of the genre of literary criticism such as found here turn up again and again in mid-Meiji writing. The year before the first publication of "The Essence of the Novel," an editorial published in the newspaper *Meiji Nippō* declared that "We believe there is a necessity for critical arguments about literature," arguing that such critical writing promoted cultural sophistication, as evidenced in the superiority of European literature.[20] Several years later Hokubō Sanji, a contributor to one of the earliest volumes of Mori Ōgai's journal, *The Weir* (*Shigarami-zoshi*), argued in "The Responsibility of the Novelist" (*Shōsetsuka no sekinin*; 1889) that the novelist must "observe life" and "pierce through to the truth of its myriad states" in order to "reveal to society its real purpose," "reform society," and "teach it what it should aim at in terms of progress."[21] For him, the novelist really functions as a *hyōronka* (critic) of society insofar as the main value of the novel lies in its capacity for social critique. Hokubō effectively adopts Shōyō's argument for novel complexity, but then conscripts the entire field of ethical inquiry back into the service of morality under the auspices of nationalism, reducing the novel to precisely the type of guide for living according to specific moral precepts against which Shōyō had argued.

In the midst of his promotion of literature as a catalyst for the "progress" of Japanese society, Hokubō directly likens the novelist to the critic, saying that the novelist's real responsibility amounts to "criticism (*hihyō*) of society." Moreover, Hokubō's own critical aims in this piece clearly parallel the goals he assigns to the novel ("discovering truth," "revealing purpose," and "setting standards that will guide its progress").[22] According to Hokubō, critics achieve these goals by making observations about novels, and novels achieve them by making observations about life.

This strong parallelism in mid-Meiji thought about the reflective functions of criticism and those of the novel also undergirds Nishinodō Koji's 1889 essay "On Criticism" (*Hihyōron*), published in *The Friend of the People* (*Kokumin no tomo*). The article represents the earliest instance of criticism wholly devoted to discussing the value and nature of the genre of criticism itself—a meta-critical enterprise that Ōgai would soon master and Kobayashi Hideo (1902–83) would later push to dizzying heights. Nishinodō begins by arguing that creative and critical writing, from opposite perspectives, engage in a dialectic whereby each impels the other to achieve greater insight about the guidance novel representation provides for real life. In the course of his argument, however, he frames the supposedly antithetical terms in much the same way: both criticism and the novel need to be based on careful and objective observation of their respective objects, and both aim at bringing to light hidden truths and thereby improving society. The key difference, in his opinion, is that the critic aims at bringing to light the logic behind what the novelist instinctively grasps and reproduces without explicitly clarifying. The objects of their inquiries differ slightly, but once again the parallel in their activity is pronounced even in the grammar of Nishinodō's formula: "The novelist interprets the natural world, and the critic interprets the novelist."[23]

Hokubō argues in "The Responsibility of the Novelist" that the novelist really functions as a "critic" of society. Nishinodō argues the same, but in reverse form: the critic really functions as a novelist. He puts this in explicit terms: "the critic in fact must place himself in the position of the novelist, think for himself those same thoughts, feel the same feelings, be in total empathy (*dōjō*) with him—in other words, he must at first become the novelist."[24] Only after he accomplishes empathetic, immersive occupation of the mind of the novelist can he "raise himself from that position" to produce "transformative criticism."[25] The novelist, then, is distinguished from ordinary individuals by his critical insights concerning real-world experience, and his sensitivity to human embeddedness in social life. The critic, in turn, distinguishes himself from the novelist through critical insights about those insights. Both, in other words, are distinguished by an ennobling self-consciousness—critics just possess an extra helping.

The ideal critic "becomes" the novelist and then surpasses him, if not in terms of the aesthetic beauty of his representation then at least in terms of his understanding of the reasons, means, and standards whereby that representation acquires significance. In Nishinodō's conception, the critic must step back to transcend his own subjectivity and so acquire a bird's eye view not only of the reality behind the novel, but also of the novelist's interpretation of that world. This echoes Shōyō's claim that the critics' work with respect to the novel requires the same sort of "objectivity" the novel ostensibly manifests in its representation of the world. Nishinodō, however, directly suggests that the critical perspective does not merely parallel, but also includes and supplements that of the novelist, providing interpretations of novel interpretations that contextualize them through an understanding of their larger significance in Japanese society. In the end, the "objectivity" both novelist and critic must seek serves the greater good of society by allowing them and readers to reflect on and frame the *shinsō* (truth) of Japanese life so as to create room for improvement.

Nishinodō's argument, like Shōyō's and Hokubō's, couches itself in nationalist terms that seek to measure Japanese literature against that of the West, invoking ideas like "progress" and "improvement." But whereas Shōyō purports to free the novel from all but aesthetic concerns, Nishinodō makes a more direct case for the connection between nationalism, ethics, and self-consciousness in novels and criticism. At the end of "On Criticism," he writes that the novel reflects reality in a stylized way that provides self-knowledge. The modern critic, he then concludes, in order to obtain the "objectivity" necessary for framing this self-understanding on appropriate evaluative terms, must turn to Western aesthetics and critical ideas about literature.[26] Extrinsic standards are necessary not because they are superior, but because they provide the proper vantage for inducing critical self-consciousness and facilitating the development of a stronger national identity. Once he has absorbed these standards thoroughly, the Japanese critic will be empowered to deploy and to critique those ideals. Through this unique vantage, the critic will be able to reflect on the present situation of literature in Japan and lead writers to greater heights, distinguishing the uniqueness of the *shōsetsu* in the process. The task of criticism, in other words, is to capitalize on its detached perspective so as to guide the novel toward promoting, on the national level, the kinds of improvements novels can engender in individual character at the personal level.

Criticism and the novel are thus theorized to perform analogous work on the ethical constitution of their readers, and through precisely the same means: the presentation of perspectives aware of the transformative work that their own representative gestures perform on their objects. As we shall see, these emphases on ethically motivated self-consciousness and detachment, as well as the critical function imputed to the novel, serve as a springboard for the early innovations of Mori Ōgai and others for whom the novel is not an artistic window onto the real world but a self-theorizing form of social and aesthetic critique.

2

A Framed Narrator: Ironic Perspective in *The Dancing Girl*

A Man of Letters

In the last decade of the nineteenth century, few writers who said anything about literature interesting enough to catch the attention of Mori Ōgai escaped the cutting strokes of his pen. Uchida Roan's 1895 satire "How to Become a Literati" (*Bungakusha to naru hō*) famously lampoons this phenomenon:

> Ōgai is the Hartmann of Japan, its number one aesthetic philosopher and critic. He's a figure so big that to wax eloquent on *Wadachi* [referring to Ōgai's 1894 essay "Kantetsuroku"] he uses four pages and two hundred lines, and to take care of Shiba No Sono [referring to his 1892 essay "On the style of Yoshiba no Sono"] he wasted around twenty pages. If you make one mistake and incur his displeasure, he may fill twenty or thirty pages on you so be careful and stay away from this danger.[1]

Ōgai earned a reputation for brandishing a critical rhetoric that invoked abstractions of Western philosophy and made claims to scientific rigor. His aggressively rationalist approach to criticism distinguished it from the more impressionistic or morally didactic work of other *bunjin* (men of letters) at the time. Through innovative, sometimes abstruse, and always authoritative declamations he often argued other critics into silence whether or not they had valid points to make.

Major studies have reinforced an image of the author as imperious critic. In his 1996 work *Ideology and Narrative in Modern Japanese Literature*, Murakami Fuminobu cites Ōgai's contemporary Kitamura Tōkoku to argue that Ōgai lacked rigor in his thinking, "treating science and aesthetics without discrimination under the general name of 'learning'" and attributing whatever was convenient to either term.[2] Isogai Hideo, in his 1979 monograph *Mori Ōgai: The Meiji Twenties* (*Mori Ōgai—Meiji nijūnendai wo chūshin ni*), argues in a similar vein that Ōgai's efforts in the early 1890s to establish an "objective" system of aesthetic criticism were predicated on naïve misreadings of German philosophy that failed to pay sufficient attention to the distinctiveness of literary art. According to Isogai, Ōgai's appeal to scientific rationalism served mostly as a pretext for establishing the authority of his ideas about aesthetics.[3]

Under such retrospective scrutiny, Ōgai has been said to use criticism and rhetoric as incidental means to the end of insisting on particular ideas about literature. Yet such interpretations represent scholarly hindsight from within a tradition of criticism and theory that Ōgai was at the time working to establish. I suggest that in much of this work the substance of Ōgai's claims was often secondary to his purpose in establishing a discursive *form* for literary criticism. The philosophical and scientific terms Ōgai wielded so fiercely may have been more important for their status *as* philosophical and scientific terms imported from the West than as rigorously investigated concepts of particular value in themselves.

There is some consensus among scholars that Ōgai's early criticism relied heavily upon rhetorical manipulation. Kabe Yoshitaka, for example, suggests that Ōgai was less interested in aesthetics than he was in the systematization of literary study and shoring up his own position as a literary critic, using argumentative tone and appeals to obscure ideas to win his points.[4] Rodica Frentiu notes that Ōgai's emphasis on rationalism in critical discourse and his pursuit of objective aesthetic standards may have been exaggerated to bolster his emergent position as a national figurehead and intellectual, one of the cultural ambassadors sent abroad with a specific mission to strengthen the nation.[5] In order to transform the methods and values of both Japanese literature and intellectual discourse on the arts, Ōgai sought to establish himself as an authority on such matters, securing for himself an identity as philosopher, scientific thinker, and creative writer engaged in a project of national advancement.

Ōgai's position as an intellectual heralding a nationally driven modernization—or, more precisely, his own promotion of himself as such—permanently shaped his public reception as an Enlightenment "Man of Ideas" rather than a doctor, philosopher, or writer in the main. Scholarship has accordingly tended to focus on the aspects of his writing illuminated by this vision. For example, critics often assess his creative writing in terms of the efficacy with which it conveys certain intellectual positions. This is readily apparent in the work of Murakami and Isogai cited above. Richard Bowring also follows this trend. For him, the *shōsetsu Youth* (*Seinen*) failed as a creative piece but succeeded as a philosophical consideration of Meiji individualism.[6]

J. Thomas Rimer emphasizes how the author's "scientific training" accounted for his spirit of "rational inquiry" whereby he explored "new ideas" conveyed by his fiction.[7] Marcus Marvin expresses awe at the sheer wealth of "factual information" conveyed by Ōgai's *shōsetsu* and sees the writer as principally a translator of experience and learning.[8] Even the rhetorical analyses of Frentiu serve almost exclusively to establish Ogai's methods of advancing philosophical and social ideas.[9] And for Frank Jacob in his 2017 "Between East and West: Mori Ōgai and the Beginnings of Modern Japanese Literature," Ōgai's literature largely "expressed his amalgamated ideas based on Western and Eastern thought, and also further emphasized an idea of freedom that was probably too advanced for his time and for the contemporary Japanese environment."[10] For all of these thinkers, Ōgai's literature served as a conduit for ideas.

Ōgai's critical work, in turn, has been critiqued for disingenuous and tendentious writing that masquerades as scientific discourse in order to win arguments by sleight of hand. This nearly converse criticism shares with critical views of his fiction the sense that for the Ōgai, writing served as a means to intellectual ends. This is explicitly the argument made by Kabe, but the sentiment is echoed by others such as Meiji scholar Hasegawa Izumi. Hasegawa argues persuasively that Ōgai's argument with Shōyō in the so-called "submerged-ideals" (*botsu risō*) debate did not only fail to contradict but in fact essentially confirmed many of Shōyō's claims—the apparent opposition revolved essentially along a willful misunderstanding of terms that became the occasion for Ōgai to launch a critique that modeled the form of criticism he wanted to promote.[11]

In recent years more nuanced attention to the reflexive undercurrents in Ōgai's writing has begun to emerge in scholarship. For example, in his 2012 study *Two-Timing Modernity: Homosocial Narrative in Modern Japanese Fiction*, J. Keith Vincent examines how the narrative form of Ōgai's *The Wild Goose* (*Gan*; 1911–13), with its twinning, Girardian structure, formally embodies the homosocial narrative it also chronicles through its "simultaneously critical … and nostalgic" consciousness—a doubled, self-conscious posture whose ethics we shall examine in considerable depth in the fourth chapter.[12] D. Cuong O'Neill also draws attention to the rhetorical reflexivity in Ōgai's work. He contends that the nearly canonical critiques of mimetic failure in Ōgai's *shōsetsu* miss the author's efforts to create a narrative form that embodies the "variable forms of temporal disorders inhabiting [modern Japanese] life."[13] For O'Neill, Ōgai's writing "offers a new language of representation, an expanded aesthetic horizon, in which the increased consciousness of the fragility of perception is transformed, with wakeful urgency, into a heightened consciousness of reflection."[14] My own work on Ōgai takes its cue from these rich analyses of the author's careful orchestration of theme and form, and of the role that literary self-consciousness plays in generating perspectival shifts that can accommodate new visions of modernity.

Although many recognize the sharpness of Ōgai's intellect and the stylistic accomplishment of his creative work, few have ever ventured the opinion that his work takes on anything like an ethical self-critique of its own narrative form. Yet for Ōgai, a writer and translator who shuttled between genres and literary traditions, the fraught relationship between language, ideas, and our commitments to ourselves and others was itself an urgent and often explicit concern. His critical and creative writing directly address the ethics of narrative representation, often by drawing attention to the very dangers of narrative self-authorization and manipulation of which he has been accused. In this chapter, I first examine a few of his earliest critical essays, especially those that have been so overwhelmingly interpreted as excluding ethical valuations, to demonstrate how they in fact ascribe to the novel a crucial ethical function and lay the groundwork for his later theories of "stereoscopic" writing. By tracing the contours of Ōgai's early theories of the novel and their resonance with what we have seen in the work of Shōyō, Hokubō, and others, and then discovering its relevance for descrying overlooked formal experimentation in his famous novella-length *shōsetsu*, *The Dancing Girl* (*Maihime*), we can discern the development of an innovative approach to novel ethics that his writing pioneers. This methodology—discovering principles of literary analysis in the author's critical essays and then considering his creative work in their light—will pave the way for subsequent work wherein we focus on the self-theorization that his later writing performs.

Ōgai's Dialectic Vision: Ethical Self-Overcoming in Critical and Novel Discourse

Ōgai's 1890 article "On Reaching a Definition of Pornography through a Discussion of the Limits of Lyric Poetry" (*Jōshi no genkai wo ronjite waisetsu no teigi wo oyobu*) attempts to distinguish "pornography" from literature. It argues against moral objections to the treatment of literary sensuousness, but only by claiming that the edifying aims of the author can qualify a work as literary and not pornographic. What matters is not the content of the work but its intended effects. By "intentions," Ōgai does not refer to the stated or imagined goals of a flesh-and-blood author or to any obvious didacticism in the content of an artwork. Rather, he maintains that a successfully edifying work of art must convert objects of licentious desire into those of disinterested contemplation for the betterment of its audience; the intentions are to be discerned from the methods of the work, its handling of the subject matter. Ethics, in other words, are more closely tied to the form of a work than to its content.

The resonance with Shōyō is clear: both authors try to shift the terms of discourse about literary value from moralism to aestheticism, both seek to dislodge represented content as the assumed measure of value, both invoke the image of a detached, self-conscious authorial figure to make their cases for artistic value, both focus on the methods of artistic representation over against its content, and both invoke European traditions of literature and philosophy. Ōgai reasons that the aesthetic accomplishment required to avoid licentiousness in the treatment of desire can only be the product of a detached state of mind, whereby creators distance themselves from keenly felt desires. In this emphasis on the detachment of aesthetics from subjectively driven interest, Ōgai draws from the tradition of Kantian aesthetics on which the German philosophers he admired predicated their work. But unlike Kant, Ōgai follows Shōyō in ascribing to aesthetics an essentially social, edifying function.

Ōgai's critical writing on literature almost always wrestles in some form or another with the problem of subjectivity in aesthetic judgment (a problem he often obliquely tied to matters of ethical or social good). He repeatedly returns to one essential question: How can a work of art transcend subjectivity and the individual desires of the author to discover more universal modes of experiencing and valuing? In the 1890s he sought the answer to this question via aesthetic philosophy, whose rational and hence presumably objective analytic framework he believed could provide a perspective that transcended that of the individual critic. Most of his essays in this period endeavor to establish parameters for scientific discourse on aesthetics. These efforts would turn out integral to his methods as a novelist as well.

In a *Yomiuri Shimbun* article "On the Novel" (*Shōsetsuron*; 1889), his first writing to focus on the genre, Ōgai addresses the compatibility of scientific and literary approaches to interpretation. Under the pretext of discussing the work of French naturalist Emile Zola, Ōgai contends that whereas in science one dissects and analyzes with the intent of revealing the true nature of the object under analysis "as it is," in literature one cannot be satisfied with the same approach. The novelist must "transform and bring to life" his observations of reality through a creative, fictionalizing faculty (*kūsō no chikara ni yorite*).[15] While the doctor strives for objectivity, the novelist must manifestly work through his subjective perspective to give his work its artistic quality. That is, he must supplement the detached observations of the scientist with the immersed sensibilities of the artist.

The "scientific" perspective advanced by the naturalism of Zola had not even reached Japan by the time Ōgai published his article, so the attack was hardly needed. The topic, however, serves a key purpose for Ōgai's debut as a scholar. It allows him to argue for the necessity of both the "objectivity" of the critical, scientific mind and the "subjectivity" of the imaginative writer, and then to leverage his unique position (as medical doctor, critic, and literary writer who has studied in both Japan and Europe) as an authority on both approaches. The essay elevates the discipline of literary criticism from that of intellectual opinion to something more like Western philosophy in its scientific rigor, all the while allowing Ōgai to claim superiority over the Western theorist he declaims.

Few if any of the specific concepts or values advanced by the Western philosophy and aesthetic theories that he imported in the 1880s were of enduring importance to Ōgai. None even rate mention in the inaugural essay for his literary journal, *The Weir* (*Shigarami-zōshi*), published in October of 1889, roughly nine months after he published "On the Novel." Indeed, most of the philosophical arguments he would make in the first decades of his critical writing, especially those introduced through imported terminology, would be abandoned within a year of his introducing them. What mattered for Ōgai was the form and methodology of novel criticism.

In *The Weir* he argues broadly for rigor and detachment in criticism without making any concrete claims for the value of either novels or criticism. Ōgai in fact prided himself on a willingness to revise any particular aesthetic or critical position, should sufficient reason ever present itself. In his 1896 preface to a collection of earlier articles on literature (*Tsukikusa no jo*) he writes:

> When I tried art criticism in Japan, I chose the aesthetics of Hartmann… and based my ideas on him… The reason why more emphasis has been placed on aesthetics, and that lectures on aesthetics take place in schools… is partly due to my promotion in the somewhat naïve articles published in *The Weir*, the journal that I and a few like-minded friends published between 1889 and

1894. Do I believe in him absolutely? Are his aesthetics my hobby horse, and would I fall if the horse were shot down? The facts give ample evidence to the contrary.... [If there is cause] I will gladly expand my present view of the arts... and even go so far as to change my perspective fundamentally.[16]

Ōgai promotes here a vision of criticism as a dialectic process whereby the clash of ideas allows new, more progressive ones to emerge. The form of the process matters more than any position within taken within it.

This view of the form and function of criticism turns out to be inseparable from (and analogous to) the view of social ethics he came to espouse later in works such as "The Tower of Silence" (*Chinmoku no tō*; 1910). The Ōgai-like narrator of that later text argues that "art" and "learning" have parallel and productively "negative" functions insofar as both destroy conventions (*inshū wo yaburu*), the reified standards of value or behavioral and social norms that must be sloughed off to make way for newer values more adequate to the age.[17] Although the characters discuss art and learning without explicit mention of ethics, the conversation about values and norms centers almost entirely on concerns about proper behavior and social responsibility amid shifting circumstances.

In *Youth* (*Seinen*; 1910), a *shōsetsu* of the same year, Ōgai again puts forward the idea that art and learning function analogously to overwrite extant aesthetic and moral structures through a productive cycle of construction and destruction.[18] He focuses in these and many other writings after the turn of the twentieth century on the cultural and intellectual processes whereby critical and creative disciplines generate new values and social systems by overcoming the norms and limitations established by previous ones. His vision of both ethics and aesthetics as driven by continual dialectic synthesis drives a continual stepping-back from ideas, the assumption of postures of reflexive detachment from his own representational gestures, that characterizes the ethics of self-consciousness we shall find operating in his creative work.[19] By standing back from his own assertions, as well as by detaching himself from former styles and other methods, Ōgai imagined that the author could transcend the contingencies of transient moralities and subjective points of view to foster a dynamic of ethical self-overcoming that would persist even as society and its moral values change.

Looking at the many shifts in ideas and style over time, critics have emphasized inconsistency in Ōgai's writing, suggesting, as Richard Bowring does, that ultimately he had to abandon his advocacy for objective aesthetic standards because of a "fundamental contradiction between the method and the idealism that lay behind the theories. Ōgai was applying logic, that tool that was so essential to the rational scientific method, to the sphere of literature where it was inappropriate. The resultant breakdown was inevitable."[20] The predominant view in scholarship is that Ōgai eventually turned to historical fiction out of disillusionment with the capacity of the *shōsetsu* to achieve the kinds of authenticity he sought.[21]

Ōgai did indeed radically change the style, voice, and genres of his writing over the years. However, he did not "abandon" his former ideas at all, so long as we recognize that those "ideas" concerned the *form* of critical and literary writing more than they did any particular philosophical or aesthetic position. Indeed, we shall see that the reflexivity incipient in his earliest critical practices (and even more palpable in his literary writing) increasingly informs his creative work as both theme and method. A remarkably consistent interest in narrative reflexivity impels the innovative stylistic transformations so often treated as "breaks" and "reversals."[22] The view presented in his early work, that of the art object as an amalgam of subjective and objective perspectives, and his sense of the fundamental homology between the aesthetic experience of novels and the ethical situation of subjects, became progressively more central to what I will show to be the "stereoscopic" vision of his prose fiction and his sense of its formal responsibilities.[23]

As I shall presently demonstrate through analysis of his first breakthrough *The Dancing Girl*, Ōgai's *shōsetsu* tend to tell two stories superimposed on one another: one that involves his characters' interactions, usually with very clear but not always admirable moral or ethical implications, and another, related story about the narrative act of representing those interactions. His narrators in fact often directly discuss the circumstances of their writing and, wittingly or not, implicate themselves in the very ethical problems from which they try to detach themselves by telling their tales. In short, the acts of storytelling that his narrators undertake are themselves subjects of narrative reflection as much as the tales. This reflexive dimension has gone relatively unremarked in the long history of work on the author.

Almost all of Ōgai's purely fictional *shōsetsu*, even his earliest, tie the production and experience of narratives directly to the ethical dilemmas his stories dramatize. By linking acts of narrative reconstruction and interpretation to the very story-world issues that his *shōsetsu* supposedly present from the detached point of view of an onlooker, Ōgai explores the ethics of the novel form. The problems of perspective and distance that readers experience become, recursively, central to the thematic explorations of his fiction. I suggest that

Ōgai's *shōsetsu* achieve aesthetic virtuosity not by mimicking Western forms nor through their intellectual weight but through the intricately wrought tensions they create between the telling and the told. We encounter in Ōgai reflexive rhetoric and self-reflective plots that require readers to consider the implications of their methods of establishing narrative point of view in relation to the themes they portray.[24]

Reflexive Narration in *The Dancing Girl*

Ōgai's first major success as a literary writer, *The Dancing Girl* (*Maihime*; 1890), addresses the capacity of *shōsetsu* to represent and engage the issues of perspective, subjectivity, and interpersonal ethics that his criticism addressed. As a novel deemed morally problematic by most of its scholarly readers, and one whose reflexive qualities have been almost entirely ignored, *The Dancing Girl* serves as a revealing example of the incipient ethics of self-consciousness that undergirds so much of his literary work.

The first-person *shōsetsu* describes government worker Ōta Toyotarō's experience abroad in Germany, where his relationship with a dancing girl causes him to fall from favor and lose the government support that made his trip possible. He takes a job as a journalist and moves in with the woman, Elise. They struggle in poverty until Ōta's friend, Aizawa, offers him a means of regaining favor with the Japanese officials in Germany. Soon Ōta must choose either to return to Japan or to remain with a pregnant Elise. Upon agreeing to return home, he falls ill, consumed with disgust at himself for his choice and unable to bring himself to confront Elise. When he finally recovers from his illness, he learns that Aizawa informed Elise of his decision, and that she went mad. The story ends with his ambivalent expression of gratitude and resentment for having such a "good friend" as Aizawa.

So goes the tale told by Ōta, which he writes in his travel journal on the way back to Japan. The form of the narrative as a memoir neatly reinforces for readers the ostensible realism of the piece. It also works for its embedded author, Ōta, by providing him with a means of achieving his stated goal of coming to terms with the remorse he feels at the way events unfolded. That is, his narrative act attempts to confer through its retrospective form a destiny upon the self (the ultimate unification of past and present selves at the close of the narrative) that will reconcile the division he feels between the consequences of his actions and his image of himself and his values.[25] Viewed in this light, it seems logical to conclude that the narrative form is complicit in its author's desire to justify the events of the plot—that it retrospectively validates Ōta's disorienting, divisive experience of the modern world, his questionable decisions, and his quest for reintegration as a Japanese subject.

In his 2001 article, "Mori Ōgai's Resentful Narrator: Trauma and the National Subject in 'The Dancing Girl,'" Christopher Hill makes just such a case, arguing that the narrative structure of the story manifests its ethical commitments to "an articulation of Meiji national identity."[26] That is, for Hill *The Dancing Girl* tells the story of an individual's realization that his duty to the state outweighs his responsibility toward, and perhaps even his love for, another individual. The narrative form complexly underwrites and legitimizes Ōta's actions because its "narrowly focused, first-person retrospection naturalizes what I will call the protagonist's accession to nationality by presenting his embrace of an identity as Japanese as the inevitable realization of qualities latent since his youth."[27]

Hill charges that the narrative form of *The Dancing Girl* is complicit in nationalist ideology by virtue of its teleology. He quotes Prasenjit Duara to argue: "The nationalist understanding of history is based upon a conception of history that is linear and progressive, in which the nation as the subject of history gathers self-awareness. The complete unfolding of the self-consciousness of the self-same people must, however, await the nation-state, which alone can guarantee this transparency."[28] According to Hill, Ōta attempts to rewrite and thereby reappraise his life in terms of a nationalist understanding of history, because the "unfolding of self-consciousness" enacted by the récit form of the narrative already implies the reinscription into the nation-state with which the story ends. Hill concludes from this that Ōgai is participating in the construction of mid-Meiji nationalist narratives that seek to co-opt the identity of individuals and reframe their ethical responsibilities on nationalist political terms.[29]

That Ōgai was himself heavily invested in this nationalist project is undeniable; he was conscious of his representative role as a national figure for all of his writing life. But if Ōgai were passively promoting an unquestioning, uncritical view of the promise of reintegration that the state offered, there would be no need even to invoke the ethical wobbles that rock Ōta on his way home, let alone to leave readers with what I will demonstrate to be resounding formal and thematic ambivalences. Hill does not address the way reflexivity undermines rather than validates the closure of this récit largely because he presupposes the closure of the form as one of the chief grounds of his analysis. As we will discover, however, Ōgai rarely invoked genre conventions merely to color within the lines; he almost always made the exposure of the narrative mechanisms of novel conventions part and parcel of the experience of his *shōsetsu*.

Hill's analysis effectively extracts the tale from its frame, without taking into account, for example, the fact that Ōta does not write from a metaphorical point of completion but literally en route to Japan, at sea in a foreign port, alone on a ship usually occupied by strangers—a setting that leaves unconfirmed the supposed promise of integration and closure afforded by the story's form. Ōta's expression of lingering resentment as the closing note of the story furthermore reminds the reader that the narrative process has *not* conferred a "necessity" on the subject's reintegration into the nation-state. It highlights the incompletion of the process of the self's authorization as a subject; Ōta has failed to come to satisfactory terms with the fundamental moral ambivalence that motivated the effort to write his story in the first place. Ōgai stages this failure for readers by explicitly remarking on Ōta's need to tell the story of himself under such estranged circumstances, detached from the moral frames of reference—and the people—for which (and whom) he is accountable.

The closure supposedly implied by the telos of the memoir finds itself challenged by yet another "remainder" left out of the equation of the story's narrative with nationalism: Ōta's unborn child, which Hill acknowledges but finds written off as "the fruit of a missown seed."[30] With Elise mad, Ōta has abandoned his own progeny to a parentless, impoverished existence. Perhaps Hill feels justified in glossing over this fact because Ōta himself does; however, the lack of a moral compass that would allow Ōta to orient himself ethically with respect to his actions is precisely the problem the narrative is supposed to be addressing in the first place. By its very absence from the story, and its presence as a loose end in the mind of the reader (especially contemporaneous readers, who justifiably wondered about the autobiographical accuracy of the story), the unborn child represents a possible future and abandoned role whose existence challenges the capacity of the narrative to confer a singular, legitimizing closure upon his actions. Both narrative structure and the elements of the story resist the implication that the narrator's choice is a settled, endorsed affair.

The *shōsetsu* thus produces a dissonance between the promise of legitimacy and security that one might assume from both the retrospective form of the narration and its narrator's (as well as author's) dutiful nationalism, on the one hand, and the loose ends, ambivalences, and questionable reliability of its narrator, on the other. Hill sees this as a failure of the author to secure the moral high ground and justify his persona's actions. The dissonance bothered a number of Ōgai's contemporaries as well. Perhaps most famously, Ishibashi Ningetsu condemned Ōta's choice to return to Japan as contradictory in light of the expectations set up by the title, descriptions of character, and the development of the story, which all seemed to demand some kind of moral growth.[31] Yet this dissonance only appears as a problem when readers or critics consider the narrative to operate transparently, conferring necessity on the plot by virtue of a structure and perspective meant to be accepted as unquestionable givens and foundations of moral value. That is, it appears problematic only if readers equate Ōgai with his narrator and read authorial intention as a project of self-justification. Such readings ignore the way this *shōsetsu* itself already calls attention to the ethical implications of the very narrative act Hill and others accuse of complicity with nationalist aims.

If we approach the text as the story of a narrative project and a reflection on the ethics of representation embodied by the narrator's use of the novel form, the apparent contradictions prove elements of a purposefully crafted, if unsettlingly dissonant, coherence. Ōgai's story is not Ōta's—the author's perspective exceeds and frames that of his narrator. *The Dancing Girl* is not only the story of Ōta's experience in Europe; it is the story of his efforts to account for himself ethically through the form of a narrative that he deliberately employs to affirm the necessity of his actions, just as Hill suggests. The act of writing, its motivation, and its ethical relation to Ōta's "quest," however, are themselves as much the subjects of inquiry of Ōgai's writing as is Ōta's autobiographical quest for identity itself.

This becomes apparent when we consider the emphasis Ōgai has placed on Ōta's own self-conscious attention to the way his writing constructs an image of himself. Ōgai has Ōta write the story of his experience in diaries in which he had formerly recorded thoughts about his trip to Europe. Ōta initially left many of these blank because, on subsequent re-reading, he discovered that the descriptions of the environments he encountered turned out to reveal more about himself and his romanticizing state of mind than about the environments he described. Ōta thus describes himself as having first read his own writing, then having imagined his readers' responses, and as now writing from a perspective enlightened by these reflections, aware of his likely reception. He informs his present reader, "I shudder to think how any sensitive person must have reacted to my childish ideas and presumptuous rhetoric."[32]

By underscoring Ōta's attention to the way his writing presents himself and solicits responses from readers in advance of giving his account, Ōgai makes it clear that his narrator invokes the memoir form as part of a deliberate, self-conscious strategy to present himself in a certain light to readers. His memoir presents itself as an honest effort to work through a troubled past, but it clearly and self-consciously has the project of self-formation in mind throughout. Clearly Ōta would not have to explain his decision to write in his travel journals if he were writing to and for himself, even if he did have to work out his more ambivalent feelings through narrative retracing. His supposed language of self-analysis is far from mere transcription of his experiences, thoughts, and feelings. It is a self-conscious effort to reorient himself ethically through projections and invocations of readers' judgment.

Ōta can no more achieve "objectivity" in his memoir than he could in the "diary" that memoir replaces. He can only hide its tendentiousness behind the veil of confession, an espoused desire not to flinch from the truth that is itself part of the self-justification his writing enacts. In this light, his use of first-person retrospective narrative is hardly transparent. On the contrary, as we have seen, Ōgai calls attention both to its self-serving aims and to Ōta's self-consciousness with respect to the way his writing promises to define him as an ethical subject. This self-consciousness proves fundamental to Ōgai's interrogation of the capacities and limits of the memoir form to accomplish Ōta's aims.

Criticism has overwhelmingly conflated Ōgai's perspective with those of his narrators, in large part because of the autobiographical resonance. And of course Ōgai thematically, even within the story, investigates the relationship of narrative fiction to real life itself, a further cause of confusion. Few scholars take pains to distinguish, and almost none set in opposition, the perspectives of the author and those of his narrator. And while a handful of critics have suggested that Ōgai may be attempting to distance himself, through fictionalized narrative, from personal decisions whose ethics he has legitimately come to question, none have suggested that Ōgai might be critiquing the ethics of his narrators' *literary* projects.

Yet this is precisely what Ōgai does throughout his literary career. He continually addresses, in both criticism and fiction, ways that the narration tends to normalize the points of view, judgments, and values of speaking selves. This happens differently in different genres, of course, and therefore yields innovative methods of implementing an ethics of self-consciousness appropriate to that form. Some even draw attention to the fact that the worlds his narrators describe quite literally come into being through the operations of their points of view upon them. While his narrators do tend to capitalize on their positioning for the sake of self-authorization, however, those failings and desires do not *transparently* reflect those of the author.

Tomiko Yōda, in "First-Person Voice and Citizen-Subject: The Modernity of Ōgai's *The Dancing Girl*," notes that Ōgai uses language to deliberately portray an authoritative speaking "I" that differentiates itself from a represented "self." She invokes Emile Benveniste's linguistic theory of referentiality to argue that:

> the "person" [as a technical aspect of narrative] is not only structural but *structuring*. The subject and its enunciatory context constitute a unique and primordial locus from which the linguistic referentiality is exercised. It is an Archimedean point that cannot be referred to in itself, yet it makes possible all references to chronological time, relative space, and differentiated identity.[33]

Yōda associates Ōta's efforts to establish himself as an externally situated speaking self, represented by the pronoun *yo*, with his attempts to authorize himself as a subject. When he speaks as a narrator to comment on his present point of view and circumstances, he uses *yo*.[34] When referring to himself as an actor in the narrative past, however, Ōta refers to himself largely through the pronoun *ware*, even when he is the grammatical subject of the sentence. In Yōda's view, this use of *yo* locates the writing subject in a sovereign position outside the field of representation:

> The novelistic first-person narration is an apparatus that forges a fictional field of representation that weave these two separate discursive planes together [the world of the story and the speaker's plane]. Correlatively, even though the pronoun *I* itself may be an empty, formal signifier that has no objective meaning, it becomes sutured to an empirical identity.[35]

The way that the novelistic first-person narration of *The Dancing Girl* brings together the abstract, self-authorizing subject-position of the speaking I (*yo*) and the real, empirical world it represents has, for Yōda, clear ethical implications. It arrogates an illusory ascendancy for the author, whose transcendental position she suggests is ultimately underwritten by the sovereignty of the nation-state to which it is sutured by this narrative gambit. Thus the validity of the narrator's choice of national identity over personal commitment is secured by grammatical sleight of hand—an analysis that echoes Murakami and Kabe's critiques of the author's critical rhetoric.

Yōda goes on to point out weaknesses in Ōgai's efforts to establish this sovereignty:

> We also see that the hero's self-transcendence as the first-person subject does not provide any resolution to the conflicts that catalyzed the quest for self-identity in the first place. Toyotarō in Berlin began perceiving his sense of self as well as his associations with others as an untenable antimony: recognizing himself as a free, autonomous and ethical individual while at the same time finding it impossible to establish a stable social identity and relations without submitting himself to arbitrary commands of authority. ... By asking the question "Who am I?" he abstracts himself from the world (and himself in the world) to better grasp it. Yet, if what prompted the question was his experience as an embodied social agent, this move is fraught with contradictions.[36]

According to Yōda, Ōta's narrative project leads to contradictions; she discovers that his effort to abstract himself from social commitments only further reveals, to perspicacious critics, his embeddedness in the physical and interpersonal relationships whose importance Ōta dismissed in his single-minded concern with self-realization. Despite the fact that Ōgai has Ōta himself become aware of the disjunction between the promise of the narrative form and its actual effects (as the ambivalence of the ending and the narrator's lingering resentment and uncertainty underscores), Yōda claims that it is her own analysis that reveals "the failure of the redemptive power invested on the first-person subject"—as though Ōgai himself, and not Ōta, were attempting to wield that redemptive power.[37]

Yōda is right, and insightful, in her analysis of the way Ōta's account aims to confer necessity upon his actions by situating them in the meta-narrative story of his own self-transcendence. She is also astute in discovering the connection between the linguistic representation of speaking and spoken "selves" and thematic concerns with the ethical gulf separating past and present selves. But following the tendency in Ōgai criticism to conflate author and narrator, Yōda assumes that Ōgai uses the first-person retrospective narrative form unreflectively to the same purpose as Ōta. Like Hill, Yōda does not distinguish between the narrator Ōta's desire to achieve the sovereign perspective of an authorizing "I," and Ōgai's aims in critiquing that desire by writing the story of Ōta's quest to achieve identity through his act of writing. Her keen awareness of the significance of the frame of the story temporarily drops out of her treatment of its language as "retrospective first-person narrative."

Without becoming more fully self-referential, as several of his later works do, *The Dancing Girl* could do little more to highlight its attention to the relation of narrative form and the ethical questions raised by its representational strategies. The *yo* may lie outside some of the field of representation with respect to past events abroad, but certainly not the passages that specifically reflect on the act of writing itself. We are told that the narrating Ōta writes with the explicitly self-serving aim of coming to terms with the ethics of his choices. We are also told that Ōta has written both professionally and nonprofessionally in a variety of forms defined by claims about their relation to "truth" and by implied contracts with readers (his published travel diaries, newspapers, academic papers, various official documents, and, of course, his memoir). Moreover, the narrator has proven a self-conscious reader of his own (professional) writing and his audience's responses to that writing. Yōda, however, examines the act of self-representation without theorizing the revelation of self-conscious purposefulness that frames the act.

Like Hill, who gestures toward the loose ends of the *shōsetsu* but then writes them off as unimportant, Yōda recognizes that the story struggles against the narrative of transparent complicity that her criticism constructs. She, too, finds that the closing lines of the *shōsetsu* present a "contradictory moment" in the text, one that runs counter to its apparent investment in authorizing the self through the deployment of retrospective narration. For Yōda, however, it is not the resentment itself but its ambivalent situation in the chronology of the story that is problematic. The final line of the story reads: "Yet, even to this day, in my mind a single point of hatred toward him [Aizawa] remains."[38] Yōda argues that because the timing implied by the phrase "to this day" may be attributed either to the writing or the represented Ōta. "We cannot be certain whether the passage represents the realization arrived at by the narrating *yo* after he has finished reconstructing his past or the narrating *yo* still projecting himself in the biographical time of the past."[39]

Yōda describes this conclusion as a radical and "disorderly" moment of indeterminacy that "hangs in midair," "weakens the unifying function of the text," and through which the "*yo* seems to lose its coherence."[40] It is mystifying why the author might end the text with such ambivalence if his project was indeed one of self-authorization. Whereas as for Yōda this critique serves as an indictment of the author, I see these indeterminacies as consistent with the author's inquiry into the ethics of narrative form. The ending only becomes problematic in both Yōda's and Hill's accounts because it reminds us that the entire story is framed by the narrator's reflexive awareness of his purpose in writing.

Yōda draws attention to the way that the potential ambivalence of the last moment leaves readers with uncertainty (are we reading retrospective projection of a subject successfully assimilated into the state or glimpsing an author lamenting the failure of his writing to achieve that goal?). This is for Yōda an aesthetic flaw which accidentally reveals the failure of the authorial project of self-justification. Personally, I find little to indicate that we are to imagine the narrator's past self was thinking this at any particular moment.[41] Regardless, ending on this note unquestionably leaves readers with remorse and ambivalence about the narrator's choice. Such ambivalence need not have been included if the goal of the author were self-justification. As the final moment of the story it seems much less likely to be a revealing mistake by the author than a note of ambivalence continuous with those of the developing meta-narrative themes.

There is no need to strain to imagine that Ōgai is trying to write off his character's regret as a previous moment of doubt now reconciled (a goal that could easily have been accomplished more competently). That the past is meant to remain a problem could not be better emphasized by the final word of the story: "nokorekeri" (remains).[42] At a thematic level, the woman, child, and future abandoned by Ōta, his sense of himself as caught between opposing configurations of the self and its ethical commitments, his resentment, and his memoir itself all remain as testaments to the failure of his quest and of nationalism to underwrite and justify it. At the level of the narrative, what remains is an odd dissonance between the romanticizing elements of the story, the promise of a single subjective perspective whose unifying effect will redeem the fractured individual's sense of self, and the self-conscious frame that refuses to allow the kind of totalizing effect on which that promise depends.

This dissonance, the tension between competing perspectives and worldviews, manifests itself in the very language of the story as part of Ōgai's formal exploration of the relation between aesthetic and ethical effects in the novel form—and not just through the contrast between the *yo* and the *ware*. At the time of writing, the Japanese language was undergoing unprecedented transformation. As discussed in the preceding chapter, *The Dancing Girl* was written when a widely popular movement to "modernize" Japanese language (the *genbun'itchi* movement) was well underway. A written language that more directly resembled actual speech was thought by many contemporary literary writers to be the most appropriate form for the modern (realist) novel, following Western models. *The Dancing Girl*, however, is written in an artful neoclassical style (J. Keith Vincent describes it as "stiff" and already somewhat old-fashioned).[43] The grammar and structure of the language is that of classical Japanese. However, Ōgai draws on a vocabulary unavailable to premodern writers, populating the text with foreign concepts and references, and describes modern situations entirely foreign to native Japanese literary and cultural traditions. The oddness of the "fit" between the classical feel of the language and the modern, cosmopolitan topics of the story reflects how literary language can produce one set of expectations and the content of a story another. It engages readers in the task of reconciling and contemplating their relation. By materializing the ambivalences and ambiguities of the *shōsetsu* as a novel form, even in its very language, *The Dancing Girl* pits novel ethos against pathos, inviting the very reflection on their relation that has been the basis of scholarly critique.

Conclusion

The frame of mind that Ōgai's *shōsetsu* require of readers is not one of passive reception. Rather, we can compare it to that of viewers of a "stereoscope," a device wherein one peers into a contraption that overlays two slightly different images to create the illusion of a unified, three-dimensional reality.[44] The scene of viewing itself, the elaborate mechanism and novelty of the device, can never fully be forgotten; indeed, the artifice of the artwork is integral to the appreciation of its experience. The effects of that artifice in Ōgai's case become the very subject of his portraits.

The tension between ethos and pathos in *The Dancing Girl* does not merely reflect the failure of its author's (or even the narrator's) project of self-justification. It produces a very different kind of novel wherein two stories are overlaid: that of the protagonist's experience and that of his efforts to convert that experience into narrative form. Where critics have found self-serving manipulation or artistic failure, I suggest we encounter an innovative and vitalizing reflection on the problems of perspective that are bundled into the architecture of the novel. If we look at the story in isolation, and then its narrative mechanisms, we find significant flaws in both. If, however, we examine the interrelation of those carefully juxtaposed flaws, we discover a nascent ethics of self-consciousness that will come to be the modus operandi of so much of his later work. By examining his subsequent works with this reflexive methodology in mind, we can come to very different conclusions about his contributions to ethical theories of the novel than his critics have proposed.

In the next chapter, I consider how the quasi-critical, quasi-autobiographical 1900 essay "Who Is Ōgai Gyoshi?" (*Ōgai Gyoshi to wa dare zo*) returns to the issues of novel perspective that his early criticism investigated. Like *The Dancing Girl*, this essay discusses the ethics of his own literary practices in a genre-crossing effort to find a language and point of view from which he might assess both the literary establishment and his ethical commitments as critic and writer more authentically and evocatively. What he discovers is his own complicity in the problematic dynamics he means to critique. I then examine the first major work of fiction after his twelve-year hiatus from creative writing, *Vita Sexualis* (*Ita seksuarisu*; 1909), to show how his literary writing struggles to free itself from complicities in objectifying discourses masquerading as confessional realism. This text materializes in two authorial personae the bifurcation between authorial and narrative points of view that creates the stereoscopic effects of his earlier *shōsetsu*. *Vita Sexualis*, we shall find, revisits the themes and methods of his earlier fiction in much the way that "Who Is Ōgai Gyoshi?" revisits his earlier criticism; it directly thematizes the dissonance that *The Dancing Girl* more subtly creates through the interaction of its narrative frames, in order to expose the relation between the form of its narrator's account and the ethics of his worldview. In the end, this text develops a methodology that runs contrary to that of its ostensible genre; instead of transparently reflecting reality, it records its own solipsistic transformation of reality into *realism*.

3

Who Is Ōgai Gyoshi?: Authorial Desire and Ethical Self-Reflection in the Aughts

The Self-Remaking of Ōgai in the Aughts

In the late nineteenth century, Ōgai fought for a rigorous and objective discipline of literary criticism that would introduce logical standards to what he saw as a chaotic field of inquiry dominated by personal taste and incoherent measures of assessment. For this task he invoked aesthetic standards largely imported from German philosophy. Yet by the turn of the century, just when he had begun winning his case, he abandoned his push for scientific and philosophical objectivity. Most have attributed the shift to other professional interests, asserting that his (then faltering) career as a medical officer, his public commitments, and his work as a translator led to diminishment in his critical productivity.

We have found that Ōgai experimented with narrative perspective and self-consciousness to reflect on the ethics of the novel even in his earliest writing. This positions us now to discern how his middle period writing intensifies rather than abandons those earlier efforts. Indeed, although he published fewer essays in the rigorously philosophical vein of his earlier critical endeavors, he barely even slowed down his writing and speaking about the novel and the state of the literary world. Rather, what changed principally was his mode of expression; he abandoned clear-cut criticism for more genre-fluid forms of discourse on the novel. From 1894 onward, Ōgai's essays about literature incorporated more informal, personal perspectives and anecdotes. His creative writing changed even more dramatically.

After publishing several *shōsetsu* that earned him fame as a writer in the late 1880s and early 1890s, his literary activity over the next dozen or so years was focused on translations of European literature wherein he experimented with strategies for rendering narrative perspectives in Japanese language. The results are an inconsistent variety of styles, all of which strongly resist the tendency toward naturalist (*shizenshugi*) writing that had become popular among the Japanese literary establishment in the early aughts of the twentieth century. After working out a range of expressive possibilities through this translational practice, he took up creative writing in earnest again in 1909, with a burst of short, mostly autobiographical fiction and some essays commenting on literature and the state of the literary field—almost all of which reflect in some way on the perspective of their narrators. Finally, after 1912 he turned almost exclusively to writing historical fiction in the years until his death in 1922.

Overviews of Ōgai's career frequently involve narratives of "breaks" and failures that led him to reverse many of his earlier positions and, finally, to turn away from fiction. For example, with the author's later, "mature" style in mind as a frame of reference, Masao Miyoshi dismisses Ōgai's 1889 *The Dancing Girl* (*Maihime*) as mere "juvenilia" that stops short of the "serious work" his later writings, and particularly his historical fiction, would undertake.[1] Richard Bowring and Karatani Kōjin both discuss Ōgai's turn to historical fiction as a partial failure of creativity, implying that the author's temperament and writing style were better suited to scholarly historical research than fiction.[2] Stephen Snyder recognizes Ōgai's success as a literary writer, but argues that he ultimately rejected the artifice (or "lies") of fiction in favor of the "truth" of historical narratives.[3] And Hasegawa Izumi notes that Ōgai's youthful enthusiasm for the ideality represented by fiction came to be replaced by a desire for the "truth" and "reality" of history.[4]

By tracing the ethics of self-consciousness at work in his writing, however, we discover a continually deepening interest in the relations of literary form and narrative perspective to ethical questions about interpersonal, social, and political responsibility. The style and genres of his writing change dramatically in part because, with each successive work, Ōgai steps back to interrogate and develop further the methodologies deployed in earlier texts. The form and structure of his own *shōsetsu* become increasingly explicit objects of interest and sites of experimentation over the course of his career. The changes wrought by his continual experimentation are indeed dramatic; however, underlying them all we find a constant focus on the ethical entanglements of narrative form and genre conventions.

This trend is perhaps most obvious in texts that explicitly discuss acts of autobiographical writing. Such works directly comment on the interrelation of the methods and ethics of his work as an author—especially the problematic ways that his writing authorizes his own judgments and sensibilities. These texts both participate in and distance themselves from described acts of self-authorizing, establishing in the process new aesthetic and ethical standards whereby his present, self-conscious writing should be valued. By focusing on two such works, the essay "Who Is Ōgai Gyoshi" (*Ōgai Gyoshi to wa dare zo*; 1900) and *Vita Sexualis* (1909), I hope to clarify the evolution of his deployment of narrative reflexivity for ethical ends, and thereby to demonstrate a clear and consistent line of development from the early *The Dancing Girl* through his later career.

In both texts, acts of self-representation and literary interpretation violently circumscribe the freedom of others to make themselves heard and recognized on their own terms. Authors desperate to establish themselves as the sole determinants of the meaning of their life stories wield narrative power to their own advantages, leading to conflict and disparity in their real-life relationships. Insofar as these texts self-consciously highlight the damages wrought by authoritative discourse and conventions of literary self-representation, I suggest in the end that Ōgai's work can both illuminate and be illuminated by theories of dialogism first formulated by Russian literary scholar Mikhail Bakhtin (1895–1975). By considering how narrative reflexivity in Ōgai calls attention to some of the ethical functions ascribed to novel narration in Bakhtin's work, and then by comparing the different ways that these thinkers explore the possibilities of a formal ethics of the novel, I hope to demonstrate how Ōgai's writing can speak to questions that have been formative for global theories of narrative ethics.

Who Is Ōgai Gyoshi? Fictions of Authorial Selfhood

Ōgai's 1900 essay "Who Is Ōgai Gyoshi" has been dismissed by Richard Bowring and others as a self-indulgent complaint about the author's severance from the literary and cultural world of Tokyo via his 1899 demotion to a medical post in the distant region of Kokura.[5] The essay certainly does represent a jarring break from Ōgai's former writing, in both style and content. But it does not simply rant; on the contrary, it orchestrates its recollections quite artfully to explore a formal ethics of literary representation.

"Who Is Ōgai Gyoshi" begins with an act of self-reading. Ōgai relates his recent surprise at seeing the name "Ōgai Gyoshi" appended to an article he wrote. This was a pen name used in literary debates of the early 1890s, which he had stopped using after 1894. His relation of the uncanny experience of seeing his recent work attributed to this persona leads to contemplation of his past involvement in the literary world (*bundan*). He then interrupts that contemplation to reflect on the circumstances that led to the writing of the present essay: the editor of the paper asked him to write about the current state of literature. Ōgai tells us with ironic chagrin that he could not comply, because he himself no longer participates in that world, and that he decided instead "to write about the literary world of the past, that is to say, about Ōgai Gyoshi."[6]

The way that the essay frames itself as a substitute for the critical perspective on the present literary world that should have been written in its place recalls the way that the subjective memoir of the narrator-protagonist in *The Dancing Girl* retells certain autobiographical experiences in a journal meant for different kinds of published observations. Once again, Ōgai describes for readers an act of overwriting that performs a kind of auto-criticism. The essay eulogizes Gyoshi as a "veteran warrior" who finally succumbed to a barrage of enemy fire (literally a "fusillade of [critical] arrows") and sank into the confusion and anonymity of the battlefield he had created.[7] Here the author openly acknowledges the combative mode of his former critical writing and points to its violent, even self-defeating consequences. Yet in the same breath he distances his present narrating self from that past persona, most obviously by pronouncing latter dead, but also by taking the occasion to reflect explicitly on the conceptual rift between writing and written selves. He notes that "Ōgai Gyoshi" was "an abstract and artificial creation" and declares that he, the presently narrating Ōgai, "chooses no longer to sign his name as Ōgai Gyoshi" and thereby assumes a new perspective.[8]

Although Ōgai's alter ego "died" (Ōgai later wryly imagines himself attending the funeral), the real writer "continued to study and learn," progressing beyond the ideas advocated in his earlier critical skirmishes.[9] The essay exposes problems in the arguments and methods through which that past "I" sought to authorize and identify itself as an authoritative enlightenment figure. Yet it also holds its own ironic and detached mode of reflection above the frays of his past. "Who Is Ōgai Gyoshi" surreptitiously claims the laurels of enlightenment for the present, self-conscious author in a process of self-overcoming that uncannily mirrors the self-authorizing strategies of his past persona—and of course that of Ōta, the narrator of *The Dancing Girl*, who tries to distance his presently writing self from a conflicted past by writing about himself. In both cases, processes of fictionalization prove tied to ethical engagements involving the authority and real-life social positioning of the author.

Ōgai's representations of himself here and in other quasi-autobiographical writing play on the indeterminant distinction between self and self-representation.[10] He invokes the term "confession" (*zange*) to describe the essay's own commentary on the literary world, playing on the contemporaneous vogue of naturalist fascination with the "truth" of confessional literature. Modern confessional literature ostensibly took material from life experiences, often experiences of dubious morality, and turned them into narrative. But here the "life experiences" and ethical engagements (represented thematically as the violence done to other critics through combative criticism) are themselves already textual, performed by what Ōgai insists we recognize as a fictional creation (literally an abstraction, a "pen name").

By rewriting criticism as critical self-reflection in the space of a literary column, Ōgai exposes the personal desires and motivations of the present as well as his past critical persona—a modus operandi that we have already found in *The Dancing Girl* and will find again in both *Vita Sexualis* and *The Wild Goose*. The tension between objectivity and subjectivity is not in this essay merely a quality attributed to the aesthetics of a literary work; it is an urgent matter of representation directly tethered to concerns with what we might call a kind of literary violence. Indeed, the essay consistently frames acts of writing on martial terms—not just the sallies of Ōgai Gyoshi. For example, it labels recent graduates of college "samurai warriors of student journals," compares two critics to "guardians at a temple gate … poised to challenge Hakubunkan's [the publishing company responsible for the eminent literary journal *The Sun* (*Taiyō*)] rule," and discusses another literary coterie (Imperial Literature, or Teikoku bungaku) as "a perpetual succession of hot-blooded warriors stepping in after one another to demonstrate their skills."[11] Here it is notably the methods and form of writing—the skills—rather than the aims of writing that Ōgai compares to instruments of violence.

The essay goes on to insist even more directly on the ethical consequences of literary representation for real lives. Ōgai claims that in the last few years his life and literary identity have become irreparably obscured, and harmed, by interpretation and rumor:

> There were novel writers known as Rohan, Kōyō … and in the realm of literary criticism, Shōyō, Ōgai, and others …. I found myself in the position of seeing Ōgai Gyoshi appear mistakenly and repeatedly as one of these celebrities of the literary world. … This exaggerated reputation began circulating in the general public, and the distinction between my critical and creative works became

hopelessly blurred. Nonspecialists outside literary circles began to refer to me as "a novelist," even though my *shōsetsu* amounted to no more than several handfuls of pages, between three and twenty each, and a week's worth of work. … I cannot help feeling that my undeserved fame works as a liability …. Indeed, I am a man whose fortunes have not been advanced by having become famous in this manner. My true face has yet to be understood by the world. That is why I have chosen to distance myself from the name Ōgai Gyoshi.[12]

Here the author asserts that his real and represented identities, as well as his work as critic and novelist, have become conflated in cultural consciousness. Misunderstandings of genre conventions—confusion over what really counts as fiction or *shōsetsu*, and the difference between critical and creative literary writing—led to misinterpretations of his work, and this contributed to his current marginalization from the literary world. He doubles down on this theme of misinterpretation by positioning himself as marginalized by the medical community as well, which he suggests illogically dismissed his medical work on the grounds of his reputation as a writer. He thus asserts on several fronts that his ideas, his work, and his own literary personae have been critically misread. More crucially, those misreadings of self-representations turn out to have had very real, material consequences for his personal life: exile. The harmful effects that misreading had on Mori Ōgai the flesh-and-blood author in fact proved fatal to Ōgai Gyoshi the critical persona, who has been "killed off by the Tokyo literary establishment." [13]

Perhaps the greatest irony of the piece is that it, too, has been misread. Awkwardly poised between critical commentary and fictional confession, and ambivalent about the relationship it paints between Ōgai himself and the literary world, the essay has lent itself to the very practices of misreading that it laments. The essay rants, but it does not *merely* rant; it insistently works out through its reflexive form questions urgently related to its theme—questions about the ethics of literary portraits of reality, authorship, authority, and complicity in literary violence. Inasmuch, the essay represents a clear link in the chain of Ōgai's efforts, in both critical and creative writing, to reflect on the power of narrative to generate subject positions that really situate the self in relation to others. This essay makes far more explicit the kind of self-conscious frame we found in *The Dancing Girl*, wherein Ōgai holds Ōta's acts of self-representation up for scrutiny by making his own writing the subject of reflexive critical inquiry. And like the later *Vita Sexualis*, it also doubles its authorial personae and critiques the methods and effects of his own writing. Even more directly than *The Dancing*

Girl, "Who Is Ōgai Gyoshi" reflects the potentially violent consequences of literary engagement—an interest that we shall see becomes the defining subject of later *shōsetsu*.

Vita Sexualis and the Ethics of Self-Reflection

It was something of a vogue in the late Meiji period for authors to produce lurid accounts of their own hidden imaginings and relations in explorations of the power of the novel to compose authentic life stories. The 1910s saw the rise of a confessional genre, usually centered on involvement in the *bundan* (literary world) that would retrospectively come to be known as the I-novel (*shishōsetsu*).[14] *Vita Sexualis* seems to follow this pattern but with a metaliterary twist: it tells the story of how desires give shape to novel forms of representation and vice versa. Like "Who Is Ōgai Gyoshi," it gives the appearance of autobiography but complicates attribution through an uncanny mirroring. The first-person account of the protagonist and Ōgai-like narrator, Kanai, is embedded within commentary by another narrator, an unnamed speaking voice whom we are invited to imagine as Ōgai himself. The assumptions that readers and scholars so often made about the relationship of the author to the protagonist of *The Dancing Girl* become an explicit question about the narrative situation of this *shōsetsu*.

That *Vita Sexualis* parodies the I-novel genre should be clear just from the description of Kanai, who, like the figure of Ōgai Gyoshi, seems to embody the author's own notoriously severe critical proclivities but in greatly diminished form that cannot even pretend to stem from detached literary or intellectual interest:

> He [Kanai] reads a great many novels .... But if the authors knew what he thought while reading, they would be furious. He does not look at them as works of art. He wanted (*yōkyū*) a great deal from art, and what they had in the middle of nowhere could not fulfill him in that way. What he enjoys is musing about the psychological states of the authors in writing their stories. When an author thinks he has written something sad or tragic, Kanai finds it extremely funny; when an author seems to have written something intended to be comical, Kanai, on the contrary, finds it sad.[15]

Kanai believes he can penetrate the veil of fiction to arrive at an understanding of the "psychological states" motivating other authors' writing. He reads this way not as the result of aesthetic standards but for the pleasing sense of mastery it provides. The scene is layered with authorial irony. Ōgai here creates a version of himself (the "I" who introduces Kanai) who creates a parodic version of himself (Kanai) who makes assumptions about the relationship between fiction and the real lives of authors who write about themselves. This doubly embedded author, the narrator Kanai, reads naturalist *shōsetsu* against the grain of authorial intent to enjoy the contrast between these writers' egoistic desires to be read in certain ways, on the one hand, and the actual effects of their narratives, on the other. He enjoys surveying the distance between what he imagines the real authors meant to reveal about themselves and the actual sensibilities he discovers in their writing. In this way he triangulates his own position as dispassionate observer—a position that will make him an odd subject for a confession of passions. Indeed, his only passion thus comes to us as a form of irony; his pleasure in reading ironically is recounted to us in the very confessional narrative form he critiques.

Kanai upends naturalist suppositions that novels can convey the real motivations and emotions of authors. He denies the ostensible premise of such writing and disbelieves the accounts of themselves that authors give. However, he nevertheless agrees that confessional *shōsetsu* do convey real human experience and emotion—not by honestly reproducing them but rather by betraying the hidden desires and mental states of authors *while they are writing*. Kanai does not read such texts for their artistic qualities, nor for the sensations produced by immersion in their sensual descriptions, but rather for the perverse pleasure of the detached critique of authors that they make available for him by the very failure of their immersive appeal. Of course, this method of reading invites readers to apply the very same interpretive criteria to Kanai's own account (and to those of his embedded and real authors).

Kanai finds himself unaffected by the sexually charged scenes in naturalist literature, but strangely stimulated by the meta-textual question "Why did authors want to write about such proclivities? He simply thought that the portraits of sexual desire painted by these individual authors were rather abnormal; perhaps novelists and poets were just exceptionally perverse."[16] The hermeneutic thrill of interpreting the intentions behind these *shōsetsu* trumps the sexual titillation at which the authors apparently aim, at least for this "frigid" narrator. For Kanai, the novel lays bare an essential narcissism; it does not provide authentic access to the lives of others but rather reveals the (authorial) desire that informs acts of writing and reading about others' lives. The perspicacious reader, Kanai suggests, can discern in the mechanisms of novel realism the real operations of power whereby authors attempt to establish themselves in positions of authority.

Of course, Kanai's desire to read this way also participates in the same dynamic of self-empowerment and leads him to take up the pen himself. Ōgai exposes his protagonist's underlying motives for this "clear" and "frank" account of his sexual "history" from the beginning. Even before Kanai thought about confessional literature, or sexuality, we are told, he expressed a desire to make himself known on the literary scene: "Sometimes he thought that he would like to write something himself .... perhaps a novel or a play."[17] Ōgai furthermore informs us that Kanai felt "stimulated" (*giyō*) by his earlier reading of Sōseki, in whom he sensed a potential literary rival whom he felt he could best. However, Kanai also felt disgusted by the failed Sōseki imitations published by other writers. Rather than end up like them, he decided to not write fiction himself.

Kanai decides instead to "set down in black and white his own desires, so that he might reflect on them. If he wrote about them clearly, he might learn something about himself [*jibun ga jibun de wakaru darō*]. And he might learn whether his own sexuality was normal or abnormal."[18] Kanai writes to grasp his life story on his own terms, and to make it available for his own interpretation, drawing on the mimetic power of prose narrative to secure the validity of his claims. But of course we have been told by Kanai's author, our frame narrator, that his interest in writing about sexual desire only became aroused by his interest in other writers' accounts of sexual desire. Both the sexual and textual in *Vita Sexualis* prove equally driven by desires to imitate, outdo, and, thereby, master others.[19]

What we learn about Kanai, then, is that he wants to distinguish himself from other would-be imitative authors whose works do not command respect but rather become objects of derision. He wants to write, like the authors he admires, but also to remain in the position of reading subject, rather than read body of work. He desires to achieve the authority he imputes to the position of the author, but cowers from the realization that once he publishes he may be subject to the critical gaze of others like himself. His strategy in the face of this is to preempt interpretation through continual acts of self-reading. This embedded author thus turns to self-consciousness as a protective rather than constructively critical enterprise—but as with *The Dancing Girl*, we shall discover that his aims are not exactly those of his author.

The desires central to the story are not so much sexual or interpersonal (indeed, this confession about sexuality seems devoid of anything tantalizing) but rather those that motivate and structure his act of confession itself. *Vita Sexualis* is hardly the inquiry into sexual desires that Kanai imagines it to be. It is, rather, an account of the desire for literary authority that inspires Kanai's *narrative* quest. The account describes itself as the prehistory of its own composition.

Kanai's story appears to have much less to do with his relations with others than with his attitudes toward himself and his desire to be the sole authoritative subject of his life story. And just as the story told by Ōta (in *The Dancing Girl*) works against his ostensible purposes, so too does Kanai's sexual confession wind up implicating his approach to literary representation in his impoverished attitudes toward and treatment of others. One of the overarching ironies of the text lies in the fact that Kanai has internalized and adopted the kind of self-absorbed consciousness modeled in the confessional literature he has read, despite his contempt for its falsity. His interior monologues take shape according to conventions of novel narration; as he lives his life (or at least insofar as he describes himself having lived his life), he imagines himself telling the story of those events, already reducing others to characters in his narrative even as he interacts in real life. Moments of potential intimacy become fodder for his story. His constant awareness of himself as the sole (narrating) subject detaches him from life, including even his triumviri of friends who themselves, along with Kanai, disdain almost all of their classmates for a variety of superficial reasons.

Kanai positions himself throughout his tale as an observer and keen interpreter of the lives of others, as we see for example when he scrutinizes his maid's features and determines baselessly that she has probably developed a crush on him. The aloof self-positioning in fact becomes almost literal in the description of his point of view: "It was as though having been caught up in a violent maelstrom I had been flung atop a cliff and was now gazing at the tumult of the waves. Everyone was mirrored in my eyes with perfect objectivity."[20] By figuring himself as a detached, transcendent subject (even noting his own past failures from his present position of enlightenment), Kanai acts very much like the exile in "Who is Ōgai Gyoshi." He in fact laments the very same confusion between real and written selves as we found in the earlier essay:

> What I wrote attracted some attention .... It had aspects that were lyrical, novelistic, and based on historical research. Some decided to call it a novel and then judge it inferior even to miscellanea in the news. Though the word "passionate" (*jōnetsu*) had not come into circulation, if it had, they would have said it lacked passion .... Similarly, the phrase "self-vindication" (*jikobengo*), used juridically with regard guilt had not come into use. But I think that there is no art of any kind that is not "self-vindication." That is because life is a form

of self-vindication. Because the life of every being is self-vindication .... [The protective] mimicry [of animals] is self-vindication. Writing is self-vindication by the same logic. Fortunately ... I did not run into criticism ... [that] cast doubt on the right of my work to exist. That was because so-called criticism, whose own right to exist is even more dubious, and which has nothing intellectual or emotional to offer anyone, had not yet been invented.[21]

Kanai writes not to communicate something to others but to affirm the superiority of his vantage. He sees all writing as an effort at "self-vindication" for the guilty offenses of its authors. Yet what is the offense that *Vita Sexualis* hopes to vindicate?

Given the ostensible topic of the story, we might assume it to have been some illicit sexual encounter, except that we are told Kanai did not feel guilty but rather "enjoyed the [few] peccadilloes he committed."[22] Furthermore, Ōgai takes pains to describe Kanai's passivity (and therefore implied lack of responsibility): "He never was moved so strongly by sexual desire that of his own accord he asserted himself aggressively."[23] There is one thing Kanai does seem reluctant to reveal (besides his passive manipulation of others to avoid the responsibilities entailed by active engagement), however: his indulgence in masturbation: "Back then I developed a bad habit. It is difficult to record, but all of this writing would be worthless if I left it out, so I must document it now," leaving this obscure note to accomplish the "documentation" it claims imperative.[24]

Kanai's guilty pseudo-confession here suggests that at least one "crime" his writing attempts to vindicate may not be any particular action toward others but rather his tendency to take pleasure privately rather than to pursue real intimacy. His masturbation allowed him to avoid contact with others and to dwell only on the images he conjured of them—as explicitly dramatized, for example, in one of the more arousing scenes when he ran from his friend Eiichi's mother's inviting sensuality, only to lie in the grass and "imagine a plethora of images."[25] In this solitary sexual practice he becomes the author of his own fantasies. What this *shōsetsu* chronicles is the way that solipsistic habits condition his literary and interpersonal engagements as well as his sexual ones.

In the story told, Kanai spends his few interpersonal sexual encounters making private and often disparaging judgments of his "partners." At the narrative level, the writing Kanai remains focused entirely on establishing the validity of his point of view without giving a thought to fleshing out the perspectives or personalities of anyone else. *Vita Sexualis* thus links Kanai's self-centered sexual practice and the detached, aloof perspective of his first-person narrative writing. The extended cogitation on both the nature of writing and his own critical reception only makes sense in light of the *shōsetsu*'s thematic conflation of his sexual and literary desire. References to books, reading, and writing as means of identifying with or defining oneself against others come up about as frequently as references to sexual desire or attraction between individuals—indeed, the "attraction" and lack of "passion" that Kanai discusses in the quote above do not concern sexuality but rather his writing. His "confession" really does uncover the truth of the mind of the author, but not by conveying his past internal states to readers. Rather, it reveals how his own investment in authorial detachment continues to preclude the kinds of authentic communication and connections that could produce more passionate and evocative writing. We will find a recurrence of this dynamic in the narration of *The Wild Goose*.

Kanai is too invested in the project of self-authorization to engage in either the kinds of writing or relationships that would allow others to emerge as interesting subjects in their own right. In his "romantic" relations, he fails to experience love (which the introduction specifically notes "is not the same as sexual desire even though it may be closely related to it") or anything like reciprocity. He discusses marriage, potential romantic interests, and intercourse solely in terms of his personal interest or lack thereof. His writing manifests these same sensibilities: he fails to represent anyone else in a way that gives them any sense of independent life or meaning beyond that which they acquire for him as elements in a self-study. Herein, of course, lies the authorial indictment of the genre of confessional novels.

The tyranny of Kanai's subjective vision, and the egocentric desire that underlies it, becomes more evident to Kanai in the course of writing the narrative. The reflective act eventually leads him full circle to contemplate the very self-vindication his writing enacts. In other words, there is indeed a narrative telos of self-discovery at work. However, it does not occur in the movement from past self to the author who begins writing from an enlightened position. Rather, this process takes place in and through the narrative level, over the course of the writing of the *shōsetsu* itself.

The "truth" of the desire that Kanai uncovers through his narrative act reflects the one that structures his writing, creating an echo chamber that evacuates his account of passion and reproduces the repetitive self-absorption of his youthful sexual habit. In the conclusion, Ōgai tells us from a presumably "authorial" perspective that "Once [Kanai] put down his pen and thought about it, he began to suspect the emptiness of writing arbitrarily about these random encounters."[26] Crucially, it is not the emptiness of the encounters themselves but of *writing about the encounters* that absorbs his attention and constitutes the denouement of the tale.

Kanai's speculation about the monotonous and mechanical nature of his own writing leads him to recognize that its failure lies in his inability to connect meaningfully with others:

> There was no possibility of passion in mere desire without love, and even Kanai had to realize that what lacked passion was unsuitable for an autobiography.
> He decided, firmly, to stop writing.... It might seem to others that he had lost his passion.... However, he knew himself too well, and his self-awareness dried up his passion in even in its incipient state.[27]

Kanai cannot commit himself to the act of textual production; he cannot denude his passionless self before the judgmental eyes of others. He discovers, then, that his acts of writing have not been creative but masturbatory. This discovery, in turn, leads to a narrative fracture: the Kanai who puts down his pen and the narrator who continues to make this act the subject of autobiographical reflection cannot fully coincide. Far from suturing together past and present self, the confessional novel form has led to irreparable rupture and the exposure of the fictional quality of the project.

The failings Kanai discovers in his personality, and consequently in his autobiographical project, are also those for which Ōgai himself has been held accountable, especially in criticism of this *shōsetsu*. Writers and critics from his contemporaries to ours have consistently maintained that Ōgai's writing in it overintellectualizes and often fails to achieve the aesthetically evocative, unflinchingly true-to-life portrait of individual experience that it declares to take as its aim. Few critics in the twentieth century even recognized *Vita Sexualis* as parody, and none has ever discussed the dissonance between narrating and authorial selves as consistent with reflexivity in his other writing. By now, however, we can see that what *The Dancing Girl* accomplishes more subtly, through its quiet tension between story and frame, becomes the explicit modus operandi and open theme of *Vita Sexualis*: a turn to self-critique as a means of mitigating complicity in the processes of self-authorization that operate through conventions of novel realism.

A Monologic Dialogism: Reflexive Critique as Ethical Posture

In his 1930s "Discourse in the Novel," Russian literary scholar Mikhail Bakhtin proposes that the novel is distinguished as a genre for its inclusion of multiple languages (in its representation of the speech and thoughts of others as well as for its incorporation of a variety of literary and nonliterary languages), and for its capacity to concretely embody multiple ideologies in the striations of language it comprises. This orchestration of different languages performs for Bakhtin a fundamentally ethical work, materializing and putting in contact worldviews and discursive systems that differ from one another, and thereby permitting and validating diverse interpretive postures. By allowing multiple worldviews and subject positions (as concretized by particular configurations of language) to coexist and exert influence on one another, while also invoking and influencing reader response, the heteroglossic plurality of novelistic writing can prevent the hegemonic operation of what Bakhtin calls "authoritative discourse." "Authoritative discourse" insists on particular modes of reception and foists upon its audience singular interpretations that are to be accepted on the basis of the authoritative ethos of the source. Such writing forecloses interpretive possibilities and insists on submission to its own discursive norms.

For Bakhtin, novelistic discourse is liberating. It maximizes the intrinsic "dialogism" of the word, the socially pluralist composition of language that causes it to ring with multiple voices and make room for heterogeneous meanings, expressions, and interpretations beyond those of any given language-user's intentions. The dialogism of the novel stands at the opposite end of a continuum from monologism, wherein discourse arranges its utterances in one clear authoritative view whose meanings are constrained by organization into stylistic homogeneity. Bakhtin's work, in particular his theories of heteroglossia and dialogism in the novel, has been at the core of formal approaches to narratology around the world, as it provides a direct link between discursive form and real-world ethics not dependent on thematic depictions or specific ideological, political, or other real-world values or circumstances.

Ōgai's work does not quite fit into the picture Bakhtin paints; it even speaks against it in some ways. Ōgai has little faith or interest in the capacity of the novel to make room for alterity within the spaces of hegemonic discursive structures. His *oeuvre* is rather both an exploration and interrogation of the capacity of the novel to delimit and authorize points of view by virtue of its instrumentation of narrative form and novel conventions. Much of his fiction destabilizes novel ethos by working through (sometimes competing) monologic registers to reveal and reflect upon the power of novel conventions to naturalize the sensibilities of narrators and authors.

In other words, Ōgai works through authorial irony and narrative frames to achieve a double-voicing accomplished by making authorial presence, and the limitations imposed by its authoritative discourse, so resonant with the story told that it cannot be ignored. In the dialogue of his characters he makes little effort to represent diverse manners of inhabiting language or subject positions with authenticity. However, by thematizing the critical desire of his authorial personae, he creates space for reflection on the complicities of novel representation. In *Vita Sexualis*, Ōgai effectively dialogizes the monologic perspective of his embedded narrator by literally presenting readers with a second authorial self whose extradiegetic presence ironizes Kanai's pretensions to authority. The external narrator and the first-person authorial character speak with the same self-centered verbosity, but the very dissonance in characterological point of view holds Kanai's monologism up for critique and implies the same for the narrative persona.

Vita Sexualis undermines the pretenses toward authenticity and realism of the *I-novel* and in the same gesture fleshes out a fuller version of the ethics of self-consciousness explored in Ōgai's earlier writing. The divorce between his narrator's desire and the author's own intent materializes in incontrovertible difference (whereas in *The Dancing Girl* the effects are much more subtle): the *shōsetsu* that Ōgai completes and publishes cannot be the one that Kanai abandons, especially not given the presence of the external narrator. The contextualizing authorial frames make Kanai's literary and sexual desires, and their relationship to his narrative act, themselves the subject of fictional authorial inquiry, and not merely the motivation behind confessional writing.

The story that this *shōsetsu* tells of Kanai's self-centered incapacity to recognize sex as a shared, relational activity, figures metaphorically his failure as a writer to achieve any kind of dialogic fullness or vibrant, polyphonic reality in his text. Kanai's ethical failings manifest themselves in the monotonous style that smothers all points of view save his own.[28] The story told by the narrative framing of this autobiographical confession, however, overshadows the insubstantial tale of Kanai's life itself and deconstructs the methods, aims, and effects of the *I-novel*. Where Kanai's project fails, Ōgai's *Vita Sexualis* succeeds, at least insofar the *shōsetsu* foregrounds the relation of Kanai's story to its narrative frame, creating what Bakhtin might call a "double-voicedness" that speaks through the monologic narration with authorial irony. *Vita Sexualis* performs through its distinctly nonheteroglossic composition what Bakhtin theorizes as one of the definitive functions of the heteroglossic novel: "dramatiz[ing] the gaps that always exist between what is told and the telling of it, constantly experimenting with social, discursive, and narrative asymmetries."[29]

The experimental, half-parodic but nevertheless sustained investment in the confessional mode along with the monologic voice of its narrator and the dissonant interjections of authorial voice in the introduction and conclusion have made *Vita Sexualis* difficult for critics to categorize. Neither true confession nor psychological study nor work of literary criticism nor genuine autobiography,[30] *Vita Sexualis* challenges readers by obfuscating the stance of its implied author toward the "history" its narrator presents. From *Vita Sexualis* onward, Ōgai created even more thoroughly and explicitly dissonant perspectives in his *shōsetsu*. His writing continued to reflect on, and thematize, its own formal and rhetorical strategies. These practices culminate in what the next chapter will show to be the pronounced "stereoscopic vision" of his last work of nonhistorical fiction, *The Wild Goose*. After that, even Ōgai's historical fiction continued to call attention to its own narrative framing, though less through the opposition of implied author and first-person narrator than through the even starker dissonance created between literary and nonliterary languages. That is, by virtue of their vantage outside the realm of pure fiction, Ōgai's historical writing revealed the novel to be what Bakhtin would later formulate as a "self-critical genre capable of revising the fundamental concepts of literariness."[31]

Setting *Vita Sexualis* alongside Bakhtin's theory of the novel reveals how the creative self-theorization in Ōgai's work claims for the novel an ethical capacity illuminated by, but running almost contrary to, the one described in "Discourse in the Novel." For Bakhtin, the potential of novel heteroglossia to liberate language from authoritative constraints that delimit its capacity to represent, express, and engage readers in experiences of otherness constitutes its ethical potential. In his work, self-consciousness and irony serve as modes and mechanisms of the novel delivery of heteroglossia via what he called double-voicing, or the way multiple points of view could speak and refract through utterances. However, such manners of style and their reflections of authorial subjectivity are far from integral ethical functions in themselves. Indeed, too much authorial presence threatens the ethical and formal foundations of novelistic writing for Bakhtin. A purely Bakhtinian analysis of Ōgai would yield the kinds of criticism that have historically been levelled at Ōgai's monologic prose. However, *Vita Sexualis* doubles down on its own monologism, ironizing through the doubling of authorial figures the tyranny of subjectivity that forecloses the potential of its narration to achieve the kinds of intimacy confessional literature pretends to portray. This "ethics of self-consciousness" works quite differently from heteroglossia but to similar ends: fostering awareness in readers of the potential calcification of narrative forms and the violent effects of such arrogations of linguistic authority on our capacity to engage others ethically. I suggest that we consider Ōgai's self-theorization of novel form as a counterpoint to Bakhtin and explore further the operations of an ethics of self-consciousness in modern Japanese fiction and other global traditions of novel writing.

4

Triangulating an Ethos: Ethical Criticism, Novel Alterity, and Mori Ōgai's "Stereoscopic Vision"

Introduction

In this chapter, I take up the last nonhistorical *shōsetsu* by Mori Ōgai, *The Wild Goose* (*Gan*; 1911), with three main purposes in mind. First, I want to challenge critical consensus on both Ōgai's supposed eschewal of ethics and the apparent failure of the work.[1] Second, I claim that this *shōsetsu* represents a culmination of the immanent ethical critique of novel form that Ōgai's earlier writing explored, rather than the break from his previous work that scholarship has generally assumed. Finally, I conclude that the *shōsetsu* anticipates methodologies being explored by criticism today and can help revitalize approaches to novel "alterity" and demonstrate the potential value of metafiction for theories of novel ethics.[2]

The Culmination of an Ethics of Self-Consciousness

Upon his 1889 return from four years in Germany, Ōgai established himself in the literary scene through critical commentaries on questions of novel perspective and aesthetics, then cemented his fame through both translations of European literature and original works of prose fiction. His work, as we have seen so far, vigilantly interrogated, critiqued, and experimented with the novel form even while interpolating it into the radically different context of modern Japan.[3]

Though skeptical of what he saw as the deceit implicit in the illusion of mimesis and "authenticity" (cast in his criticism as *shinri*, *shinsō*, etc.) on which the novel seemed to depend for its production of pathos, Ōgai recognized the power of ethos in producing such illusions. He sought to capitalize on the power of ethos to move and compel judgments from readers while experimenting with reflexivity to expose and critique the ethics and effects of narrative manipulation that produce such ethos. In his earliest prose fiction, such as *The Dancing Girl* (*Maihime*; 1890) and *Foam on the Waves* (*Utakata no ki*; 1890), Ōgai produced this reflexive critique more subtly, creating faint disjunctions between his embedded narrators' points of view and those of his implied authors. In contrast, Ōgai's mid- and later career fiction (e.g., the 1909 *Vita Sexualis* and the 1911 "Delusions" [*Mōsō*]) becomes more explicit about its critical exploration of how formal problems of *shōsetsu* writing may be implicated in ethical ones. *The Wild Goose*, his last work of pure fiction, foregrounds its construction of narrative ethos so jarringly that it has met with widespread criticism in Japanese and English language scholarship. Even proponents of *The Wild Goose* largely argue that it represents an interesting and insightful failure to achieve an objective perspective in fiction, a turning point in the career of a man who subsequently abandoned fiction for the "truth" of historical novels.

Speaking broadly of Ōgai's final works of fiction, Shiokawa Tetsuya typifies this perspective by arguing that "the point of view of Ōgai's narrators no longer remained fixed, and a fissure irrupted into the authenticity of his narration," resulting in deep "flaws."[4] Such critical response stems in part from the long-standing notion that for Ōgai, whose thinking was informed as much by Confucian ethics of honesty as by critical study of novel aesthetics, the aim of novel representation was the authentic reproduction of experience through realism. It may also stem from the fact that until recently, the terms of ethical literary criticism applied to modern Japanese writing within the Japanese tradition differed greatly from those of formal and aesthetic criticism, making it difficult to recognize *The Wild Goose*'s unique insights: that the aesthetics of the novel emerge as part and parcel of the ethics of its formal approaches to the representation of alterity, and that both ethics and aesthetics might be enhanced, rather than undermined, by self-conscious reflection on the methods through which they are produced.

The Wild Goose directly concerns the ethics of narrative manipulation. It tells the story of individuals who establish and vie for power in their relationships by appropriating the lives and discourses of others in self-serving narrative performances. The narration sometimes becomes absorbed by its own empathetic portrayal of characters whose thoughts and voices literally take over the first-person narration (at times effacing the narrator). At other times, the narrator's reflections on himself and his act of writing take over the story, foregrounding his narrative manipulations of other characters and raising questions about his own credibility as a writer let alone moral agent. As it happens, the story itself concerns problems of manipulation and appropriation; at every level, then, we confront questions about the capacity of discourse to represent perspectives and desires of others. In the end, *The Wild Goose* turns out to be *about* the ethics of narrative representation that it investigates through its formal experimentation.

The Wild Goose's Formal Ethics: Complicities of Novel Perspective

Ōgai consistently interrogated even as he sought to expand the novel's capacity to represent the world with authenticity and to transcend the subjective points of view of an individual narrator or author. In *The Dilemma of the Modern*, Dennis Washburn notes that Ōgai had a strong suspicion of "the relativistic sense of knowledge implied by the reliance on the validity of each individual's understanding of life" promoted by novels.[5] As he continued to experiment with the genre throughout his career, Ōgai became increasingly concerned with the limits of realism and subjectivity in novel point of view. *The Wild Goose* represents a struggle against those limits; as Washburn puts it, Ōgai turned to "parodic narrative that turns the convention of the romance on its head in order to deal with the issue of credibility or reliability of fiction as a means of conveying truth."[6]

The anti-romance parody of *The Wild Goose* takes effect chiefly through the mock-heroic plot. Our narrator retells a story told to him by the protagonist: Okada. In that story, the handsome protagonist Okada discovers a beautiful woman, Otama, at the mercy of the selfish moneylender Suezo. Okada slays a snake that attacked Otama's lovebirds and thereby appears to gain her heart. In the end, however, Okada fails to act the part of the romantic lead. On his last day before heading overseas, he wanders off with the narrator (who may have purposefully thwarted a tryst) and winds up killing a wild goose instead of taking Otama up on an obvious invitation. These elements all play on romantic conventions and genre expectations. Yet they are framed in a displaced, unstable, confessional "realist" mode that raises its own set of "modern" expectations which are never satisfyingly integrated with the romantic elements.

The first-person narrator of the main story frequently makes remarks designed to establish his credibility and the reality of his account. He situates himself in real life by mentioning Japanese landmarks near the familiar haunts of the flesh-and-blood author, claims to have witnessed much of what happens, and establishes himself as a close acquaintance of the protagonist. Yet midway through the *shōsetsu*, the narrating "I" disappears almost completely and the narration shifts into the perspectives of Otama, her father, Suezo, and even Suezo's wife with the perspectival freedom of earlier forms of Japanese *gesaku* or *monogatari*. This unsettling, unjustified change to more free-form and omniscient storytelling cannot be justified by the illusion of first-person confessional realism the narrator cultivated so painstakingly from the start, a mode which had taken root as a paradigmatic form of novel "authenticity" in Japan during the first decades of the twentieth century (especially in the form of what have retrospectively been called *I-novels*). The narrator's promotion of himself as character-witness to real events is undermined by the employment of his narrative omniscience, forcing readers to consider questions of his reliability and motivation in telling the tale itself.

Washburn argues that the formal contradictions in *The Wild Goose* are deliberate; for him, they signal Ōgai's pessimism about the possibility of achieving truth in fiction. He sees Ōgai's work as the embodiment of a struggle against the ambiguities of literary form and language in hopes of achieving the closest thing to authentic representation. On Washburn's view, *The Wild Goose* represents a final purely fictional assay against the problematic relation of fiction and reality, which Ōgai then went on to address through meticulous fidelity to historical documents in his *rekishi shōsetsu* (historical novels).

This assessment of *The Wild Goose* as orchestrating the failure of romantic and realist conventions is generous compared to more canonical views. Ikeuchi Kenji notes that most critics have read *The Wild Goose* as riddled with abortive digression and internal contradictions, which, they argue, represents Ōgai's frustration with the enterprise of writing fiction that he subsequently "abandoned."[7] The inconsistencies in its narrative structure, coupled with the apparently inexplicable shift in focus to characters on the periphery of the main story, have led to condemnation of the story typified by Richard Bowring and Masao Miyoshi's views that the novel's awkward, disjointed structure belies its failure.[8] Yet as my analyses in the previous chapter suggest, narrative perspective in Ōgai's novels often aims to produce the kinds of discordance these critics lament, for both ethical and aesthetic purposes. *The Wild Goose* simply does this more boldly and self-consciously than his earlier fiction.

The novel begins with the line "Furui hanashi de aru" (This is an old story), which, as Stephen Snyder notes, recalls the formulaic opening from traditional Japanese fiction *Ima wa mukashi* (literally "Now it is then").[9] The traditional phrase is generally used to situate a story in a distant, perhaps mythical past (much the way the phrase "Once upon a time" functions in English); it also creates expectations for fantastic or romantic elements in the story. With *The Wild Goose*, however, Ōgai puts the ancient phrase in modern vernacular, signaling the *shōsetsu*'s ambivalent positioning vis-à-vis opposing modes of literary representation: those of classical Chinese or Japanese tales and those of the "modern novel." The tension between these modes bears directly on the ethics of the story. Are we reading a fanciful tale whose fabrications bear no responsibility to be credible or authentic, and need only contribute to an aesthetically or ethically rewarding "design"? Or are we reading a story about contemporary reality in which we are to invest our sympathies and judgments as we would in real life?[10] *The Wild Goose* foregrounds its ambivalent relationship to genre from the beginning, prompting readers to reflect on the very interpretive conventions that structure their apprehension of the ethics of its representations.

The *shōsetsu* ties the problem of its genre to the problem of its narrator's perspective. As noted, the narrator takes great pains to emphasize the realism of his tale, repeatedly noting that he himself witnessed events and often invoking the existence of some real landmark or shop to further establish authenticity. "What Okada would do on these walks was nothing more than to stop in briefly at one used bookstore and then continue along his walk until the next. There are even two or three of those bookstores from that age … still standing today …."[11] Tellingly, his claims to have merely transcribed "reality" wind up situating the story more squarely in the *bundan* (literary world) than the real one. The landmarks supposedly situating the novel in the real world are all book lenders. Furthermore, the narrator marks the time in which the novel takes place by discussing literary rather than political or cultural history. He comments, for example, on the difference in literary sensibilities between the time the story takes place and the time of writing, and then uses those literary references to describe Okada.[12] Indeed, even Okada views the world through a literary lens: "Okada's literary taste amounted to nothing more than an interest in reading about new happenings in the world through poetic forms."[13] Indeed, we are told that the chief motor of desire in the embedded story, Okada's view of women, developed from his sentimental literary taste.[14]

The narrator further establishes the credibility and reliability of his knowledge of Okada by explaining that he used to share a wall with the protagonist, in a dormitory situated at the epicenter of several circular routes to the book lenders. The story would not even exist, the narrator continues, had he not gotten to know Okada by virtue of their mutual habit of strolling by and patronizing those shops, and through a particular episode in which they bid for the same book of fiction.[15] This transaction literally gave them their first occasion to exchange words, in two senses: insofar as they address each other for the first time, and insofar as the narrator lends Okada the book in question after winning the bid.

Even if we accept at face value the narrator's claim that he has faithfully rendered reality (a claim made more dubious by later revelations), that reality itself proves at every turn underwritten by the literary. The gestures with which the narrator establishes his presence and credibility all turn out to depend on the circulation of written texts. The route between book lenders is the main thoroughfare of the novel, the only orbit along which any of the main characters connect. Despite having lived in the same dormitory for months, and despite the narrator's interest in this "other" with similar habits and personality traits, they did not cross the wall separating their rooms (or the social customs and habits of character preventing spontaneous intrusion) until their mutual desire to possess a work of literature made the interaction (or transgression) possible.

Through its constant literary references, the narrator's discourse works against his claims of immediacy and presence to foreground its narrative transformation of reality into fiction. We cannot but recognize its deferred, retrospective, and *written* quality. This transformation is highlighted by the slide it enacts from the opening to closing sentences, whose parallelism itself speaks to carefully controlled literary design, especially in a serialized novel written over the span of a year. The novel begins by describing itself in the first sentence as an "old story" using the word *hanashi*, a term for speech, conversation, informal "news" about someone—literally "something to say," grounding the tale in the vernacular of contemporary reality. In the last sentence, however, the narrator refers to the tale as a *monogatari*, which (like *hanashi*) literally means "something told," but has been employed since antiquity to designate crafted stories or works of prose fiction, highlighting its intentional structure as a literary work.

The Wild Goose thus works in several ways to dispel the illusion of self-presence on which its realism seems to be premised, destabilizing the implicit surety of its narrative perspective. The prominent evidence of literary design, in conjunction with the shifts between first-person and other narrative points of view, calls into question the authenticity of the narrator's reportedly journalistic account, and consequently his own motives in presenting it as he does. Why has he taken such pains to produce reality effects and to justify his imaginative leaps into other minds when the novel itself lays so bare the fictional qualities of those endeavors?

By so effortlessly constructing an atmosphere of first-person realism and then violating the conventions on which this mimetic illusion is predicated, *The Wild Goose* calls attention to the technical problems of novel representation that it fails to smooth over. As Washburn notes, "The ambivalent quality of the narrative voice in *The Wild Goose* represents a crucial step in the development of Ōgai's concept of fiction: it makes central the difficulties created by the influence of the narrative voice—even a detached, supposedly objective voice—asserts on the story."[16] The tensions in point of view have led many critics to dismiss it as a failed aesthetic experiment, incapable of either surmounting "the problem of fiction" (Stephen Snyder's term for the problematic relationship between the artificial rhetoric of realist fiction and the truth or reality it strives to represent) or even establishing some kind of aesthetically coherent point of view. Yet I suggest that it is the very power of the novel to hold its various modalities in tension, and thereby to reframe and self-consciously work through the "problem of fiction" itself, that epitomized the genre for Ōgai.

Keith Vincent, in his excellent study *Two-Timing Modernity: Homosocial Narrative in Modern Japanese Fiction*, draws attention to the overlaying of dissonant narrative perspectives accomplished by the shifts in focalization to ask ethical questions about how the writing discloses the operations of power through social and literary conventions. He notes that the narrator's judgments of Okada often emerge most from moments when we follow, omnisciently, the experiences of Otama: "As Otama watches the students, the reader senses not just her perspective, as a woman, on this culture of male students, but also the narrator's own. Thus ... *The Wild Goose* is mediated by a perspective that is simultaneously male *and* female."[17] Vincent's work reminds us that what few voices are allowed to emerge in the *shōsetsu* are overshadowed by the narrator's own, but also that the effects of their presence reverberate into theme and storytelling, making the ethics of representation central to the narrative handling of alterity that the authorial persona cannot acknowledge on its own terms.

Ōgai emphasizes the role that desire plays in both conditioning writing and structuring novel plot. What we encounter in *The Wild Goose* is a distinctly *triangular* desire strikingly consonant with what French literary theorist René Girard sees as the essence of the novel in *Deceit, Desire, and the Novel* (1961). Girard argues that the purpose of the novel is to "reveal the presence of the mediator."[18] When a hero pursues a love interest or other goal, Girard suggests, this is not merely a linear desire. Rather, the "object" of affection has become desirable because the hero sees it as having been desirable for another, one to whom the hero imputes authority. The hero's imitative or "mimetic" desire to occupy the place of this "mediator" sets into motion the plot of the novel. The accomplishment of the novel on this view is in fact to reveal to readers that the hero's ostensibly spontaneous, object-oriented desire is really an effect of social mediation, a metaphysical desire for a position of authority represented by another subject who is not consciously the object of attention.

The plot of *The Wild Goose* indeed revolves around a triangular relationship between hero, heroine, and narrator. Yet Ōgai's object here is not to reflect like Girard on the psychology of desire by dramatizing its revelation in a love triangle. Rather, he brings into view the (triangular) desire for literary authority that inheres at the narrative level of the story. What Girard would call metaphysical desire turns out to structure the narrative frame of this *shōsetsu* far more powerfully than it does the relationships in the story told, where Girard looks for it.[19] As Vincent puts it, "the rivalry between the two men has been transmuted and absorbed within the very form of the narrative itself."[20]

Parallels in the way the narrator positions himself with respect to both the story and its telling turn out to betray a metaphysical desire. At the narrative level, he positions himself partially within and partially outside the plot of the story he tells, claiming to have been present for some parts and only learned others retrospectively, secondhand. He draws on real biographical details from Ōgai's life (locating himself in the same dormitory during the same year Ōgai lived there, for example) and mixes them with fictional inventions, hinting at his "real" identity but then deliberately donning a fictional mask. With respect to the events of the story, he declares himself an uninvolved bystander but then hints at a deeper relationship with Otama. He calls himself Okada's friend, but then deliberately withholds information that could help him, and casts his "friend" in an increasingly skeptical light. The narrator's desires ambivalently condition his mode of writing in the same way that they condition his representations of himself and others.

Observing the odd resonances between his writing and written personae, Atsuko Sakaki notes that the narrator has conflicting desires to be both author and hero.[21] She draws the conclusion that there are in fact two distinct narrators, suggesting that the central dynamic of the story is the contest between a "narrator-character," who desires to assert himself over Okada by winning Otama, and the "encoded author" who wants to establish his authority over the entire narrative as such, even at the expense of the credibility of his character-self. The need for such a stark and artificial division disappears, however, if we consider the ambivalence in the narrator's self-presentation as expressing one and the same metaphysical desire for a kind of narrative authority. The narrator is not a separate character from the self he represents, nor does he have two different and wholly distinct desires (interpersonal on the one hand and authorial on the other). Rather, what differs is the field of reception of what is in both instances an essentially *narrative* desire.

The claim of narrative desire is easy to make for the writing persona, but what of the self he describes, who seems to have a more strictly object-oriented desire? First and foremost, we have seen that "reality" in the fictional world of *The Wild Goose* is in fact an essentially textual world whose reality is underwritten by reference to literature. Accordingly, the narrator's rivalry with Okada is not merely for the position of the hero (and possession of Otama). To assume this is to overlook the key role narrative itself plays in instigating their rivalry. The very occasion for their relationship is the fact that they both bid for possession of the same book (which the narrator won). Moreover, although the narrator had already seen Otama, he thought nothing of her until he heard Okada's *tale* of a potential romantic connection with the beautiful woman. Only the transformation of the woman into an object of Okada's storytelling—an object further compared to the love interest of an old Chinese tale—arouses the narrator's desire to retell the story on his own terms (a dynamic we have now seen structuring the narrative form of *Vita Sexualis* as well). What Okada represents for the narrator is not simply the place of the hero but equally a position of textual authority—the place of the author. The story of the narrator's actions is the expression of the mimetic desire he feels upon his encounter with Okada's embedded *story*; what we read is the aggressive wresting into the narrator's own words of a tale originally belonging to Okada himself.[22]

The narrator applies the same methods to achieve his ends in both the story and narration: he dissembles (and indeed the act of dissembling through fiction is the real subject of this tale). After hearing how Okada wound up killing a snake that threatened Otama's lovebirds, the narrator realizes that Okada has found himself living one of the romances that he so avidly read, and that Okada may have even found the very type of heroine he so idealizes. Yet the narrator stifles his urge to tell Okada of this revelation, probably because he realizes that Okada might then recognize the value of pursuing Otama. Within the story world, then, the narrator reserves the exclusive right to orchestrate and make sense of the unfolding story of their relationship at the expense of his "friend's" understanding and potential romance.

The narrator manipulates the narration of *The Wild Goose* to the same ends that he prevaricates in his discourse with Okada, and with resonant ethical implications. Early in the novel, he uses his retrospective insight to point out Okada's blindness to his own desire, showing his rival's failure to understand Otama's feelings or to act on his own. The narrator thus implicitly positions himself as the better suitor and more perspicacious reader of both self and situation. He also points out the moral deficiency in the way that Okada later failed to reveal certain information to him (something he has just let us know he also did within the story world). He then takes a kind of narrative-level revenge for Okada's efforts to keep the narrator on the periphery of Okada's story by claiming a position of superior insight, aware not only of everything Okada knew but also of Okada's duplicitous intent in withholding information. The narration becomes a means of ensuring that the narrator has the final word. By using reported speech rather than direct quotes to represent Okada's dialogue, he quite literally takes over his rival's position as narrator of the man's own tale. The narrator's interactions with Okada and his construction of the text of *The Wild Goose* itself thus both prove structured by the same methods of self-assertion. Consequently, we should be alert to the ways that his attitudes toward characters and actions in the represented world correspond with his narrative activity in the text itself, both in the story, with respect to his *narrative* treatment of other characters, and in terms of his engagement with his readers.

In the end, the narrator dissembles with respect to *readers* as well as his supposed rival in the text. He directly refuses to address questions about his own involvement with Otama through a final injunction against the reader's curiosity. In the last sentences of the story, when he claims to have heard part of the story directly from Otama herself, the narrator insists that the matter of how he came to know her lies "outside the scope of the story" and that readers should "refrain from idle speculation."[23] He limits the reader's ability to question his claims and his motives, maintaining the authority of his account and shielding himself from accusations of bias or betrayal. In other words, he tries to make it as difficult as possible for readers to wrest from *him* the tale he wrested from Okada, preventing readers from contextualizing it in ways that could undermine his authority or reveal him to be driven by same desires he claims to be observing and revealing from an unaffected, objective distance. He hides his desire from the reader (who implicitly winds up occupying the role of "rival" over the narrative itself) in precisely the way Okada attempted to hide his own desire from the narrator.

The deceptive narrative practices mirror rather precisely the methods through which Okada previously attempted to deceive the narrator. And just as Okada's efforts at dissembling end up exposing rather than masking his desires, so too do the narrator's various strategies to maintain control over the narrative of *The Wild Goose* fail to cohere in ways that reveal to readers how personal desires structure his purportedly objective storytelling activity. The story the narrator tells turns out to reflect precisely the kinds of ethical problems that condition its telling. Exploring the ethical entanglements the narrator maps out in the parts of the tale that seem least related to or even consistent with the main storyline, then, may help us understand the effects of the novel's dissonant structure and see how our experience of its (aesthetic) form ultimately depends upon its ethical positioning vis-à-vis the representation of others.

A Colonizing Imagination: Suezo as Reader

The reading preferences of Otama's father, the acquisitive moneylender Suezo's strategies for dealing with his wife Otsune, and Otsune's mental reflection on her own responses to Suezo have almost no bearing on the central story of the romance (or anti-romance) that the narrator insists, in his own words, is "the story of which I must make Okada the protagonist."[24] The scenes on which the novel lingers so long have emotionally compelling dimensions, and the narration itself adroitly leads us through the various points of view in ways that round out our understandings of characters who seemed one-dimensional from narrator's perspective. Yet there is no obvious aesthetic justification for their inclusion. These side dramas do not wind up coming together with the main storyline through plot twists that make them relevant, and the shifts in narrative perspective required to tell these tales are never satisfyingly justified. It is only by recognizing the ethical dimensions of their concern with narrative form that we can discover how these long "digressions" attain their relevance. For in these scenes we find dramatizations of the ethics of narrative performance, scenes of "reading" and interpreting the accounts of others that bear directly on methods and ethical inquiry of the *shōsetsu* as a whole. For the sake of expedience I will focus only on some of the attention paid to the character of Suezo.

Through the omniscient narration we observe Suezo as a voyeuristic spectator of the lives of others. Even Otama's moving account of her difficult past, "the joy, anger, pathos, and humor [*kidoairaku*] she and her father had experienced over the years," becomes to him merely a pleasing aesthetic effect: "Rather than listening to the substance of her story [*hanashi*], he listened to her voice, like the chirping of bell-crickets in a basket, and smiled without thinking at the twittering sound."[25] The contentment he feels comes not from greater understanding or intimacy but from the sensory pleasure of his experience of the telling itself. The pathos of her account becomes for him the arbitrary content of the form of experience he seeks, which confirms his privileged position as listener with no responsibility to respond sympathetically.

The scene bears little relevance to Okada's story. However, the ethical questions raised by it resonate uncannily. Okada's translation of Otama from a potential subject of interpersonal interaction into an object of aesthetic appreciation (there is a strong suggestion that he abandoned her to her fate to enhance his own image of her tragic beauty) mirrors Suezo's own treatment of her. And of course Okada's attitude has its origins in his reading of fiction: he found a Chinese tale of a heroine's pathetic struggle against fate so beautiful that it shaped his vision of ideal femininity. In both cases, the men apprehend the stories of women and their oppressive circumstances as aesthetic pleasures modeled on what they knew from reading experiences, rather than as occasions to respond or consider their own roles in those circumstances. Both Suezo and Okada, then, ignore Otama's real needs and transform her distress into the substance of gratifying tales—as, perhaps, our narrator does as well. In Suezo's case even more prominently than in Okada's, however, it is clearly the *form* of the story and not its content that sets his desire in motion.

Through the characterization of Suezo as a reader of the lives of others, *The Wild Goose* shines a grotesque light on the ways its other characters, narrator, and perhaps readers may take purely aesthetic pleasure in the privilege of getting to know other points of view, rather than ethically transformative experiences.[26] Despite his apparently stereotypical role as a villain in this romance, Suezo turns out to reflect aspects of the protagonist and narrator that may help us establish a clearer understanding of the self-critique the *shōsetsu* performs. His business in fact depends upon his Machiavellian ability to deduce the desires of others from their speech and behavior, allowing him to adopt whatever attitude that will be most profitable in manipulating them. This applies to his personal life as well: at one point, he reads subtle changes in Otama's manner, deduces that something in her attitude has changed, and strategizes to keep her in line. He responds to another moment with his wife by defensively imagining an entire conversation with her, usurping her ability to speak for herself and using his "knowledge" of her likely feelings and responses to anticipate and deflect potential criticism the next time they do talk.[27] He then engages her in actual dialogue only to calculate the extent of her knowledge about his affair, using his understanding of her point of view—which he partly articulates to her as though it were (and because in fact it is not) not her own—to extract information by feigning ignorance or anger. He then deceives her by weaving whatever true facts she knows into a narrative tapestry of lies that she cannot prove false. This rhetorical approach to dealing with his wife reflects some of the manipulative methods of the narration itself, which frequently presumes the right to articulate the unspoken thoughts and feelings of others.

Suezo insists that his wife clarify and justify the vague sense of outrage for which she can find no discursive expression, and he refuses to recognize the validity of feelings that cannot be expressed on the terms he prefers, those of rational debate. Moreover, he shifts a potentially incriminating conversation about his infidelity into economic language of profit and loss, explaining his whereabouts and the necessity of his actions in a register of business dialogue that he knows she cannot fully understand, and therefore cannot deny: "Just as when she was told something about social sanctions, whenever Suezo used those difficult words he read in the newspapers, she felt intimidated and yielded in her ignorance."[28] His wife simply doesn't have the words to represent herself or her feelings on the terms he establishes.

It is not any specific argument, misrepresentation, nor even his unfaithfulness that inflicts such deep suffering on his wife but rather the way his account of himself implicitly establishes normative requirements of relating that leave little room for other positions or modes of response. His ability to construct seamless (and duplicitous) narratives oppresses his wife in ways that exceed mere deception. He controls what we might call with Judith Butler the "scene of address," or the "primary relationality on which any act of representation depends for its ethical orientation."[29] According to Butler, in the process of narrative self-construction, one "recreates and constitutes anew the tacit presumptions about communication and relationality" through which that account establishes its relation to an "other."[30] On her view, narrative acts always risk doing violence to the freedom of others. They may prevent others from accounting for themselves in ways incommensurable with the normative assumptions underwriting the initial narrative act. This is precisely the case with Suezo. His speech suppresses his wife's freedom of expression, causing inner turmoil and forcing her into silence as a means of protecting herself from his "defensive" self-positioning.

The narrator might be said to commit a similar kind of narrative violence against other characters (and, as we shall see in the conclusion, his readers as well). He decides the terms through which they appear as subjects, literally speaks for them or translates their discourse into his own words, deliberately withholds information from them (and from readers), and he emphasizes other characters' manipulations to hide his own. He secures his own position as narrator through his insight into both their desires and the discursive methods through which they seek to realize those desires. These gestures all establish *narrative* control as the condition of authority as a subject, a condition he singularly meets. In this light, his insistence on the reality and authenticity of his account proves a means not only of assuring the aesthetic coherence of the novel as a realist work of art but also of securing the sovereignty of his subject position, at the expense of the freedom of other characters to express themselves differently and, were he to have his way, readers to interpret differently.

By "disorienting" the narrator's first-person account with its perspectival shifts, and by exposing the way the *shōsetsu* is structured by the very metaphysical desire it reveals through its dramatization of triangular relationships, Ōgai problematizes *The Wild Goose*'s narrative coherence and its narrator's aesthetic project in ways that lead us to ask questions about its ethics. The narrative shifts highlight the parallel between the way characters like Suezo presume to understand the perspectives of others, in some cases projecting entire conversations that do not take place (for the purpose of manipulating them later), and the way that the narrator imaginatively constructs the stories of them doing so. This is more than a problem of the narrator's reliability; it is critical to the issues of genre and interpretation that frame our approach to the text and its ethics. The first-person realist confessional novel depends on belief in the authenticity of the confession (and hence the limits of the narrator's knowledge); the omniscient novel conventionally depends on the pretense that the account is reliable, free of the biases of characters in the diegetic world of the work. The narrator's presentation of others' thoughts and speech at times he was not present, the novel's abrupt shifting from obviously first-person narration to something like third-person omniscience and back, and the surfacing of first-person point of view markers in the third-person, virtually omniscient sections destabilize conventions that were rapidly coalescing at the time.

Such disruptions may have intrinsic ethical value insofar as the very coherence of the narration itself "may foreclose an ethical resource—namely, an acceptance of the limits of knowability in oneself and others."[31] As Butler argues, coherence is part of the problem with narrative accounts; it implies the exclusion of other accounts through the illusion of self-sufficiency. The narration of *The Wild Goose*, however, by disrupting its own illusion of coherence, prompts readers to piece together fragments of other perspectives against the narrator's apparent intentions. It thus incorporates within itself contrastive impulses; it invites sympathetic identification with characters at the same time that it calls attention to fabrication and potential bias in the perspective that invites such emotional investment.[32] The story told by the plotted events and those told by the emplotting narration produce a kind of structural interference that leaves us ambivalent about how to invest our emotions.

In the end, the narrator gives us a figure for imagining its various dissonances—and, indeed, the rhetorical strategy of Ōgai over the long course of his career:

> Half of this story comes from intimate exchanges with Okada, but the other half, since his departure, comes incidentally from what I heard through my later acquaintanceship with Otama. It is somewhat like a stereoscope through which we look at two superimposed pictures as if they were one; I created it by casting together in one light what I saw before and what I heard afterward. Readers may want to question me about this. "How did you become familiar with Otama? Under what circumstances did you hear all this?" But the answer to this, as I said already, falls outside the scope of this tale. I will only add that it should go without saying that I lack the necessary qualities to have been Otama's lover; readers are better off avoiding pointless speculation.[33]

This account puts the incommensurability of *The Wild Goose*'s narrative methods in almost synaesthestic terms, combining the *mita* (seen) of immediate personal experience and the retrospective *kiita* (heard) of second-hand dialogue that allows him to transcend the limits of his first-person point of view. The emphasis on the sensory difference is completely unnecessary as a practical justification: the narrator must certainly have *heard* what he "saw" firsthand as well. Whereas for something to be "seen" implies immediate experience, for it to be "heard" in this context suggests mediation through the story of another.

The juxtaposition here highlights how in both fiction and real-life experience we constantly translate different modes of perception into coherent models of reality that ignore the seams, whereby we stitch together potential differences and incompatibilities. The trick of the stereoscope is that it plays upon this habit of apprehension and invites us to forge the *illusion* of a coherent whole out of the juxtaposition of two different images, similar in content but in fact slightly at odds with each other in their perspective. The narrator, too, hopes to play upon the conventions of realism to convince us to ignore the incommensurability between the two perspectives, and to apprehend the text as coherent, even exceptionally "true to life," precisely because it transcends one particular perspective. The self-conscious reflection here invites us to overlay the different points of view and thereby produce a more compelling, realistic effect that is just that—a reality effect.

Ōgai's invocation of the foreign technology of the stereoscope here also plays on the tendency in Western humanities and sciences to privilege the experience of the individual. The illusion of realism and "depth of field" a stereoscope produces is won at the expense of centering perspective on a singular, privileged point of view one must adopt. Maeda Ai's brilliant critique of a resonant interest in perspective and "panoramas" in Ōgai's *The Dancing Girl* corroborates the likelihood that this perspectival technology serves as a metaphor for the *shōsetsu*'s critique of its own narrative structure. Yet it is not merely the first- and third-person points of view that this ending juxtaposes. The self-conscious reflection on narrative structure here also creates a kind of palimpsest wherein the story that plays out in the diegetic world has been overlaid by the story of its own rhetorical, constructed dimensions. Narrator and reader both find themselves having experienced this textual world through two lenses—the immersed "realist" experience of the events of the story and the self-conscious "reflexive" experience of the self-conscious narrative—through which they must, perplexingly and recursively, bring into focus the significance of the composite experience. The story told does not lose its importance in light of the reflexive impulses of the narration; on the contrary, the thickening of novel ethos here makes it even more urgent to attend to the relations and interactions among characters. We need to grasp them in order to fathom the narrator's (and behind him, the author's) intentions in positioning readers as he does, as well as the potential ethical consequences of our responses. In this way, *The Wild Goose* vivifies in the process of dispelling the illusion of mimesis upon which the modern novel seems to depend. By shuttling readers between immersion in the story it tells and self-conscious reflection on the consequences of accepting the premises of its modes of representation, it functions more like a well-executed specimen of novel criticism than a novel per se.

Ōgai's Ethical Aesthetics

Two decades before the writing of *The Wild Goose*, Ōgai insisted that ethical considerations had no place in novel criticism and that aesthetics—as he understood the concept through his exposure to German aesthetic philosophy, particularly that of Eduardo von Hartmann (1842–1906)—alone determined the value of the novel. As I have argued in the previous chapter, his dismissal of novel ethics aimed at scholars who critiqued prose fiction based entirely on its illustration of ethical principles in the *plot*, whereas Ōgai's later critical investigations and experimentation with novelistic writing would lead him to discover an ethics intrinsic to the form and language of the novel. That later writing, which plays heavily on the literary conventions associated with particular kinds of novels, foregrounds the ethical potential of various forms of novelistic writing with increasing clarity—a point also made in Dennis Washburn's convincing argument about manly virtue and the bildungsroman form in Ōgai's second to last work of pure fiction, *Youth* (*Seinen*; 1911), implies. This is not to say that ethics replaced aesthetics as the raison d'être of the novel in Ōgai's view. Rather, his growing insight into the way the novel positions itself ethically through its form led him to think about the way ethics might play a role in constituting the aesthetics of the novel itself, and vice versa, as I will now argue his *The Wild Goose* makes clear.

The Wild Goose achieves its dissonant aesthetic effects by overlaying two stories of manipulation: that of the characters (including the narrator) and that of the narration. The narrator attempts to suture together his claims to first-person experiential authority and third-person authorial omniscience. He does this in such a way as to occlude the mechanisms of his own desire while telling the story of his insight into the workings of the desires of others. The fact that he gives this description of narrative structure in the same breath that he insists readers should not speculate about his involvement with Otama, however, belies the apparent disinterest of his methodology. Questions about the narrator's motivations and the relationship between the narrator and protagonist cannot be disentangled except through the equally imbricated and codependent problem of the narrator's relationship to readers.

By reflexively calling its own methods into question and tying them to the manipulations it exposes, *The Wild Goose* emphasizes the way its ethics inhere as a function of its discursive modes and not merely the story it tells. It thus directs readers toward conclusions that can help us reframe some of those at which contemporary ethical theories of the novel have arrived. Blakey Vermeule, for example, concludes that we read novels in part because the practice of developing and then detaching from our imaginative projections of others, independent of the particular responses we make, cognitively prepares us to meet the ethical and emotional demands of social involvement.[34] Vermeule's argument assumes that "detachment" is the process of turning from novels to engage real life; *The Wild Goose*, however, produces this detachment as a problematic internal effect of the *shōsetsu* itself, one that it demands readers experience and reflect on. It highlights this process through both thematic representation and formal manipulation: each main character projects, engages, and then detaches from projections about other characters in a narrative that itself oscillates between points of view, leaving no alternative for readers but to do the same even if they desire to remain fully immersed. The *shōsetsu* thus involves readers in the shuttling between immersion and reflection that critics today so often undertake in their effort to tease out novel ethos. In other words, *The Wild Goose* does not leave readers in a state of emotional attachment from which they must disengage, but rather keeps them in a perplexed state of oscillation, caught between involved and detached (also first- and third-person) perspectives, as well as between story and narrative frame.

This state defines ethics itself for Geoffrey Harpham, who argues in *Shadows of Ethics* that "ethical inquiry is dominated by two questions: How ought one live? What ought I to do? ... The first reflects the distanced perspective of some deindividualized and ideal being free to consider laws and norms as such; the second, the particular perspective of a real person confronting an actual situation."[35] Harpham claims both perspectives are necessary, and yet also incommensurable and in irresolvable tension, so that the best we can manage is to shuttle between them. He concludes that "[e]thics is about articulating perplexity, not guiding the perplexed."[36] *The Wild Goose* does not merely articulate this perplexity, however, but also draws attention to the very methods through which that articulation takes place, undertaking its own ethical self-theorizing. The *shōsetsu* brings to the fore of readers' consciousness the very problems of perspective and position whose complexity ethical criticism attempts to elucidate. The heavy-handed symbolism of the final scene in *The Wild Goose* could not highlight these operations any more clearly, and therefore makes an ideal point of conclusion for this chapter.

Having just passed Otama's house and arrived at the turning point of their walk, the narrator and Okada encounter a classmate who intends to kill one of the geese in the nearby lake. Before he does, Okada accidentally kills one with the rock he throws in an effort to frighten them off. The classmate, then, asks the narrator and Okada to stand apart from one another and guide his movements as he swims out to the goose. The two take complementary positions according to the principle of *parallax* (which word appears in Roman letters as *Parallaxe*), the idea that an object apparently shifts in position relative to the angle of observation, and that simultaneous observation from two vantage points can work to triangulate its location. There could hardly be a more explicit model for the narrative function of the Girardian paradigm: the object upon which the narrator and hero each fix his gaze is the titular "goose" of the story itself, an obvious substitution for the ostensible love object, Otama, and, of course for the narrative that bears the title. This stark symbolism fuses into one image the thematic interest in triangular desire and narrative interest in perspective, clearly underscoring their parallelism through the parallax view of the story's "stereoscopic" form. The narrator finds himself physically situated in a triangular dynamic that is specifically identified as such, in symbolic contrast to his insistence on the singularity of his detached and uninvolved vantage point.

The unintentional violence with which Okada destroys the goose literalizes the ethical offenses of his having internalized conventional literary representations of women and consequently apprehended Otama as an aesthetic object whose distress renders her beautiful. But the narrator's apparently more insightful apprehension of Otama as a richer figure with her own complex internal life no less relegates her to the status of an object to be "possessed." In fact, his distanced vantage as the "objective" narrator of a realist *shōsetsu* together with his redeployment of the conventions of the romance genre combine to objectify Otama as the (tragic) vanishing point of a stereoscopic vision. What the two men obtain through their triangulation is not the living beauty they desire but the destructive consequences of the colonizing force of that desire, symbolized by the battered and broken goose they proceed to purloin and consume.

The all-too-literary feel of this climactic scene has rankled critics. Such obvious and convenient symbolism only further strains the premise of true confession on which the narrator bases his account. It also strains the efforts of any critical account to give the episode much weight, since there is certainly a self-conscious, tongue-in-cheek element to the accidental death and subsequent struggle to smuggle the unwieldy creature, hidden under Okada's coat, past a nearby policeman—all the while discussing mathematical formulas so as not to appear suspicious. But the scene makes an effective point: that novelistic representation risks reducing alterity to the status of there-for-us objects and covers the violence of its operations through the formulas of convention. *The Wild Goose*'s parodic exposure of its own dependence on the same operations marks its self-conscious resistance to complicity in that violence, whose benefits it nevertheless reaps.

The contradictory impulses of the text, the pull of its sympathetic portrayal of Otama and the distancing push of its self-conscious reflection, engage readers in the oscillation we have seen posited by new ethical theories' accounts of an ethics *of* and *while* reading. At the same time, the narrator's and characters' problematic failures to sympathize and understand the lives of others, on the one hand, and their manipulative narrative appropriations, on the other, leave readers poised uncertainly between an ethics of identification and an ethics of letting be (see note 32). Balancing careful attention to the ethics of narrative representations of alterity through its illustration of social consequences in the story it tells, on the one hand, with an awareness of the degree to which the narrative form of novelistic representation itself bears an ethical responsibility, on the other, *The Wild Goose* puts two of the foremost (current) perspectives on the ethics of the novel in tension in order to create a unique ethics of self-consciousness.

Ōgai's *shōsetsu* makes an exemplary model for contemporary ethical criticism precisely because it both dramatizes and reflects on the situation constitutive of the field of inquiry of ethics itself: the difficulty of negotiating the problems of perspective encountered through our simultaneous and fraught relations to abstract ideals and real individuals. It shows us that novel aesthetics depend upon the same negotiation, and it warns us of the ethical consequences of unreflective acceptance of literary conventions that prove complicit in the same kinds of self-serving narrative manipulations its characters and narrator perpetrate. The ethical imperative of the novel genre, according to *The Wild Goose*, consists in its self-conscious critique of the very interpretive conventions through which it makes itself legible. *The Wild*

Goose demands that readers both engage the text and reflect on the ethics implied by their mode of engagement as part and parcel of the experience of its narrative.

In this sense, *The Wild Goose* incorporates into itself the task that much Anglo-European ethical criticism has reserved for the critic. Even contemporary emphasis on the agency of the reader and the ethics of reading practices depends upon assumptions that the ethical imperative of the novel is to present readers with engaging representations of alterity upon which criticism can reflect. This dependence seems to me a reminder from the pathos-oriented tradition of European and American traditions of realism. Few major contemporary ethical critics, regardless of whether or not they promote ethics of identification or ethics of letting-be, turn primarily to metafiction or surrealism to ground their claims. There are practical reasons: ethical criticism typically posits readers' apprehension of characters as real human subjects in order to substantiate claims about the way literature fosters readers' capacities for "caring" or developing human understanding (whether or not that understanding develops from sympathetic identification or from an acknowledgment of the other's irreducible alterity). Wayne Booth in fact describes the ideal texts for ethical criticism as those in which "the story itself *consists* of the conflict of defensible moral and ethical stances; the action takes place both within the characters in the story and inside the mind of the readers as he or she grapples with conflicting choices that irresistibly demand the reader's judgment."[37] For Booth, resonance between our response to dramatized ethical conflicts and our understanding of the ethical stakes of those conflicts relative to the aims of the novel model the relationship of (realistic) literary representations to real-world ethicality.

Booth's sense of the importance of ethos for ethical criticism depends upon his prioritization of pathos in the representations of novels themselves—on his view, it becomes the task of the ethical critic to derive the ethos of the narration from readings of pathos in the plot, and then to adjudicate whether that ethos conforms with whatever ethical values the critic holds. One way that oppositional ethical theories might attempt to resolve their differences, however, would be to focus on texts like *The Wild Goose*, which deliberately problematize their own representations of human relationships, foregrounding the operations of the novel itself over against those of its characters upon one another. *The Wild Goose* calls attention to the scenes of address, the genre conventions, and the narrative structures through which such representation occurs in ways that raise ethical questions as productively as do those representations themselves. This *shōsetsu* asks ethical critics to follow its own intrinsic, formal critique of the role of ethos in structuring the novel's ethical commitments. By attending to the workings of ethos in fiction that consciously resists or plays upon the tradition of realism from which most pathos-oriented approaches to literary ethics have developed, we may find models for contemporary literary ethicality more conducive to simultaneously and seamlessly engaging in an ethics *of* and *for* reading.

In short, *The Wild Goose* offers a model more than an object for ethical criticism. It performs much of what ethical criticism itself undertakes. Recognition of its accomplishment can help us apprehend the ways novel narration might actively engage ethics through its formal rendering of perspective and positioning of readers; it also points to the possible centrality of self-conscious novels for studies of novel alterity.

5

Akutagawa's Affective Ethics

An Ethics beyond Understanding

Ōgai layered realism and reflexivity in his stereoscopic *shōsetsu*. He employed narrators who frequently reflect on and interpret their own acts of writing even in the process or presenting a novel reality. Perhaps this penchant for overdetermining his narration is part of what Akutagawa Ryūnosuke (1892–1927) decried as a lack of a "poetic spirit" in the older author's work.[1] Through its tightly controlled, chiseled prose and forays into philosophical speculation, not to mention the epigraphic (instances wherein the author speaks through characters) commentary about his own intellectual goals, Ōgai's more self-conscious modes of narration risk reducing the very feelings and desires that motivate it to objects of intellection. Over time, and especially once he begins writing historical fiction, one finds in his work a flattening out of what would become one of Akutagawa's chief concerns with novel writing: literary affect.

We have seen how Mori Ōgai's (1868–1922) last work of nonhistorical fiction, *The Wild Goose* (1911), exposes the manipulative potential of its own invocations of ethos and pathos. Just four years after the publication of that work, Akutagawa broke onto the literary scene with a story that provides its own play on ethos and pathos, and its own brand of ethical self-consciousness, to quite contrastive effects. The 1915 *shōsetsu* "Rashōmon," like Ōgai's *The Wild Goose*, experiments with formal innovation that establishes a parallel between the ethical questions raised in the story it tells and those raised by its telling. Unlike *The Wild Goose*, however, "Rashōmon" does not present a self-conscious critique of novel realism. Rather, it accentuates the fictional quality of its representation and capitalizes upon the capacity of novel aesthetics to engage readers in ethically effective affects. Ultimately, "Rashōmon" explores how aesthetics may give shape to ethical identities in ways that resist or exceed our judgments or beliefs about what is right and wrong.

We can think of the difference between Ōgai's and Akutagawa's treatment of novel ethics in terms of a contemporaneous divide in intellectual approaches to the field of ethics itself, which both writers addressed in critical essays. Two decades prior to the publication of "Rashōmon," German thinkers had begun to distinguish schools of thought that approached ethics as a matter of rational reflexivity from those that considered ethics primarily a matter of affect. German and British philosophers Oswald Külpe, Walter Bowers Pillsbury, and Edward Bradford Titchener categorize philosophical thinking about ethics in their 1895 primer on the classification of philosophical schools, *Introduction to Philosophy*, as follows: "Affective ethics defines the motives of moral volition and action, in accordance with their psychological character, as feelings, emotions, etc. The ethics of reflexion, on the other hand, sees the impulse to morality in deliberation, a reflective process of the reason or the understanding."[2]

The latter understanding of ethics, as a matter of reason and reflection, dominated German philosophical approaches to the field through the latter half of the nineteenth century, while "affective ethics" was more or less relegated to the realm of burgeoning psychoanalytic study that would come into much fuller force in the early twentieth century. As a rigorously scientific thinker who studied German medicine and philosophy in Germany in the late 1880s, Ōgai worked from within the former tradition. He maintained a strong suspicion of psychologized understandings of human experience and the emotions throughout his career. In his late historical fiction, Ōgai almost completely eschewed representations of anything like interiority in favor of detached descriptions of the decisions, comportment, and actions of his heroes. His *shōsetsu* figure good conduct as a matter of bringing the will in line with rational understandings of ethical principles through self-reflection. In his thinking, the novel played an ethical role insofar as it could prompt readers to become conscious of the way their desires and habits were situated within greater networks of power and responsibility. It could make readers cognizant of the ethics of their attitudes toward others through its formalization and aestheticization of the language and narrative acts through which commitments and relations with others, senses of selfhood and subjectivity, and larger values took shape.

In essence, ethics was a matter of real-life responsibility for Ōgai. The novel was an occasion for bringing about contemplation on the way acts of representation could restructure perspectives on real-life decisions and actions. Akutagawa, by contrast, emphasizes aesthetic experience. "Rashōmon," as we shall see, fleshes out the role that affective responses to aesthetics play in the formation of ethical identity. The story expresses deep skepticism about the possibility or wisdom of subordinating affective response to rational judgments or beliefs at all.[3]

The complex relation between representation and real life is the essential thematic, existential, and ethical concern of much of Akutagawa's work. Despite his reputation as an art-for-art's-sake *aesthete*, Akutagawa wrote extensively about what it means to live well and in harmony with others. He sometimes invoked the ideals of *biteki seikatsu*, or "beautiful living," laid out as part of the ethical vision of that other influential importer of German philosophy, Takayama Chogyū (1871–1902). On those views, art became a model for life rather than the reverse. To comport oneself toward aesthetic goals was the essence of the "good life," in contradistinction to following the dictates of moral precepts.[4] Although, like Ōgai, Akutagawa rejects prescriptive morality, the idea of ethical flourishing as both a personal and collective goal remains critical to his vision of literary value.

Art provided a form for and was integral to the notion of ethics in Akutagawa's thinking. Even his most straightforward efforts at articulating theories of real-world ethics almost always refracted understandings of real life through literary sensibilities and references. In his 1925 "The Morals of Tomorrow" (*Ashita no dōtoku*), for example, Akutagawa tries to explain what he sees as the future of moral thought in Japan. He is characteristically dismissive of the idea that moral laws are transcendental rather than contingent; what is transcendental, for Akutagawa, is the transformative experience of beauty—an experience has to do with shared human experience and its expression as well as transmission.

To make his case, Akutagawa draws what appears at first simply an analogy between the development of morality and the development of literary approaches to the representation of realism. He demonstrates how movements and countermovement from romantic to naturalist and then "back" to neo-romantic literary schools not only mirror but directly embody what he sees as the historical development of a dialectic "critical spirit" of morality, one that forms itself in opposition to the morality of preceding ages. The conservatism of realism and the progressive idealism of romanticism each renew the other, as do emphases on collective versus individual bases of identity and value. Theirs is an ongoing argument about how we engage reality and transform it into shareable meaning. His conclusion is that this dialectic itself needs to be transcended and that the novel can serve as a vehicle for reimagining values and catalyzing new perspectives on social reality.[5]

Akutagawa's turn to *shōsetsu* as a means for discussing modern Japanese moralities shows how thoroughly integrated the genre and ethics were in his thinking. He saw the novel as modeling and reshaping the narrative forms through which subjectivities form and values coalesce. Such reshaping was not for him so much a matter of will or reason as it was a consequence of immersion in the transformative experience of aesthetic expression. Indeed, for Akutagawa aesthetic experience represented one of the only domains available to the modern subject for assuming any kind of ethically grounded identity beyond what he saw as the stultifying false consciousness of the age.

Akutagawa writes often of subjects cut off from the social world—marginalized for their social rank, crimes, physical characteristics, talents, or simply by accident—who cannot imagine or achieve any kind of satisfactory integration into society due to their abject statuses. These stories concern their efforts to reconcile themselves to roles and responsibilities vis-à-vis a society from which they feel alienated. In the end, only moments of intense affective experience—usually of the stories, gestures, or images created by others—propel Akutagawa's literary subjects into new identities and relationships. For example, in "Suspicion" (*Giwaku*; 1920) a professor of ethics confronts a powerful blind spot in his self-image as a result of listening to the disturbing tale of an audience member. Likewise, in "Handkerchief" (*Hankechi*; 1916), a professor of colonial studies' satisfaction with his own empathetic nature shatters after reading of a theory of artistic expression of the emotions that challenges his interpretation of a grief-stricken woman's story. In "Yam Gruel" (*Imogayu*; 1916) an accusatory phrase causes a character to discover an unsettling spiritual connection with all of humanity. And as we shall see in this chapter, in "Rashōmon," it is the story of an old crone that propels the protagonist into a new social and ethical identity.

The transformations in values and social positioning that his characters experience do not come about through acts of will or deliberation and decision-making. Whereas Ōgai arrived at self-conscious as an ethical end, for Akutagawa self-consciousness was an anxious point of departure, a condition of the modern subject that potentially precluded authentic relations with others. Rational thought was not a means of marshaling self-interested emotion in the service of a greater good but an entrapping and alienating mode of representation. We find this to be the case most obviously with the protagonist of "Rashōmon," who is paralyzed by the very effort to think about himself or reason his way through an ethical dilemma. But even the narrators of Akutagawa's last works confront the limits of logic and reason as they try to establish more authentic understandings of themselves and others.

Akutagawa insists time and again that ethics gathers its force in something that resists cognition. We find in his writing a continual effort to reach beyond the domain of the intelligible to render present a *nani mono ka* (something), an experience of alterity that threatens the fragile and provisional self-satisfactions that the intellect cultivates through its narrative constructions of self and others. The term "*nani mono ka*" itself occurs in two of the stories noted above: the professor in "Handkerchief" feels the unsettling and threatening presence of *nani mono ka* at the end of the story, and "Suspicion" describes how a *nani mono ka* led one audience member to a fateful ethical decision, one whose unsettling effects are fully transmitted to the stunned and silenced ethics professor by the end of the story. It features dramatically in Akutagawa's last works of fiction as well.

This radically other *nani mono ka*, which manifests as a kind of linguistic aporia, disrupts expressive possibilities and threatens the integrity of the self that experiences it. It negates the very modes of representation through which characters attempt to identify themselves and others. Yet encounters with this alterity have positive valence as well, especially in Akutagawa's earlier works, insofar as they shake subjects out of protective egoistic solipsism and narratives of social identity in which they find themselves captured, and which delimit their capacity to recognize and respond to others. Indeed, the experience of alterity is the defining condition for ethical transformation in these tales. By fracturing the security of the self, the intensity of such experiences makes understanding and identification with others possible—at the risk of a breakdown in self-coherence and with no guarantee that these understandings will be put to good use.

Akutagawa's work throughout his career explores both the potential and the danger of experiencing alterity. Part of this danger is not only that the self may not be able to withstand such experiences (as we find in his last *shōsetsu*) but that it may withstand them too well. Such intense states cannot be maintained, and so the ethical identities achieved through them are plagued by instability. If these experiences do not so overwhelm the self as to lead to madness, there is the opposite risk of their being subsumed by the reflections of an intellect incapable of recognizing alterity except by translating it into something more familiar and self-serving. His narrators, writing from detached or retrospective positions invested in creating a coherent narrative, tend to cast experiences of affective intensities as transient epiphanies extinguished by modern life, perhaps ultimately no more than fantastic projections or hallucinations produced within and experienced by the self. Since they are antithetical to the kinds of sustained identifications through which the metonymic logic of novelistic narrative tends to construct its versions of selfhood, such experiences are frequently ironized or framed by jaded narrators as subjective fantasy or what we might consider psychosis.

Part of the stories that his *shōsetsu* tell, we will find, concerns the efforts of storytellers to transmit rather than merely describe to their audiences the powerful experiences of alterity that transform characters. By putting the self-consciousness of his narrators in tension with their efforts—and those of characters—to represent or respond to alterity, Akutagawa's writing attempts to render the radically other *nani mono ka* present for readers as an affective and potentially transformative force. Knowing that any effort to dramatize the ethical potential of intense affective experiences could only appear an idealistic fantasy of social integration—knowing, in other words, that portraying a state is not the same as evoking one—Akutagawa sought to create from the juxtaposition of the pathos of his characters' often powerful emotional experiences and the ethos of his self-conscious, highly stylized narrative voices, the same kinds of intensely self-aware and often unsettling affective responses as those experienced by his characters who encounter other forms of alterity.

Akutagawa's work on the ethics of the novel remains obscure and undertheorized in part because his aims and methods center on what remains inexpressible and unrepresentable in novel experience. We do not find clear models or lessons about ethics in his *shōsetsu*. As ensuing chapters shall argue, his stories do not occasion ethical reflection in readers so much as they disturb readers by demanding urgent responses to what refuses to fit into our cognitive frameworks of judgment. That very unsettling, I will argue, is given significant ethical value through the interrelation of story and narrative that constitutes Akutagawa's ethics of self-consciousness.

To come to terms with his approach and express its potential contributions to contemporary thinking about literary ethics in this chapter, I draw on Charles Altieri's theory of lyrical ethics. Altieri provides us with a vocabulary for valuing literary affect without reducing its effects to the categories we already have for describing ethics. After first discussing the way that "Rashōmon" both dramatizes and produces for readers unsettling tensions between cognitive and affective values, I will consider how its innovative form of ethical inquiry can help us to refigure the relationship of ethics and aesthetics in both scholarly and novelistic writing.

From the "If" of Reason to the "As If" of Stories: The Novel Ethics of "Rashōmon"

Akutagawa's early *shōsetsu* won fame for their highly stylized aesthetics and carefully wrought plots. They tell tales culled from ancient texts but given distinctly modern psychological and literary inflections. Two of his earliest tales, "Rashōmon" and "Yam Gruel," take up the stories of nameless outcasts who struggle to maintain the meager lives they have staked out for themselves. The substance of the tales might appear sentimental or allegorical in isolation. Yet the rich language and self-conscious narrative perspective through which Akutagawa frames them produces a complex and distinctly literary affect that reminds readers, even as they work through emotional responses to the pathos of the represented stories, that they are engaged in an essentially aesthetic activity framed by the ethos of an artistic sensibility at odds with those of the characters and contexts portrayed. In this chapter and for the sake of expedience I will focus on "Rashōmon," but find that "Yam Gruel" works in very much the same vein.

On the surface, "Rashōmon" describes the way that a moral crisis faced by a recently fired underling resolves itself in dramatic fashion. The tale takes place in an abandoned gate during a period of earthquakes, fires, and famine in the eleventh century. The structures of society have broken down. People steal from one another and break down cultural edifices for the meager benefits of the raw materials they provide. As the story opens, a former servant has just been dismissed from his position and is standing out the rain by a dilapidated two-story gate that serves as a way station along a popular travel route. Unbeknownst to the man, he stands below numerous corpses and the unlikely presence of an old woman stealing hair from the dead—more evidence of a decaying social order. He is trying to decide whether he will starve to death or do the unthinkable and become a thief, with no success. Eventually he ascends to the second floor, meets the crone, hears her story, and makes a fateful decision to rob her and leave her for dead.

The story is derived from a centuries-old *setsuwa*, or spoken tale, often used in Buddhist teaching for the purposes of illustrating principles. The *shōsetsu* signals through this form an edifying resolution, one ultimately denied by the manner of narration and the twist in its conclusion. In analyzing this story, I will first draw out the uncanny parallels between the ethical situation of the world described and the aesthetic features of the story itself, both of which are not merely subject to but constituted by erasures and ambivalences. I will then discuss how ethical reasoning fails to help the protagonist respond to his circumstances, whereas aesthetic encounters propel him into new positions. Finally, I will argue that Akutagawa's retelling of the tale shifts our focus from the pathos of that story to the tension between the substance of the tale and the ethos of its telling. The contrastive juxtaposition between pathos and ethos will prove to be Akutagawa's signature method for involving readers in unsettling experiences of alterity that refuse to resolve into clear moral stances (but may for that very reason be ethically effective).

The protagonist of "Rashōmon" has no control over the circumstances of his expulsion from society. He has trouble thinking through his limited options, and he applies very simple reasoning whenever he decides anything. By contrast, the narrator often shows off his agency, intelligence, and judgment. He belittles the protagonist for crudity, cowardice, and moral turpitude. Yet the very gestures with which the narrator asserts his superiority and authority over his subject and tale turn out to situate him in a position analogous to that of the character. By recognizing this parallel, we can uncover a significant aspect of the ethics of self-consciousness at work in the architecture of *shōsetsu*.

Deteriorating physical and ethical structures described in the world of "Rashōmon" turn out to have clear parallels in cancelings carried out at the narrative level. In the story world we find traces of symbolic institutions that no longer serve their original functions or command respect for their moral or social authority. Temples have been destroyed for their raw materials and the official gate itself bears the remains of ornamentation long since stolen. At the narrative level, we find retractions and erasures in involving descriptions of what turns out not to be present. The narrator tells us, for example, that "in addition to the man there might have been a woman in a straw hat or a man in a soft black cap sheltering from the rain. But there was no one besides the man."[6] The reality effect provided by the detailed evocation of the objects worn by others proves undone by the absence of the very scene it calls to mind. The narrator soon makes a similar gesturing, noting:

> a great number of crows gathered here. In the afternoon, they could be seen circling the high fish-tail ornamentation on the roof, crying as they flapped about. Especially when the sky above the gate reddened with sunset, the crows stood out like a scattering of sesame seeds. The crows, of course, came to peck at the flesh of the dead on the upper floor of the gate. Today, however, perhaps because of the late hour, not a crow could be seen.[7]

These oddly beautiful narrative erasures compose the story world out of an absence compelling for its particularity, creating haunting afterimages of what is not present and reminding readers of the power of the narrator both to determine and to recast the reality of the tale.

An even more obvious narrative vanishing act is performed soon after this moment, one that deconstructs not so much our image of the diegetic world but rather our experience of the narration itself:

> This writer said earlier that the servant was "waiting for the rain to end," but in fact even were the rain to end, the servant did not know what he would do .... Instead of saying that the servant was "waiting for the rain to end," it would have been more fitting to write that "a lowly servant trapped by the rain had nowhere to go and no idea what to do."[8]

Here both the reality of the fictional world and the textuality of the story find themselves refigured in a moment of narrative reflexivity. The narrator acts as though his original act of narration possesses a finality that can be dismantled but not erased, one that leaves its traces even in a future that proves its undoing. The gesture conflates the nature of the situation described (a world in decay) with the character of the narration, marking the discourse as subject to the same uncertainty and ambivalence that characterizes the protagonist's situation. It requires readers to consider the rendering of point of view rather than simply to experience it; narrative perspective becomes part and parcel of the subject of the story.

This statement of course invites us to wonder why the narrator did *not* choose the "more appropriate" description at which he now arrives, or why he did not simply go back and change it once he came to this conclusion, leaving readers none the wiser. It is as though the narrator has become trapped by his own narrative gestures and must struggle to come to revise the terms through which he situates himself vis-à-vis the world of the story—as though the story of the narrator telling the tale is in fact part of the story being told. And, of course, the act of self-reflection here makes this so.

The need for self-revision is precisely what the protagonist faces. The narrative retraction at once revises our understanding of both the protagonist's sense of his situation (he is not waiting but trapped) and the analogous position of the narrator. This already sets the story apart from conventional Buddhist *setsuwa*, wherein a moral message is delivered by recounted events whose narration matters not as an integral part of the tale told but rather for its capacity to engage audiences in an immersive moment and to deliver a moral message. Like the image of crows at the gate or the woman in the hat, the expectations raised by the kernel of *setsuwa* at the heart of the tale are erased even as they linger in the minds of readers.

At both story and narrative levels, then, "Rashōmon" comprises haunting erasures and ambivalences. Even the titular gate, a waypoint in the process of being dismantled on the outskirts of civilization, now home both to corpses and a remnant of the living, seems to hesitate between possibilities.[9] Everything in the story proves as subject to erasure and disappearance as the security of the protagonist, lost as he is in social, financial, and ethical limbo. The narrator who relays these details might himself seem above the fray, playfully ironizing the plight of the lowly servant. Yet he turns out to occupy strikingly similar position. Like the protagonist who swings from one resolution to another, the narrator makes assertions and tries out stances only to revise them. Both vacillate between moments of immersive involvement in the world of the story and moments in which reflexive cogitations about their own thinking blot out that world. Both still imagine identity according to conceptual apparatuses that no longer obtain. The narrator, we should recall, continues to refer to the protagonist as the "lowly servant" despite the fact that the man has lost even that meager title. And both seek a resolution that will confer a *telos* on their ambivalent activity: the servant works toward a resolution to his identity crisis, and the narrator a resolution to his tale.

These resonances make their contrastive approaches to resolving their situations all the more striking. The servant proves remarkably ignorant of his own dispositions and motivations. He responds more or less instinctively to his surroundings, moved by feelings over which he has little control. The narrator can dismissively parse the servant's motives by explaining, for example, that he was "moved by six parts fear and four parts curiosity," but the servant himself is merely driven by his experiences of the world around him (he came to the gate to take shelter from the rain, with no other plan) rather than by conscious decision.[10] He has thoughts about what he should do but hesitates to act on his moral ruminations largely out of cowardice. A lack of willpower renders his reasoning useless as a guide to action. The servant thus vacillates between the two possibilities before him (to starve or to become a thief) without approaching any kind of resolution:

> If he didn't choose—the servant's thoughts kept aimlessly ranging back and forth between along the same path, ultimately leaving him in this situation. Yet this "if," no matter how much time passed, remained an "if." While affirming that he would have to do whatever was necessary, he could not muster the courage to affirm those words that necessarily followed this "if," namely, that "there was nothing to do but become a thief."[11]

When he proposes it to himself as a matter of rational decision-making, in the logical form of an "if" proposition, the dilemma proves intractable. His thinking is caught up in an obsolete episteme of conventional moral reasoning that offers nothing but a self-destructive paradox (as the narrator says, "he had to do something in a situation for which there was nothing to be done"), from which no amount of thinking can free him.[12] A coherent ethical identity, and the force of will required to realize that identity in the current social milieu, is not achievable through rational reflection on the options available in the failing social and moral frameworks of society. The servant can only cease to exist or abandon the social system from which his very sense of selfhood derives.

What moves him toward one choice and then another is not logic but his involuntary, affective responses to the appearance and situation of another person and, ultimately, her story. When he first discovers the crone picking at corpses, the servant experiences a surge of emotion that wells up into an ethical stance, one that explicitly defies rationality.

> A burning hatred for evil rose in his breast like the torch the old woman had set on the floor. Of course, he had no idea why she was pulling hair from the dead, and so had no idea how to judge the good or evil of the situation logically. However, to him, on this rainy night, on this Rashomon gate, the act of pulling hair from the dead was by itself already an unforgiveable evil.[13]

It is notably the servant's aesthetic reaction to the repulsiveness of the scene, and not logic, that moves him to assume an ethical attitude and push past the impasse of his reasoning.

He decides that he will become righteous and just in the future.

The servant's response to the crone's actions moves him to imagine himself taking a particular ethical stance. However, this projected self-image remains abstract and unrealizable. He does nothing. The moment lacks the force required to propel him beyond the gravity of his paradox and to assume the role of a barely imagined ethical self through concrete choice. For that to occur, the *story* of the crone is required. Once she tells him the story of her own ethical crisis, ostensibly to solicit sympathy for the circumstances that drove her to the evil act of stealing from the dead, the servant finally leaps into action.

The difference between these moments is crucial. In the latter case, the imaginative identification built into the conditional "as if" of her tale, its invitation to put himself in her place as if he were experiencing what she related, transports him beyond the impasse of the logical "if" of his reasoning. Courage spontaneously builds within him as he listens; her story realizes for him, through the repositioning required by its summons to identify and sympathize, an identity position he could but vaguely imagine earlier. His loathing of her ugliness and that of her actions coalesces into a passionate fury that her tale allows him to marshal in the construction of a new attitude and, finally, an action.

The narration follows closely his posture of listening, showing him "fingering his pimple" (an index of his ugly humanity) as "courage formed in his heart while he listened."[14] He is transformed as the tale progresses, and not simply by the flawed logical reasoning he gives as a rationalization in the end. This courage gathers itself as a physiological force and viscerally moves him, though "in the opposite direction" to his earlier resolve. It is through his participation in the "as if" of her story that he leaps into action, robbing and leaving the woman for dead by claiming, "Well then, you won't blame me for stripping you of those clothes. I, too, am a body that will starve to death if I don't."[15] The inadequacy of his own self-justification at the end serves only to underscore the impoverishment of reasoning and its falsification of the rich array of human experience, perception, feeling, and thought that gives rise to our ethical identities.

That the servant's ultimate decision to abuse and rob a destitute and defenseless old woman violates most moral standards need not lead to the common conclusion that Akutagawa simply cared more about aesthetics than ethics. This is almost exactly what Sako Jun'ichiro concludes in his study *Ethical Explorations in Modern Japanese Literature* (*Kindai nihon bungaku no rinriteki tankyū*; 1966). According to Sako, Akutagawa saw human nature as depraved and flawed; therefore, he turned to aesthetic art as refuge rather than means of engaging reality.[16] Yet the ethics of Akutagawa's art has less to do with the moral choices modeled by characters in his stories than the multivalent states of affective engagement and self-reflection in which those stories engage readers.

In so much of Akutagawa's writing, affective responses to expressive forms, and to narratives in particular, allow dramatic personae to make projective identifications and thereby—for better or worse—radically transform their senses of themselves and their relationships with others. His *shōsetsu* also explore their capacities to engage readers in similarly unsettling and potentially transformative moments. "Rashōmon" is not only the story of the servant's experience but also the story of the narrator's stance toward that experience, and inasmuch faces readers with the challenges of working out their interrelation and coming to terms with the very different kinds of valuing they invoke. The force of the story's ending comes not simply from the germ of life that begins to grow within the protagonist's breast but from the contrast between that brutal vivacity, along with its terrible consequence, and the quiet conclusion in which the servant escapes the purview of the narration by fleeing the gate, as though the detached narrator were bound to the liminal discursive space of Rashōmon, permanently subject to the very undecidability to which he had condemned the now-escaped servant precisely because he could not marshal the will to take a stand himself.

The ambivalence of the narrator's attitude toward the servant's decision, and the narrator's own performance of ambivalence (the retracing and vanishing acts) in the writing of "Rashōmon," confronts readers with a dilemma analogous to the one in which the story situates the servant. We face vexing options in working out our responses to the ambiguous implied values of the work. We can hardly valorize the attack on a destitute and infirm old woman without dismantling or abandoning whatever value systems we brought to the text. Merely condemning the decision, however, is to ignore the significant tensions in the story, to discount its vitality and insistence on an indomitable animal will to survive in the face of an oppressive and opaque ethical quandary, as well its systematic undermining of precisely the kind of rational value judgments no longer effective in the broken age of the story-world. Our ethical values and aesthetic sensibilities thus find themselves in conflict, making it difficult to fathom how we feel about the experience of the story, let alone how we are invited to feel.

The story has prepared us for this ambivalence by having shuttled us from sympathy with the servant's plight to amusement at his self-righteousness to bemusement at the emotional adjustments he must make with each new event in the unfolding story. The contradictory crosscurrents of feeling and judgment that the protagonist experiences both cause and resonate with those occasioned by the contradictory demands of the narrative representation. There is no simple way to construct an attitude toward the story that both responds adequately to its aesthetic demands and situates itself stably within an implied ethos. "Rashōmon" thus embroils readers in ethically and aesthetically ambiguous territory analogous to that in which the servant finds himself. We face, as he did, the problem of translating our affective responses into stances that accord with both our ethical sense of ourselves and our desires for (aesthetic) satisfaction.

An Affective Ethics

How can we understand the contrast between the story's ultimate refusal of ethical resolution and the careful story-level and narrative-level plotting that make conflicts among feelings and ethics both the means and object of experience? It is too simple to conclude that Akutagawa simply showcases the failure of ethics, as embodied by the failing social order and the polarized idea of justice in the protagonist's thinking. That is, after all, the starting point of the story. To draw more robust conclusions and create fuller accounts of the energies the story expends on the relation between ethics and aesthetics, we must consider more carefully the role of affect in his work.

Akutagawa employs an ethics of self-conscious that works quite differently from that of Ōgai despite some essential similarities. Both writers ironize the perspectives of literary personae and leave readers with ambivalences about their own sympathies.[17] In Akutagawa's *shōsetsu*, however, the narrator stands above the fray of the diegetic world and has no clear agenda in expiating guilt or justifying choices. Readers of his fiction are not led to ultimate revelations about authorial manipulation or even their own complicity in wielding narrative or interpretive authority. Awareness of authorial mastery and manipulation is impressed upon us from the opening moments of many of his stories, if not as directly as in "Rashōmon," then through the wry reflexivity of artfully fashioned prose that so strikingly contrasts with the personalities and worldviews of his protagonists. In Akutagawa's hands an ethics of self-consciousness does not work to interrogate the formal commitments of novelistic narration. Instead, it brings into focus the conditional, fictional qualities of novel experience itself. The reflexivity at work in the narration clouds the transparency of realism throughout its thickened experience of literary aesthetics. It calls to consciousness its own formal artifice and the unreality of its story even while depending for its effects on our investments in the diegetic world. "Rashōmon" insists that much of what matters to us is our own consciousness of the pleasures of its experience *as* unassimilable fiction.

By complicating moral judgment (especially but not exclusively through its potential endorsement of an ethically deplorable action) and by insisting on the unreality of a story that exists at the whim of the author, "Rashōmon" vexes the conventional approaches of most ethical criticism. It tends to leave readers perplexed as to how to marshal their affective responses into acceptable or even coherent dispositions toward the story told. If we recall, however, Geoffrey

Harpham proposed that what literature can contribute to ethics might have more to do with "articulating perplexity" than with providing guidance or rational propositions for contemplation. On his view, literature can help us engage ethics by involving us in modulation between first-person moral dilemmas ("what should I do?") and third-person ethical uncertainties ("how should one live?").[18] The experience of the incommensurability or irreconcilability of the different demands made by each of these approaches has value, for Harpham, insofar as it provides supplementary terms and contrastive perspectives for expanding our capacities to respond to otherness. The kinds of fictional projections required of ethical reasoning (imagining from other points of view, for example) suggest for Harpham the value of literary experience that can provide terms and grounds for self-reflection and working through confusion.

In *The Particulars of Rapture: An Aesthetics of the Affects*, Charles Altieri echoes this sentiment but suggests that scholarship in general has emphasized conscious reflection over against the more immediate practices of feeling and affective response that compose our ethical orientations. He highlights the emotional and conative difficulties we face vis-à-vis our situations within limited perspectives and networks of social and political power that may foreclose in advance possibilities of ethical comportment. In addition, he points to the failures of language even in describing let alone engaging such difficulties, noting that the terms on which we regard ethical questions have generally privileged cognitive understanding and those emotions predicated on identification or sympathy. In the process of analyzing Foucault's advocacy for an ethics of care of the self, Altieri echoes but reformulates Harpham's perspectivalist approach so that it no longer implies rational choice as the measure of ethicality. He suggests that an ethical goal which the experience of art can foster is to "develop modes of identification that enable us to modulate from first-person intensities to second- and third-person forms for adapting ourselves to social demands and social values."[19] In other words, we need both the immediacy of our felt enmeshment in the presence of alterity and some vantage grounded in the social world, and we need to experience these vividly and without capture within stultifying illusions or ideologies.

For Altieri, this is where literary affect can play a crucial role. Affects are part and parcel of our ethical situation insofar as they "emerge as immediate aspects of the kind of attention we pay to the world and to ourselves."[20] Literary affect in particular, because it occurs as immediate personal experience but also takes shape through the representation and invocation of social norms and other points of view, and because it has been arranged as part of a worldview whose composition matters for its aesthetic efficacy, can involve us in ethical modulation between perspectives. It can move us into states of caring and identification while also requiring us to check those feelings against the ethos of the text which provides frameworks for valuing our responses. Novelistic fiction like Akutagawa's that intentionally shuttles us between immersion and reflection can perform particularly useful ethical work because it incorporates reflexive attention to the differences in perspective and valuing that its opposition of pathos and ethos engenders.

So far we have come to see how, in general, literature that employs an ethics of self-consciousness and keeps us suspended or shuttling between immersion and reflection might help us develop an ethically useful plasticity in our habits of imagining and responding to otherness. Now I want to consider the value of what "Rashōmon" accomplishes through its invocation of certain affects and what it casts as an urgent but unresolvable ethical dilemma. What does its articulation of ethical perplexity yield for readers, and how can it help us understand the potential of an ethics of self-consciousness to produce innovative forms of novel ethics?

Akutagawa, as we have already seen in "The Morals of Tomorrow," found scientific and utilitarian argument about ethics pernicious. He preferred to explore the capacities of literature to move subjects into new existential and social frames of experience. "Rashōmon" makes a particularly useful case study for such explorations because it dramatizes the very dynamic (that of a subject ethically reshaped as a result of encounter with a story) in which it seeks to engage readers, providing a form of self-theorization against which we can compare its narrative effects. The story's challenge to epistemes of morality can prove especially instructive for scholarship that struggles to do justice to the ethical accomplishments of literature without reducing them to what can already by recognized within given frameworks of value.

We can learn from both the methodology and thematization of the relation between literary affect and ethics in "Rashōmon" once we call into focus the roles that affect and imagination can play in ethics more broadly. Affects motivate but precede the conversion of our responses to stimuli into recognizable stances. They "call our attention to how those states [assemblages of feelings not yet organized into stances] take on significance for the imagination …. Feelings become affects when they introduce *asness* into the core of sensation."[21] Crucially, it is the conditional modality of metaphoric transformation, the *asness* which feelings can bring to experiences, that mobilizes them as affect by staging their relevance for the imagination. The imagination translates aesthetic experience into ethical potential; it is "our way of opening ourselves to being affected" and "our means of escape from hermeneutic views of expression into performative ones," whereby we take action rather than merely exerting a will to understanding.[22] Sensations and feelings become socially relevant as affect.

"Rashōmon," as we have seen, directly contrasts the effects of rational reflection with those of feelings and, ultimately, affects occasioned by the experience of the crone's tale. The lowly servant's imagination fails him when he tries to reason through his situation; he cannot muster the will to act on the options he envisions. His feelings of revulsion upon seeing her do indeed move him closer to assuming a new ethical identity. However, they lack the cohesiveness, longevity, and conviction to transform him; they offer no social ground for staking out a viable subject position. The crone's story, however, stirs his imagination powerfully through its invitation to imagine the situation *as* another. It is quite explicitly an invitation to organize feelings aroused by aesthetic response into a socially meaningful emotion like sympathy. The results she intended may have been controverted, but the very reversal of expectation illustrates the power of the storytelling medium (over against intention) to transform affect into ethical consequence.

This dramatization of the relation of storytelling to the production of affect in the story told provides us with a basis for theorizing the ethical value of the *shōsetsu*'s own engagement of readers and its contributions to our understanding of novel ethics. It models for us an experience of the relation of ethics and aesthetics that it places in mise-en-abyme relation to the one that it occasions in readers. Like the servant, however, critics have found it difficult to formulate the methods and stakes of its engagement in vivid and meaningful terms.

In part because of its commitments to the language of philosophy, scholarship in general has an impoverished vocabulary for expressing how literary affect engages us ethically. As Altieri explains it:

> At one pole, there is a range of states open to self-reflection that are too subtle or transient to have much to do with cognition or with rational appraisal.... [T]hese affects simply enliven our participation in moments as they pass.... At the other pole, ..., there are many self-dramatizing possibilities within affective life that tend to establish their own rewards and to be difficult to reconcile with efforts at rational assessment.[23]

Literary experience can shake us from the strictures of moralizing imagination, whereby we conceive of ethics as principles and precepts for conduct rather than an openness to the immediacy and contingency of the demands and effects of encounters with alterity. Part of what can be distinct and ethically effective about literary experience is the vividness with which it can involve us in the processes whereby sensations and feelings cathect into affect and attitude.[24] Literary affects that entail powerful reflexive dimensions, furthermore, can help us to attend and therefore take responsibility for those processes, even if they do not offer any clear-cut application to behavior or principles. By giving readers experience in attending to the ways that affective responses build into attitudes, and then by affording opportunities to reflect on the differences between those attitudes and both the solicitations of novel ethos and, separately, our own beliefs, literary works that employ an ethics of self-consciousness can be uniquely effective in prompting readers to comport themselves differently in addition to providing new perspectives on our own ethical dispositions.

"Rashōmon" celebrates and involves readers in affective states much more in tension with our ideals of judgment than those forms of understanding that best lend themselves to discourse on ethics. The *shōsetsu* troubles rather than clarifies our efforts to come to terms with its ethics even while it requires us to feel and reflect on them. Yet the refusal of literary affect to resolve into legible ethical stances may have substantial value for readers. Altieri makes the case for the ethical value of lyricism not despite but because of the difficulty of identifying the kinds of ethical positions it makes available. "The sudden sense of finding oneself vividly aware, but not cogently positioned, offers strong incentives for trying to understand how one might then formulate a position for the self capable of incorporating phenomena for which one has no belief categories."[25] Literary affect, in other words, can induce us to construct for ourselves new ethical postures to accommodate the unstructured feelings that move us, and so can be a force for ethical transformation precisely because it does not fit into established schema or self-images.

Conclusion

In "Rashōmon," the tension between the pathos of the protagonist's plight and the ethos of the reflexive storytelling precludes the easy deployment of literary affect into clear attitudes. The story neither evades its problematic entanglement with ethical commitments nor diminishes its aesthetic force by resolving those entanglements. Indeed, it makes the difficulty of coming to satisfying terms with its effects on both the subject and mode of its experience. At both story and narrative levels, the *shōsetsu* draws attention to the processes whereby aesthetic response may give rise to ethical attitudes without the involvement of will or conscious reflection. As such, "Rashōmon" affords readers a vantage on how ethical stances come to be composed by the experience of literary affect through the perspectival apparatus of narrative fiction.

Ethical criticism typically endeavors to clarify the frameworks of judgment appropriate for adjudicating the ethics of novels and our responses to them. "Rashōmon," however, reveals the ineffectualness of such an approach. It acknowledges the powerful and insistent role that cognition plays in our efforts to thrive even while it refuses to subordinate ethics to reason. As we have seen, part of what the *shōsetsu* accomplishes is the fostering of self-consciousness with respect to the ways that our dispositions form and take on ethical valence. However, the *shōsetsu* insists that the kinds of identifications we make through reflection on our values and identities play at best a second-order role with respect to our ethical orientations. What moves us is the organization of feeling into the kinds of affects and emotions that propel us into orientations toward others.

The ethics of self-consciousness at work in "Rashōmon" engages readers in multivalent states of simultaneous feeling and reflexive consciousness that may move us beyond the perspectives we can imagine for ourselves. It also distinguishes itself from the methods of Ōgai, who also created tensions between the ethos of narrative perspective and the pathos of dramatized story. Ōgai employed reflexivity to call into question the ethics of novel realism, ultimately subordinating pathos to an ethos of self-critique. By contrast, Akutagawa plays upon the manifestly fictional qualities of his stories ("Rashōmon" is framed by its own narrative as a found tale) to embroil readers in irresolvable conflicts between feeling and judgment, immersion and reflection. By keeping us poised between possibilities, and also keeping the conditional qualities of his worlds, their status as fictions, in plain view, Akutagawa investigates the possibilities of a distinctly novel affect to involve readers in ethically freighted experiences that have more to do with dismantling the (largely cognitivist) assumptions we may have about our ethical identities than with dramatizing any particular lesson.

"Rashōmon" ultimately leaves readers both to consider and to feel the way that aesthetic responses marshal themselves in ethical attitudes that exceed the categories we have for apprehending them. Over the course of Akutagawa's career, the works that most deeply explore the relationship of affect and ethics do so with increasingly metaliterary inflections. The tale told by the mocking "Yam Gruel" narrator resonates uncannily with the actions taken by a young lord who forces the lowly protagonist to enact a fantastical story of desire. The 1920 *shōsetsu* "Green Onions" (*Negi*), which we shall examine in the next chapter, makes an even more overtly metafictional turn, whereby an intrusive narrator reminds us continually that we are reading a short story cobbled together for his own purposes. And in his final works, autobiographical personae seem to intuit the fact that they exist as fictional characters in an all-too-literary worlds. With each successive work, the narrative situation becomes further embedded within increasingly self-reflexive metaliterary frames, with fraught implications for the kinds of relations and ethical reorientations that novel affect might facilitate in readers.

Over the course of his career, Akutagawa pushes toward the farthest edges of this technique, testing its viability in increasingly complicated variations until the form can scarcely maintain the kinds of tension between ethos and pathos that prove ethically and aesthetically transformative. If Akutagawa despairs in the end, it is not because of his failure as an artist. Rather, it is because the tensions he explored could not be sustained indefinitely. Yet the very failure of an ethics of self-consciousness in his work opens the door for a dramatic and powerful new turn. As we shall find, his later and especially his final texts employ a devastatingly reflexive ethics of self-consciousness that compellingly engages the *nani mono ka* beyond the self which had always haunted his writing.

6

The "Real" Tears of Fictional Readers: Akutagawa's "Green Onions"

The Unreal Ethics of Mimetic Worlds

As I have argued in previous chapters, theories of novel ethics overwhelmingly assume that the ethical efficacy of the genre derives principally from its mimetic representations of human beings in particular situations.[1] It is our cognitive and emotional responses to the pathos of novel realism and its representations of alterity, our engagements with characters *as if* they were real human beings, that situate us in the realm of ethics for most critics—even if they differ widely on what that means or how we should respond to novel representation. In presuming so, however, ethical criticism renders itself particularly vulnerable to objections like those raised by Candace Vogler in her 2007 "The Moral of the Story." Vogler takes the provocatively contrarian position that the novel cannot model or engage ethics at all. She agrees that novels seem to offer ideal opportunities for ethical critics, especially since for any given dramatized situation, novels make every relevant detail available for analysis, including sometimes the thoughts and feelings of all involved parties. Novels thus provide controlled environments wherein readers can test their judgments and draw conclusions whose accuracy or value can be assessed against the designed outcomes and ethos of the story. This view aligns what Catharine Gallagher argues in her claim that the rise of the novel corresponded with urbanization and the need for readers to experiment risk-free with the consequences of their judgments and emotional investments in strangers. It also accords with Blakey Vermeule's argument, in *Why Do We Care about Literary Characters?*, that literature provides an "offline" forum for exploring our theories of mind and ethical identities.

For Vogler it is the very attractive ideality of novel experience that constitutes its fatal flaw: real human beings simply are not knowable in this way. Characters, she reasons, are mere images, aesthetic elements in a fictional artwork that exist for the sake of readerly apprehension and gratification. To believe that our understandings of dramatized experiences give us ethical insight, for Vogler, is positively frightening, since it implies that it may serve our ethical interests to acquire the kind of totalizing knowledge of others that readers are invited to have of characters. It would be monstrous, she jokes, if we tried to apply novel ethics: we would have to follow our friends into intimate moments, read their diaries, hide under their beds, and access their inmost thoughts and feelings. Significantly, Vogler denies the novel real-world ethical value without contesting the assumption that the novel engages ethics primarily through its mimetic representations of human agents—in fact, her position equally depends upon this assumption. But this is precisely what the ethics of self-consciousness developed by modern Japanese novelists contests.

The *shōsetsu* of Ōgai and Akutagawa complicate and at times directly undermine their invitations for readers to imagine characters as real people. Ōgai calls attention to the complicities of narrative perspectives in falsely representing the lives of others and reflecting the subjective biases of authors and narrative personae; Akutagawa keeps the fictional qualities of his stories as literary fabrications always in view, sometimes by having his narrators discuss their source material in prior literary texts (as in "Yam Gruel"). Yet for these authors, reflexive attention to the desires, methods, and structures that create characters as aesthetic elements can prove ethically transformative precisely because of the challenges they pose to mimetic illusions.

Ōgai insists on oscillation between immersion and reflection that never permits the delusory self-satisfaction of wholly immersive sympathy with characters. In his view, self-conscious reflection can temper and redirect the colonizing impulses of authors and readers and thereby triangulate a more intersubjective approach to the apprehension and interpretation of others. Akutagawa employs reflexivity for ethical ends as well, but through different means and to contrastive effect. In "Rashōmon," we found that readers confront an ambivalence produced by the tension between pathos and ethos that proves homologous to the ethical uncertainty experienced by the protagonist. By refusing to resolve the contradictions and problems raised within and by his storytelling, Akutagawa explores the potential of literary aesthetics to command attention to the ways that our ethical dispositions form through perceptions, affective responses, and other processes inimical to the kinds of cognitive reasoning and decision-making that has traditionally constituted the discipline of ethical inquiry. To draw out the usefulness of Akutagawa's approach for theories of novel ethics today, and to provide a framework for understanding the later turns of his fiction writing, I will follow up on my earlier consideration of the resonance between Akutagawa's methods and the work of Charles Altieri by examining in more detail the ways that literary affect has been theorized to involve ethics. I will then demonstrate how the reflexivity in Akutagawa's most obviously metafictional work both complicates and addresses some of the contentious and challenging questions raised by efforts to theorize novel ethics, while at the same time providing a unique response to Vogler's challenge.

Lyrical and Narrative Ethics

Altieri argues that modernist writers explored the capacity of aesthetics to involve audiences in multivalent states of affective engagement and reflexive consciousness.[2] For Altieri, such states are not reducible to mere cognition or emotion, and for that among other reasons are not readily subsumable in abstract ethical systems. Nonetheless, the experience of such states mobilizes complex interactions between our desires, feelings, values, habits of thinking, and self-image, on the one hand, and the representations, contexts, formal structures, and the values implied by the relationship between pathos and ethos that we encounter in literary texts, on the other. Recognizing the complex ways that literary art can engage us in ethically relevant experiences can help us to attend to the innovations of Akutagawa's *shōsetsu*. Fortunately, and unlike most of the writers that Altieri examines, Akutagawa dramatizes, within the worlds of his fiction, the very kinds of affective responses Altieri theorizes as effects of reading. Several of his *shōsetsu* thus provide, in their stories, models of the ethical effects of literary experience against which we can then consider the methods and effects of the selfsame *shōsetsu* in which they are represented.

Akutagawa rarely if ever aims at anything like transparent realism. He tends to throw a veil of wry self-consciousness between reader and text, diffusing the very intensities of sympathetic involvement that his stories on their own might cultivate. His work never dramatizes straightforward lessons for readers to learn, even when they draw explicitly on moral parables for the substance of their tales. Instead, Akutagawa confronts readers with tensions between the kinds of responses made available by extant frameworks of ethical judgment and feeling, on the one hand, and the kinds of transgressive, reflexive awareness of the inadequacies of such frameworks to do justice to the literary experience of the stories conveyed by his *shōsetsu*, on the other.

As we have seen in the previous chapter, "Rashōmon" allegorizes the tension between the immediate demands of experience and the imaginary constructs (such as self-image or value systems) whereby we understand and evaluate those experiences. The servant struggles to reconcile his desires, his sense of himself as an ethical agent, with his emotional responses to the presence of another—a struggle that takes an explosive turn once he is presented with the story the other tells of herself. "Rashōmon" produces an analogous tension for readers by pitting narrative ethos against pathos, a method operative in much of his oeuvre. To theorize the value of these odd effects I will build on a theory developed in response to Altieri's insistence that a lyrical rather than strictly narrative theory was required for ethical criticism to do justice to both the ethical and the literary.

For James Phelan, one key to literary ethics lies in narrative *positioning*, the situational force whereby narration establishes possible forms of relations for characters within diegetic worlds and for readers beyond them. For the most part, Phelan agrees with Altieri's critique.

> [E]thical criticism's attempt to fit the concrete experience of reading with the abstract generalizations of ethics leads ethical critics to emphasize pathos over ethos. Sympathy and compassion are readily linked to moral abstraction, but the complex intersubjectivity that follows from attention to the overall character of literary communication does not lend itself to such abstraction.[3]

However, Phelan feels that the challenges Altieri sets to ethical criticism can be surmounted through more attention to the narrative dimensions of literary experience and not just a turn to lyricism or affect. He suggests that the form of narration itself, independent of the meanings it may convey, can situate subjects in intersubjective or objectifying relations to one another. Narrative relationships establish dynamics wherein interpretive authority, understanding, exposure, and many other forms of social power position readers vis-à-vis diegetic and extradiegetic demands on attention, judgment, attitude, and response. Phelan argues that a "rhetorical ethics" that attends to narrative positioning can provide much fuller models of literary ethics than those more dependent on pathos and mimesis. Such models can also make strong claims to ethical relevance because readers really engage fictional narratives and find themselves positioned vis-à-vis other narrative subjects regardless of their ontological status. In this sense there are real rather than simply imaginary dynamics of power that play out in our encounters with the narrative representation of fictional worlds.

In this chapter I explore how Akutagawa's "Green Onions" (Negi; 1920) develops its own implicit theory of novel ethics that directly concerns the complex relationship between affect and narrative positioning. I take my cue from Phelan in attending to the various ways that the rhetoric of the story—in particular, the overt addresses to readers and remarks on characters made by the narrator—embroils readers in problems of ethical positioning. My focus, however, will be on teasing out the ethical implications of the story's metafictional turn and not on applying ideas developed by Altieri or Phelan. To frame the value of this for theories of novel ethics, I will consider how the role Akutagawa ascribes to literary affect *within the story he tells*, as well as at the narrative level, compares with some of our most rigorous efforts to understand the relationship among affects, literature, and ethics. I will then consider how deconstructionst theories and subsequent work by Rei Terada on the social relevance of affect illuminate the dynamics at play in this *shōsetsu*. I invoke their work not because they explain Akutagawa's methods but rather because they provide a language for translating the value of his work into the terms of contemporary conversations on novel ethics.

Ultimately, I argue that the affects that "Green Onions" both represents and produces may engage ethics not despite but because of their overtly fictional qualities. The *shōsetsu* shuttles readers between modes of responsiveness whose very irreconcilability may provide a means of circumnavigating Vogler's objection to the very possibility of novel ethics—that novels cannot actually engage ethics because they do not authentically represent autonomous human subjects.

"Real" Readers and Fictional Emotions

"Green Onions" concerns the relationship between literary sensibilities and real-world relationships. It begins with reference to its own status as fiction written by an unnamed first-person author desperate to make money. His characters, we are made to understand, are not only unreal but mere means to a very pragmatic and self-serving authorial end. Within the story that this embedded author (hereafter, "narrator") tells, the heroine O-Kimi is introduced as a sentimental reader of fiction who takes such comfort in the depth of her own "literary feelings" that she spends an entire night tearfully writing a letter to the unfortunate fictional heroine of a Russian novel, out of sadness for the character's emotional state. In stark contrast to her willful apprehension of literary characters as real others, the narrator repeatedly reminds us that she has no existence save as the fictional character he must create to finish a story for a deadline. Yet "Green Onions" paradoxically *depends* upon our caring for her despite this knowledge, as the plot concerns the dangers that a predatory suitor poses for her innocence and safety—as well as the narrator's voiced concern for the propriety of his heroine's conduct.

The story's reflexive attention to the way we impute reality to literary representations manifests itself in the structural tension between the narrator's self-conscious irony and O-Kimi's credulous sentimentality. It also turns out that the "danger" O-Kimi faces in the story arises from the difficulty she experiences reconciling the illusory quality of her beliefs about herself and others, which are derived from her habits of reading sentimental fiction, on the one hand, with the demands of the real social and economic circumstances in which she finds herself positioned, on the other. Like "Rashōmon" (and "Yam Gruel" and others), "Green Onions" allegorizes in its plot some of the difficulties of the complex relationship it establishes between pathos and ethos, and between protagonist and narrator. Working through the plot, therefore, can prove instructive for our efforts to come to terms with the relationship between ethics and aesthetics that the *shōsetsu* explores.

What puts O-Kimi in danger is her habit of projecting into the real world the values she has cultivated through sentimentalized reading practices: "O-Kimi would ... read *The Cuckoo* ... indulging in an artistic ecstasy (*geijutsu-teki kangeki*) far more steeped in *sentimentalism* (*santeimantaaru na*) than even the moonlit-shore scene in the movie-version of the book."[4] Her failure to discern the true nature of her suitor stems directly from the regular practice of willing herself into romantic moods through encounters with amateurish literary works designed to prey upon her lower-middle-class aspirations. The predatory suitor himself, Tanaka, embodies the ideals peddled by the tawdry works she reads:

> Tanaka was an unknown, well, artist. We'll say that because Tanaka was the talented sort who could write poetry, play the violin, work with oil paint, work as an actor ... and play the Satsuma lute. There's not a person who could tell which of these were his real profession and which were hobbies. As for the man himself, his face was smooth as an actor's, his hair had the sheen of oil paints, his voice was as gentle as a violin, his speech as careful as poetry ... and his ability

to skip out on a loan rivaled the bravado of his Satsuma lute playing .... If I think about it, he is really one of an already well-known type, the kind you might find sitting (in the cheapest seats) at local music academy performances, or in cafés and bars, with a look of scorn for the vulgar masses. So if you would like a clearer portrait of young Mr. Tanaka, you should go look in one of those places. I am done with writing about him.[5]

Tanaka exists as pure performance, both "literally" as a character whose fictional nature the story emphasizes and more figuratively insofar as he seems to have no true substance or profession save his purposeful staging of these novel signifiers of masculine ideality. He cultivates just enough demonstrable "talent" in conventional measures of sophistication to produce an image of himself as a kind of ideal literary hero, and this is precisely how O-Kimi perceives him. "To O-Kimi, Tanaka was like none other than Ali Baba, who knew the secret spell for unlocking the doors to that cave of treasures. What paradise would appear before her when that spell was uttered?"[6] Tanaka disguises worldly motives in the same veneer of romantic idealism that O-Kimi has learned to pursue in lieu of more substantive and less self-deceptive experiences with "reality."

Tanaka's cultivation of a distinctly fictional image of himself merely exaggerates in more perfidious manner the kinds of romantic self-projection in which O-Kimi engages. We are told early in the story that the heroine

> appears to have stepped out of one of Takehisa Yumeji's illustrations for a novel. Which seems to be one reason why the café's regulars long ago chose to give her the nickname "Potboiler." She has other nicknames, too, including ... "Miss Mary Pickford," because she looks like the American movie star ... O-Kimi is also quietly contemptuous of [coworker] O-Matsu's low-brow taste. She is convinced that O-Matsu has done nothing since graduating from elementary school but listen to *naniwa-bushi* "folk-tale style narrative songs", eat *mitsu-mame*, and chase after boys.[7]

O-Kimi makes pretensions toward the fine sensibilities of high-brow literati, and her own performance of this identity casts her in the eyes of others as a quasi-fictional character or even a work of fiction herself; her patrons in fact call her "potboiler." The image of the potboiler, an often hastily produced work of relatively poor quality designed to make money, has both thematic and metaliterary resonance with O-Kimi's role in the story (in addition to the obvious metonymic and metaphoric ones regarding her reading habits and sensibilities). It reflects how on a daily basis she must sell an image of herself in the café to make enough tips to survive, without the luxury of time or money to cultivate any deep literary sensibilities or to accentuate her beauty with elegant and tasteful clothing. It also makes her a figure for the "Green Onions" text itself, which began with its author's admission of his need to sell it: "I plan to write this story in a single sitting in time for the deadline I'm facing tomorrow .... So then, what am I going to write about? All I can do is ask you to read what follows."[8]

The apparently frivolous frame proves essentially connected with both the realities of the protagonist's social life and her engagements with fiction. The narrator's cavalier attitude toward the value of his work is belied by the carefully wrought structure of the story itself, including the story- and narrative-level emphases on the relationship between literary and real-world concerns. There is also an irony—reminiscent of that more subtle version we encountered in "Rashōmon"—in the quiet contempt of the narrator's own condescending description of his heroine's unwarranted condescension for what she sees as the less refined sensibilities of her coworker. Both narrator and heroine define themselves in the story vis-à-vis their superior aesthetic insights and literary taste. This irony magnifies to the point where the narrator himself plays upon it in the subsequent discussion of O-Kimi's apartment:

> Ah, all alone in Tokyo, on a night after the sounds of the city have faded away, O-Kimi raises eyes wet with tears to the electric lamp, dreaming of Namiko's seabreeze and the oleanders of Cordoba. When I conjure this image of O-Kimi— damn! It's not just that I don't bear her ill will; if I'm not careful, even I could get caught up in her *sentimentalisme*! And I'm the one that worldly critics always accuse of having too little sympathy and too much intellect.[9]

The narrator of course is not falling into the same kind of "*sentimentalism*" as his heroine; the thickened irony here is that the very gesture of concern invokes the very sentimentality he scorns. By exposing the affectations of her literary sensibilities through the pose of sympathy, the narrator asserts the difference between his self-conscious awareness and her immersive credulity. Yet this distancing functions as a self-protective mechanism not much different from O-Kimi's sentimentality. Both character and narrator use affectation to cultivate an air of taste, to create aesthetic effects for audiences and thereby promote a certain image of themselves, and to fabricate a world and a worldview that they believe to be more insightful and fulfilling than the vacuity they see in what passes for reality in others' views.[10]

As we found in "Rashōmon," the subtle parallels between narrator and protagonist invite us to peer beneath the veneer of self-consciousness with which the narrator veils his created world, just as he peers beneath the veneer of sentimentalism in which O-Kimi enshrouds her own. The narrator's contempt for literary pathos represents a blindness similar to O-Kimi's—an anxious refusal to accept his dependence upon prosaic realism. The story exposes the real class and financial pressures pushing O-Kimi to take refuge in the idealism of romantic fiction, pressures also exerted on the author and conditioning his *narrative* response and refuge in novel conventions of sentimentalism and irony.

The narrator makes it clear that O-Kimi steeps herself nightly in a dreamy pathos conjured up by artificial flowers and romanticized readings of melodramatic texts as a balm against the prosaic shabbiness that surrounds her. She adorns her walls with what "art" she could cut out from magazines (an image of Woodrow Wilson hangs in her mistaken belief that it is Beethoven); her "desk" proves a rickety table covered in a thin cotton cloth; even the artificial lily she prizes is really just a damaged ornament no longer needed by the café where she works. The very details that make her seem affected also attest to the limitations imposed on her sensibilities by social and economic conditions. The narrator acknowledges as much when, with characteristic reflexivity, he plays up the pathos of her situation by pointing out the effects of his description of her:

> While I write this story, the fact is that I cannot suppress a smile at O-Kimi's sentimentalism. But there is not a trace of ill will in that smile. Lined up in O-Kimi's second-floor room, in addition to the artificial lily, the collection of Tōson's poetry, and photograph of Rafael's *Madonna*, are all the kitchen tools she needs to survive without eating out. There's no way to say how much the harsh realities of her Tokyo life symbolized by these kitchen tools continually heap oppression upon her. Yet when you look through a mist of tears, even a desolate life can develop a world of beauty. To escape the oppression of her real life, O-Kimi hid herself in her tears of aesthetic ecstasy.[11]

The narrator effectively beats readers and would-be critics to the punch, calling out his own heavy-handed symbolism (the kitchen tools "symbolize the harsh realities of Tokyo life") as part of his tongue-in-cheek critique of the kind of affected potboiler world that attracts O-Kimi's sympathy. Yet the double-consciousness O-Kimi must cultivate in order to preserve her sense of herself against those harsh realities, even rendered as it is through the thick melodramatic irony of the narration, strikes me as a deeply human response to the difficulty of reconciling aesthetic ideals and sensibilities with real situations. There is pathos behind the bathos; her absurdity is also an index of her desperation. If it were not, readers would find very little to engage them and the narrator's potboiler would not sell.

The story achieves its powerful if contradictory effects in part because, as we have seen in Akutagawa's earlier works, it creates feelings for O-Kimi even while revealing her unreality. Her capture in the narrative of someone so flippant about her plight is perhaps one more (absurd but real) feature of her character that solicits our sympathy. The story invites readers to experience their own form of double-consciousness, working as it does through the dual valence of the narrator's meta-story about the production of the text and the nested story of the dangers that lurk behind O-Kimi's perhaps willful misconstruction of the literary ideality she discovers in Tanaka. We read her as illusory and real at the same time, willfully setting aside our awareness of her fictionality for the sake of the aesthetic experience of the story. How this double-consciousness plays out in O-Kimi's own negotiation of literary and real-life experience, therefore, may serve as a guide for apprehending the value of how it plays out for readers.

O-Kimi turns out to be not quite as naïve as the narrator at first portrays her. She possesses her own measure of self-consciousness about the disjunction between how she interprets Tanaka and the true nature of his character:

> Across the vision that O-Kimi was picturing for herself just now, dark clouds would pass sometimes as if to jeopardize her entire happiness. True, O-Kimi loves young Tanako. But the Tanaka she loves is a Tanaka on whose head her artistic ecstasy has placed a halo…. Nevertheless, O-Kimi's fresh, virginal instincts are not entirely unaware that her Sir Lancelot has something highly dubious at his core. Those dark clouds of anxiety cross O-Kimi's vision whenever such doubts come to mind. Unfortunately, no sooner do those clouds form than they melt away.[12]

O-Kimi proves a willing participant in the idealization of her suitor. She ignores the symbolic "clouds" that trouble her fantasies. Indeed, because she is young and lives almost entirely for artistic ecstasy, "she rarely takes note of clouds except when she is worried about rain on her kimono."[13] This attitude models the one into which the narration pushes its readers; it solicits our imagination despite occasionally "clouding" our vision of the story told by withholding key details, by manifesting ambivalence in its posture toward its heroine, and by reminding us that the whole thing is a fiction. We ignore the symbolic clouds, however, and persist in following the "real" action of the story despite them.

"Green Onions" goes further than any previous story in reflecting on the conflicts between aesthetic sensibilities and ethical positions that it both dramatizes and produces. The "character" Tanaka has all-too-literary designs on O-Kimi. He deceives her by playing the part of a romantic hero, leading her astray with compelling fictions: the story of the date they will have at a circus performance, and then, after she accompanies him, the fabricated tale about why they cannot go to the circus and that of their real destination. Her willful credulity in the fantasy he presents puts her in danger of very real emotional and physical violation. Her readiness to see in him literary-ideal qualities reflects the solipsistic tendencies of characters (including the narrator) to regard others on the same terms that they regard characters in works of fiction.

It turns out that every character mentioned in the story approaches others this way—a phenomenon all the more striking for the relatively little information we receive about most of them. For example, the patrons of O-Kimi's café all devise various nicknames (most related to some mode of literary or artistic production, such as "potboiler" and the appellation "Mary Pickford," for the Western actress) for O-Kimi, treating her as nothing more than the amusing object of attention that her role as waitress invites. O-Kimi and her co-worker, O-Matsu, mutually scorn what they perceive as the other's vulgarity, each making assumptions about the other without actual knowledge of the other's private life or values, on the basis of surface signifiers that serve as coded indexes of character and value in contemporaneous fiction. And we have already discussed O Kimi's imaginative projection of Tanaka as the literary ideal of a suitor. At the end of the story, however, it turns out that even the realist and scheming pragmatist Tanaka has been peering at O-Kimi through his own veil of fiction.

Once they are close to Tanaka's goal of getting O-Kimi to a secluded house, he muses with satisfaction on how he has presented himself as an ideal lover in O-Kimi's imagination. He begins to fantasize about their destination and how things will proceed. But his own fantasy shatters unexpectedly when she stops on their walk to buy the titular green onions.

> The image of the cozy little house he had been imagining had strangely begun to fade little by little. In its stead, the image of a pile of green onions with the tag "1 bunch for 4 sen" stuck into them gradually appeared before him. Then, suddenly, these images were all shattered when the next gritty gust of wind passed by, as penetrating as real life and full of the eye-stinging stink of green onions, which literally punched Tanaka in the nose.
>
>   … Poor Tanaka, looking at the world through such pathetic eyes, stared at O-Kimi as if he were seeing a completely different person.[14]

In the excellent surprise twist of this story, what saves O-Kimi from the ominous destination of her date is the fact that the overpowering smell of reality issuing from the economic onions shatters not her fantasy, as we might have expected, but what we are shockingly made to realize has been the predator Tanaka's fantasy all along—his fantasy of her as a romantic character who has been dreamily imagining *him* as an ideal literary hero. *He* is the one "punched in the nose" by the pungent force of this encounter with bottom-line reality—along with readers. The destruction of his fantasy takes place through a metaphoric substitution in which Tanaka's image of the house (itself a perversion of the fantasy of domesticity that O-Kimi imagines) becomes transformed into an image of green onions, and then obliterated by the green onion's overwhelming olfactory presence. Tanaka's experience of the powerfully real sensation quickly translates into a disappointment that renders his fantasy unsustainable, literally nauseating him. Real life has intruded on his imaginings not, as it may seem to do for readers (who are reminded by the narrator of the reality that the story is a fiction), as a matter of awareness or cognition but through visceral contact whose physiological dimensions lead to an emotional state contrary to his original arousal.

Like the servant in "Rashōmon," both Tanaka and O-Kimi find themselves moving in one and then opposite directions toward immoral conduct, as a consequence of affective states brought about by their responses to powerful sensory stimuli that also bear symbolic weight for them. In "Green Onions," however, the kinds of experience that produce these affects explicitly concern conflicts between fantasy and reality. The pleasurable fantasies that O-Kimi internalized through her reading practices lead her to ignore the real qualities and perspectives of others, so that she looks down upon her coworker and projects an image of Tanaka that leads to a liaison that may violate her own ideals. The surprise is that it turns out that Tanaka, too, nurtured a complementary fantasy of O-Kimi as a reader of the literary ideals he projected—an image of her enraptured naivety and willingness to sacrifice reality for the sake of the fantasy he represented.

In the end, however, affective responses to the reality presented by the bunch of green onions prove more powerful than either of their romanticized projections. "In O-Kimi's happy heart, which until that moment had been intoxicated with love and art, latent real life woke from its torpid slumber."[15] O-Kimi's response abruptly reminds readers that her fantasies take place within the province of a pressing social reality that has always conditioned them, despite the appearance of her credulous absorption in an imaginary world. Even one of the most meager pleasures that real life offers easily trumps her romantic fantasy. Perhaps, then, some sense of social reality haunts our experience of the narrator's (and Akutagawa's) own insubstantial illusions.

Indeed, the *shōsetsu* "Green Onions" concerns the romantic fantasies of an imaginary reader of potboiler fiction whose own hardships are veiled from readers through her self-delusion and the narrator's ironic mockery. In the end, however, the reflexivity of the story heightens, even as it undermines, our feelings for its heroine. Deep concern with the pressures exerted by social reality underlies this tale of solipsistic escapism. These pressures and the realities they reflect provide the *shōsetsu* with a real affective force, not despite but because it insists that we respond to such pressures through fantasies sustained by the fictions purveyed and required by the (bourgeois) cultural situation of readers.

In almost all of Akutagawa's *shōsetsu*, social worlds produce alienation and anxiety for characters. Readers, however, come upon this pathos refracted through literary self-consciousness. The dissonance between the perspectives of his characters and those of readers provides some of the productive tension of his early works. "Green Onions," however, ratchets up this self-consciousness. It is no longer strong-but-subtle homologies between narrative acts and those represented in stories that remind readers of authorial consciousness at work. Nor is it the selection of classical material retold in a carefully wrought neoclassical or contemporary register. In this story the relationship of readers to fiction is the explicit subject of numerous narrative utterances that render the narrative-level effects far more dominant than in previous work.

"Green Onions" ends, in fact, not with the surprise twist and dénouement of the story it tells but rather with one that the writer of that story achieves. Following the description of Tanaka's disillusionment and O-Kimi's banal bliss, we encounter a graphic line, a bookend that marks our crossing from the representation of the story to the reality of its narrative framing.

Well, in the end I finished writing after all! … But what is this feeling of oppression weighing on me even though I actually managed to finish? O-Kimi made it back again to that room over the beauty parlor without harm. But unless she quits waiting on tables at that café, there's no way to say she won't end up going out with Tanaka again. When I think about what might happen then— no, whatever happens then will happen. It's not as if my worrying about it now will change anything. Well, I suppose I should just lay down my pen. Goodbye, O-Kimi. And so, tonight then, just like that other night, go out lightheartedly and bravely—and be conquered by the critics.[16]

The narrator here plays on the divide between the self-conscious frame of the story and the "reality" of the world he constructs. In one breath he dismisses it all as a fiction concocted for a deadline and in the next describes a feeling of oppression and anxiety for the protagonist of the story, as though she were a real agent beyond his control. The (tongue-in-cheek) gesture conflates the heroine with the text itself, suggesting that the kinds of violence performed on textual bodies by critical readers might not be so distinguishable from those that might befall O-Kimi. This echoes the ending of Ōgai's *The Wild Goose*, but without the underlying realism on which that text depended, and with a shift in emphasis that implicates readers rather than authors in responsibility for textual violence.

The story told by "Green Onions" concerns the author's stance toward his characters as much as it does his characters' literature-mediated navigation of their fictional reality. From start to finish, the story ties attitudes toward fictional characters to real-life ethical concerns with actions and dispositions toward others. "Green Onions" in this sense directly addresses, through its metaliterary turn, the essence of Vogler's complaint against novel ethics. It creates its own literary effects not simply through the illusion of mimesis that Vogler finds problematic for ethical theories of the novel but by exposing that illusion as such, effectively undertaking the theoretical work that Vogler herself performs. And yet it seems to insist that the feelings evoked in response to fictional beings are not merely aesthetic but have at their core an ethical dimension.

"Green Onions" essentially grants Vogler's objection that literary reality cannot substitute for real ethical experience. The text culminates, in fact, with the contrast between the anemic fantasies of the characters and the powerful smell of real life. Fiction cannot attain the substantive, immediate presence of green onions; it cannot represent reality except *as* a fiction. Yet here, surprisingly, Akutagawa draws almost the opposite conclusion as Vogler. It is precisely the refusal of mimesis that empowers his *shōsetsu* to engage ethics, because it forces readers to attend to the real ethical effects of the kinds of fictionalizing that we really undertake.

Real Effects of Fictional Affect

Instead of representing characters' lives in *shōsetsu* as occupying some credibly verisimilar reality, "Green Onions" confronts us with the imbrication of real life and fictional reality. More radically, it drives home the extent to which fictional narrative might structure the everyday interactions of real life. To parse out this latter claim, and to suggest the relevance of Akutagawa's work for new theories of novel ethics, I will draw on work that deals with the relationship between literature, ethics, and affect as theorized by Jacques Derrida (1930–2004) and other deconstructionists. Like Akutagawa, Derrida evinced deep skepticism about ethics as an institution, one often invoked as a disciplinary framework for the operation of hegemonic power. Nevertheless, he devoted his career to exploring the various effects of our capture within domains of linguistic and ideological power he cast in terms of "textuality." For Derrida, "textuality" was no mere figurative term for the various regimes of understanding within which acts of identification and communication become possible—it was the very condition of human subjectivity. Derrida famously gave priority to the "graphocentric," to the "written," over against a "phallogocentric" illusion of presence and oral or ontological immediacy as the ground of human activity and identity. While I do not claim that Akutagawa was a proto-deconstructionist, I find strong affinities with his conviction and anxiety about the degree to which we are linguistic beings, composed in a framework of textuality that in moments of doubt came to feel like a "false enamel" between himself and some transcendental ground of identity.[17] The work of Derrida and his successors, I feel, can provide a conceptual framework that can help us to discern the effectiveness of Akutagawa's ethical reflexivity.

In her book *Feeling in Theory*, Rei Terada explains Derrida's position on affect in a way that clarifies its relevance for Akutagawa's text and for ethical theories of the novel. She argues that as Derrida saw it, continental philosophers had been inclined to attribute immediacy and self-presence to the physiological dimensions of affect, assuming them to be "first-order" experiences. Derrida suggests instead that we recognize affects as second-order projections. In short, and as consistent with the sense we have ascribed to the term following Altieri in the previous chapter, every "affect" is already a representation that takes place through the domain of sociality. What we feel is, for Derrida, always already an interpretation of sensory input apprehended as meaningful in social context and based on a projected identity in which the self apprehends itself as seen by others. On this view, even in what we might consider wholly private moments we interpret and engage the social world vis-à-vis our conversion of the physiological and affective experience of phenomena into signs of distinctly social significance.

Affect proves the domain through which we translate personal experience into an emotional "language" of shared values. "Emotions emerge only through the acts of interpretation and identification by means of which we feel *for others*."[18] The process of staging affect as emotion has ethical valence in part because it constitutes the very possibility of recognition that allows ethically salient affects like sympathy or pity to take shape in attitudes or relations. Terada argues as much when she notes that "Pity, the arch passion in Rousseau, is itself, as Derrida has very well perceived, inherently a fictional process that transposes an actual situation into a world of appearance, of drama and literary language."[19] This insight provides grounds for challenging Vogler's argument that literature cannot represent real-life ethical situations. We may counter that in real life we arrive at ethics only through a process of fictionalization that construes the actual as though it were in fact "fictional."[20]

"Green Onions" underscores the theatricality of the staging of emotions, perhaps most obviously in O-Kimi's private but thoroughly stylized performance of sympathy for the fictional character of the novel she read. Moreover, it points out the ethical risks that fantasies about our own emotional lives might pose if not tempered by self-conscious attention to the fictionalized dimensions of that staging—that is, the dangers of sentimentality. Sentimentality, Terada suggests, is the name we give to emotional responses that refuse to recognize the performative nature of affect and persist in delusions of un-self-conscious and unmediated orientation toward others. In "Green Onions" O-Kimi's sentimentality underscores a willful blindness to the performative quality of her own feelings, a blindness that extends to her failure to recognize others as anything more than elements in the drama in which she acts as heroine.

Through its refraction of O-Kimi's self-deceptive feelings into the ironic, self-conscious emotional response of her narrator to those feelings, "Green Onions" allegorizes its own translation of O-Kimi's sentimentality into a literary pathos. Terada draws on Derrida's "Cogito and the History of Madness" to define pathos as a second-order emotion, a feeling about the representation of feeling, specifically an "emotion for *another*."[21] Pathos in itself is not necessarily a form of sentimentality; however, what "Green Onions" puts on display is what de Man calls "ostensible pathos," the deployment of pathos as means of establishing the authenticity of emotional appeal—a tactic shared by the media O-Kimi consumes as well as the man she sees.[22]

According to Terada, de Man associates "ostensible pathos" with credulous, "entirely thematic readings" and the idea that "keenly affecting texts must be based in the real—in real, not fictive, emotions."[23] Ostensible pathos, in de Man's view, is an illusion produced by the "reality-effect" of literary representation, a kind of self-deception which assumes that realism secures the authenticity of affective response. Such responses suppress the self-consciousness of pathos for self-indulgence in emotions that secure one's own self-image. This is of course what O-Kimi feels for the suffering heroine of the work she reads, and what translates into the projections about her own life that lead her to misrecognize others and, critically, herself. "Green Onions" exposes the illusory nature of literary reality-effects and the affects those projections generate; the text thus reads as an allegory of the reading processes it seems to invite.

In de Man's view, "any narrative is the allegory of its own reading," and therefore about the "appearance of its own undoing."[24] Yet Akutagawa's reflexive framing of the problems of literary reading in "Green Onions" theorizes its own allegorical function and provides us means for valuing its contributions to literary ethics. Through its attention to the effects of literary affect on both character and narrator, "Green Onions," more like de Man's *Allegories of Reading* itself than any text that de Man reads, makes us cognizant of the misrecognition that gives way to sentimentality in literature—what de Man calls the tendency to construe pathos as ethos.

Nietzsche, on whom de Man draws to elaborate his marginally more generous theory of literary pathos, held that pathos tends to masquerade as ethos for those within its embrace: "We always assume that it is the only state that is possible and reasonable for us and … an *ethos* and not a *pathos*."[25] As in the case of O-Kimi, fictional feelings give rise to the belief that they are grounded in real, not second-order, emotions. "Green Onions" adds a complex twist to this insight by acknowledging the power of this effect but further revealing the way that even "real" feelings have their bases in fictions. For all dramatic agents in the work, including the narrator, feelings are predicated on fictions: those they read, those through which they filter their views of others, and those that circulate in stories told. Becoming self-conscious about the role of fiction in the formation of their attitudes and interactions with others is an ethical good insofar as it provides knowledge of the contextual frameworks within which their emotions are produced as social fictions of real consequence. While the characters themselves never recognize the extent to which they interact through veils of fiction, that dynamic is laid bare for readers in the very process of their participation within it.

If even supposedly primary affective responses prove mediated by expressly literary representations, and these produce real pathos not despite but because of their consciously fictional qualities, then Akutagawa's self-conscious and all-too-literary *shōsetsu* can make far greater claims for ethical value than his critics have assumed. In fact, analysis of this work points toward the powerful metafiction can play in theories of novel ethics more generally. If real life involves negotiating the relationship between fictive ideals and reality, as it does for characters, narrators, and readers, then the fictional "Green Onions" may be much truer to life than Vogler assumes possible. By presenting itself as fiction, "Green Onions" paradoxically takes one step closer to the real through its refusal to permit the self-delusion of ostensible pathos. This possibility does not contest the assumptions of Vogler's argument (that literary representations of real life can never exceed their aesthetic dimensions as there-for-us objects), but leaves answers to the question she poses more open than Vogler herself believes.

Conclusion

Akutagawa in the end would surely agree with Vogler's position that literature does not provide equivalents to real-life ethical situations, and that the particularity of literary representation cannot without violence be aligned with general ethical principles or schemata. Yet in his work an avowedly literary pathos, defined as an emotion "for another," may be no less real or ethically inflected than the presumably primary emotions (pity or infatuation, for example) that arise from our immediate encounters with others, because it acknowledges the extent to which fictions form the basis of other-oriented emotions constructed from our affective responses. "Green Onions" may engage the real, social world all the more for its apparently self-absorbed refusal of the reality-effect that would seem necessary to ground its affect in real-world relations.

It appears that "Green Onions" maintains the same kind of tension between pathos and ethos as Akutagawa's earlier work—the pathos of its story world (which consists of O-Kimi's allegorical oscillation between reality and fantasy), on the one hand, and the ethos of its narrative frame (which consists of the ironic portrait of the narrator's oscillation between reflexive undoing of the tale's mimesis and his repeated insistence on its emotional appeal), on the other.[26] In the end, however, the text appears to subsume its pathos within the ethos it generates, crossing back to the authorial side of the dividing line with its conclusion. It insists that we recognize its pathos as a literary effect in the service of a narrative ethos, which in this case itself proves a fictional trope of the framing story of the narrator. "Green Onions" thus makes explicit this insight that underlies all of Akutagawa's writing, which always foregrounds its narrative effects over against sentimental absorption in the pathos of its dramatizations: that pathos can only be made available through an ethos that determines its value and effects, and that it is in the establishment of ethos that what he will come to call the "poetic spirit" of the text operates (see next chapter).

We find in this text that real life turns out to consist in negotiations between fictional projections and real situations, as it does for all of the story's embedded characters, narrators, and, perhaps, readers. The *shōsetsu* does not merely offer an allegory of reading but also provides an experience that undoes the possibility of straightforward thematic reading—much as de Man theorizes Rousseau's *Julie* to work by foregrounding questions of authorship and authenticity in its prefaces.[27] "Green Onions" boldly situates ethics within the domains of literary language and affect rather than those of real-life behavior or rational judgment.

Even at the physiological level of affective response, the worldviews and stances of his subjects toward one another prove thoroughly mediated by literary representation (the characters view each other on distinctly literary terms and the narrator literally possesses the power to subject his heroine to ethical or unethical treatment by virtue of his literary writing). That all of the dramatic agents in "Green Onions" are framed as fictional representations themselves does not make them unavailable for ethical inquiry as Vogler suggests. Rather, it renders all the more human for their production as narrative beings.

Like Vogler, "Green Onions" takes issue with the kinds of sentimentality that imagine novel mimesis as the essential field of ethical value. Yet it surprisingly suggests that to imagine real-life subjectivity as wholly distinct from fictional representations is to profess the same kind of naiveté that Vogler ascribes to credulous readers and theorists of mimetic fiction. The wry dismissal of tears shed for fiction betrays its own failure to grasp the realities of both reading and the real fictions that compose our experiences of self and others.

In Akutagawa's subsequent work, especially his last writings, metaliterary self-consciousness culminates in a complete collapse of diegetic and ontological levels, resulting in the powerful fragmentation of the form and style of his language itself. *Cogwheels* (*Haguruma*) and *A Fool's Life* (*Aru ahō no isshō*) go considerably further than the ironic representation of fictional characters whose blindness to the difference between real life and literary representation threatens their integrity and livelihoods that we find in "Green Onions." Whereas the present text very tidily tells the story of fictional beings experiencing crises of sensibility and interpersonal relationships, in the late quasi-autobiographical works, the structure and coherence of the narrative itself is threatened by the disintegration of boundaries between the literary and the real. The effect is so totalizing that subsequent scholarship has since struggled with the complex task of distinguishing the author from his acts of self-representation.

7

A Novel Theory of Literary Affect

An Art of Aporia

Akutagawa Ryūnosuke's *shōsetsu* weave together moments of epiphany, disillusionment, whimsy, agony, and rapture through passages that produce haunting novel ethoses. His work arrested the attention of his generation by artfully intertwining neoclassical and contemporary language that blended conventions of the contemporary Western novel with traditions of Japanese literature. Yet his writing in the year before his tragic suicide seems to exhibit little of that celebrated orchestral virtuosity. It fragments and fades into uncertain equivalencies, redoubles on itself with repetitions and questions marks, and trails off into elliptical moments of aporia and paralysis. The mental preoccupations of his narrators occlude the plotlines of his final stories, sometimes to the point where his fictional worlds themselves dissolve into obscurity behind skeins of existential questions. According to scholarly orthodoxy, the anxious prose and failure to portray a convincing fictional reality belie deterioration in the author's mental and literary faculties.

Noting that the Taishō period (1912–26) was largely coextensive with Akutagawa's literary career, critics have portrayed such deterioration as both symbol and symptom of a decline in Taishō intellectualism. Akutagawa's suicide represents for many the end of a certain spirit of the age, as had General Nogi's (1849–1912) just after the end of the Meiji period. His turn to what appears to be naked self-reflection in his final works serves for many as an index of the author's incapacity to grapple with anything outside his own collapsing sense of selfhood. Given the consistent experimentation with novel ethos and the ethics of self-consciousness that we have discovered in Akutagawa's earlier fiction, however, this commonplace narrative bears revisiting. Viewing his late writing as the culmination of lifelong experimentation with reflexive narration can help us to recover contributions this work makes to the development of the *shōsetsu* in Japan and to theories of novel ethics more broadly. The very failure of his late writing to produce certain kinds of coherence may in fact make possible a transmission of affect and experiences of alterity that many contemporary writers have only recently begun to explore.

In this chapter I examine the reception history of Akutagawa's late work to trace through it a consistent assumption that the ethical efficacy of the novel depends on its construction of compelling and self-consistent mimetic worlds. For an alternative approach, I suggest that we attend to Akutagawa's own theory of the novel through examination of some of his overlooked and unpublished corpus as well as the late essay, "Literary, All-Too Literary" (*Bungeiteki na, amari ni bungeiteki na*; 1927). In it, Akutagawa defines the genre of the novel in terms of its potential to produce affective responses in readers rather than its capacity for mimesis. This essay lays the groundwork for a formal ethics of novel narration whose goal is the transmission of ethically relevant affect rather than the compelling representation of verisimilar situations (and whatever ethics such simulated encounters might entail). His theory of the novel, generally neglected for the disarray of its presentation and the illogic of its expression, provides a robust framework for valuing the accomplishments of his late prose and perhaps new ethical metafiction today. In the next chapter we will consider his final works in the context of that framework.

Storied Failures: Critical Orthodoxy on Akutagawa's Late Fiction

As George T. Sipos notes in his 2017 essay on the "modernist temptations" of Akutagawa Ryūnosuke, "With very few notable exceptions, Akutagawa's contribution to Japan's modern literature in search of different modes of expression is still little analyzed and even less understood and appreciated."[1] Sipos continues to lament that "although his modernist contributions have been … reevaluated for their importance … Akutagawa remains mostly identified by his early creative stage, the 'art for art's sake' writer of the short stories."[2] Despite this insistence that Akutagawa remains undervalued, Sipos finds the author's late work of diminished quality. He echoes a critique made by Donald Keene to write off *A Fool's Life* as a "plotless and disjointed text meant to mirror the writer's state of mind at the time of its writing."[3] Sipos concludes that "From a literary point of view, except for isolated instances, the [late autobiographical] stories do not do justice to Akutagawa's earlier artistry and, shrouded in nostalgia and melancholy and touched by desperation as they are, they paint a rather desolate overall image of the character's life."⁴

Scholarship has widely assumed that Akutagawa's late *shōsetsu* fail as coherent literary texts. As Seiji Lippit points out in his 2002 *Topographies of Japanese Modernism*:

> during the 1920s, the conventional boundaries of literary practice were assaulted by various cultural developments, including the growing emphasis on class consciousness and the increasing demand for literature to engage social reality ... [Akutagawa's *A Fool's Life*] reveals his inability to create a novelistic narrative of his life. He instead had to reduce the story to a succession of separate moments in time stitched together to form a somewhat disjointed, patchwork personal history.⁵

Lippit's account reflects nearly a century of scholarly consensus in determining that Akutagawa's late "intellectual crisis" reflected the author's "inability" to produce mimetic coherence.⁶ Such critiques overwhelmingly assume that conventional forms of coherences in plot and writing should serve as standards against which the work is to be measured. They also overwhelmingly arrive at the same conclusion, one attractive for its broader explanatory power: that the author's personal breakdown and failure were symptomatic of a larger ethical failure of intellectual literati "to engage social reality." To challenge these assumptions and conclusions, I want to examine their emergence in critical history to trace within the various modalities of ethical critique levied against the author persistent and misleading assumptions about the ethics of novel mimesis.

In 1929, scholar and rising figure in the recently founded (1922) Japanese Communist Party Miyamoto Kenji sharply denounced the work of Akutagawa. In his essay entitled "The Literature of Defeat" (*Haiboku no bungaku*), Miyamoto reads both the life and art of the author as symptoms of an intellectual bourgeois consciousness that ignored material reality in favor of art, and which could not in the end transcend history. For him, the celebrated artistry of Akutagawa's writing amounts to no more than a veneer of aestheticism covering the absence of genuine understanding of the social world. On his view, and those of many subsequent scholars, modern Japanese absorption with the literary construction of subjectivity reflects an anxious solipsism born of intellectual idealism. He contends that Taishō intellectuals turned to art for imaginary salvation rather than face the hard work of engaging real-life problems.⁷

Miyamoto builds his critique by referring to Akutagawa disparagingly as a "man of letters" (*bun-jin*), emphasizing the lexical play of this compound to suggest that Akutagawa was trapped in the "artificial" (*jinkō*) armor of his highbrow literary art (*bun*gei), and therefore incapable of authentic relations or any kind of genuine representation of reality.[8] Conveniently forgetting the veil of fiction separating author from self-figuration, Miyamoto assumes that Akutagawa speaks authentically and transparently with his own voice in his fiction. He refers imprecisely to the "literary life" of the author and draws as much on views expressed by his narrators and characters in fiction as on those of the flesh-and-blood author (240) to cast Akutagawa's detachment from real life as simultaneously an aesthetic issue in his fiction and a moral problem inherent in the real author's worldview.[9] Ironically, Miyamoto relies for much of his argument upon a Marxist critique of the distinction between the real labor of flesh-and-blood individuals and the abstractions of literary representation that alienate individuals through the production of illusory subject positions detached from the real circumstances of their lives. By conflating the authorial personae of Akutagawa's fiction and the flesh-and-blood author, Miyamoto himself winds up performing the very obfuscation whose critique forms the basis of his judgment against Akutagawa's literary aestheticism. As my analysis of *A Fool's Life* shall show, moreover, the gulf between self and self-representation remained consistently, and intentionally, in the foreground of Akutagawa's late writing.

Miyamoto aims at cleaning up literary history for an emerging "literature of the proletariat" and so criticizes Akutagawa's literature for its isolationism, egocentrism, and highbrow elitism. He claims that the author's greedy intellectualism led him "to think of reality as only his own self."[10] Thus trapped in his own solipsistic, bourgeois world of ideas, Akutagawa could no longer authentically portray anything in the world: "'He' could not even satisfactorily write a single dog. … [T]he only thing he got from his self-reliance [his intellectual literary production] turned out to be powerless and easily damaged, since 'his' world was no longer bright."[11] This was not merely a problem of aesthetic quality or authenticity for Miyamoto but a social, political, and ethical one that the critic makes emblematic of the Taishō period. In failing to represent others or society adequately, Akutagawa's literature served to reproduce and codify further an oppressive bourgeois worldview, validating the elitist points of view of his narrators.

Miyamoto reads the fragmentation of Akutagawa's later work as symptomatic of the dissolution of the intelligentsia itself. The moral vacuity that appears so horrific in Akutagawa's works turns out, in Miyamoto's view, merely to reflect the inherent corruption and essential emptiness of the whole bourgeois project in which Akutagawa participates. In the end, Miyamoto implies that both the author and his writing were doomed to be driven, by the proletariat, to "surrender to life"—through death and dissolution.

This portrait of Akutagawa's life and literature as culminating in failure persists even in criticism considerably more sympathetic to Akutagawa. For example, in his 1941 article "Akutagawa Ryūnosuke," Japanese literary critic Fukuda Tsuneari tries to work out the relation of Akutagawa's personal anxiety and his writing. In the end, Fukuda finds that the fragmentation of the author's literary work directly reflects a psychologically fragmented experience of the world from within an unstable mental outlook occasioned by impoverishment in his personal life and worldviews.[12] Unlike Miyamoto, however, Fukuda recognizes that the literary "problems" that arise in Akutagawa's work were not mere symptoms of personal circumstance but intentional subjects of theoretical interest in Akutagawa's interrogation of the relationship between literary representation and human values: "[Akutagawa realized that] the problem of literature is not reflecting reality. It is the relation of the will to the world it sets up."[13] He argues that the elusive goal of Akutagawa's work was to construct a fictional world which could satisfactorily represent the effects of the self's efforts to express and impose its desires on reality.

This goal, according to Fukuda, was unattainable because the "self" and the "reality" that Akutagawa sought to realize through literary representation made contradictory demands. Representing the self required abstract formulation, whereas representing the world required something more "realistic" (*genjitsuteki*). On Fukuda's view, Akutagawa's work alternates from one perspective to another—from describing represented worlds in granular realistic detail to commenting ironically on their unreality from the perspectives of detached narrators—because the author could not find the proper balance between his commitments to a shared objective reality and to the ideality of subjective imagining.

Fukuda notes the dissonant effects occasioned by oscillation between the immersive, embodied experience of stories and the narrative-level intellectual reflection afforded by Akutagawa's writing. And he recognizes in this oscillation an effort to connect literary ideality to material reality and thereby to find some kind of authentic, mediating role for literature to play with respect to real-life values. Yet Fukuda imposes on this oscillation preconceived judgments about novel ethics. For him, ethics remains squarely in the domain of shared objective reality; hence, novel ethics can only consist in the mimetic representation and evocation of real-world situations. Akutagawa's failure to "reconcile" his subjective imaginings and literary methods with a concrete, realist approach therefore seems to reflect the ethical failure of an aesthetic vision too absorbed with abstraction and self-reflection. Although Fukuda gives far more credit to Akutagawa's aesthetic abilities and ethical impulses, he follows Miyamoto in the end, finding Akutagawa's literature ultimately solipsistic and at ethical fault for not engaging reality more directly.

A decade later, prominent scholar of modern Japanese literature Yoshida Seiichi (1908–84) takes the theme of bifurcation between Akutagawa's self-reflection and his sense of obligation to a shared reality all the way back to Akutagawa's birth—a vogue in mid-century Japanese scholarship. In his 1953 essay "Akutagawa Ryūnosuke's Life and Art" (*Akutagawa Ryūnosuke no shōgai to geijutsu*), Yoshida begins by addressing the "doubt" which has been cast on the circumstances surrounding Akutagawa's naissance and early life, mapping out something like a history of the "nervousness" (*shinkei-shitsu*) that informs Akutagawa's subsequent life and work. One of the main pieces of evidence Yoshida submits to show the depth and extent of Akutagawa's sense of the self as an essentially fragmented construct comes from a line in the author's late critical essay, "Literary, All-Too Literary": "Born in contemporary Japan as I was, in a literary way as well I cannot help but feel within myself an infinite splintering (*bunretsu*)."[14] Yoshida argues that a pervasive uncertainty about the constitution of the "self" and the lack of transcendental or social grounds led to a breakdown that undermined the author's ability to create coherent literature toward the end of his life.

Although it largely defends the artistic value of Akutagawa's earlier literary accomplishment, Yoshida's scholarship assumes a "downfall" at the end of his career predicated on binarisms imputed to Akutagawa's thinking, particularly those between the real social world and consciousness of the self, and between real life and literature. "Among the many problems—domestic, political, literary, moral—that hounded Akutagawa, perhaps the rupture of generational consciousness of the self (*jiko-ninshiki*) was the most critical" in determining the course of his late life and literature.[15] Yoshida finds the fragmented form and structure of Akutagawa's final works representative of a crisis of identity beyond Akutagawa's individual situation—the struggle of the self-conscious modern intellectual to come to terms with the self as a social being burdened with moral responsibility. Yoshida ends his account by once again making Akutagawa a symbol of the problematic condition of his age: "Yet when we set him against the backdrop of the Taisho period, we can see that ... [more than any other literati or intellectual] Akutagawa possessed a demeanor suited to absorbing the troubles of his time, as well as those of humanity."[16] Like so many other scholars, Yoshida sees the explorations of fragmented experience in Akutagawa's writing as evidence of a symptomatic abstraction from reality; the author's failure to ground his sense of selfhood more authentically in shared experience makes him in such critical accounts a tragic figure of Taishō intellectualism.

Even those who disagree with both Miyamoto's politicized notion of literary history and his actual judgments of Akutagawa's writing, such as Makoto Ueda, still reiterate the core principles of Miyamoto's criticism. In his 1976 book *Modern Japanese Writers and the Nature of Literature*, Ueda claims that "Akutagawa made a religion of art" and that the ultimate failure of art to provide a transcendental ground for the self led to Akutagawa's loss of faith in that religion, and life as well.[17] Instead of concluding that Akutagawa's intellectualism doomed him to ethical and aesthetic failure, however, Ueda lauds the author's effort to find a constructivist solution to the modern loss of faith in the security of the self and the social institutions that govern self-other relations. Ueda draws nearly the opposite conclusion from Miyamoto about the value of Akutagawa's work. However, the terms on which he examines Akutagawa, the binarism imputed to his thinking about self and world, and the method of conflating worldviews of the real author and those of his narrators repeat the patterns established by Miyamoto's work. Precious few scholars, especially those who treat ethics, acknowledge that the confusion between subjective apprehension and objective experience was a consistent and deliberate metaliterary object of inquiry rather than a side-effect of personal crisis. Because Ueda maintains the binarism of Miyamoto's imagined opposition between Akutagawa's ideals and a presumed "real life" with which the author fails to reconcile himself, he arrives at the same conclusion: that the author's last works are symptoms of the failure of his ideals to surmount the difficulties of the real world.

Even critics who admire Akutagawa's work find themselves reproducing the logic of critical orthodoxy that condemns its ethics. Sako Junichirō, for example, devotes over 150 pages to Akutagawa in a study entirely focused on *Ethical Explorations in Modern Japanese Literature* (1966), but not once attributes deliberate ethical intention to the author's work. Sako instead describes Akutagawa as an aesthete who created moving portraits that keenly reflected the decay of modern life with intellection dispassion. Akutagawa's aestheticism serves in this account as a point of contrast to other, more ethically invested modern Japanese authors, rather than as his very means of ethical innovation. Sako's critique of Akutagawa rests like so many others on the commonplace that Akutagawa despaired of securing any ethical understanding of real life, preferring instead the perpetual recreation of an imaginary world through increasingly recursive, self-involved acts of poiesis that further detached him from actual social conditions.[18]

The failure of Akutagawa's art to engage social life remains a dominant narrative in criticism in part because it provides a convenient explanation for the changes in Akutagawa's writing. It links his spiritual crisis to the intellectual climate of the modern period. It also weaves his life and work into a cogent whole, whose tragedy critics can interpret as symptoms of literary and cultural history. With Akutagawa's suicide and the end of an era as foregone conclusions, scholarship has framed the disorienting effects of those texts in largely pejorative terms, casting them as symptomatic of his inability to write coherently with the same command of artistic expression that he had achieved in earlier work.

Yet if anything attests to the mastery of those final works, it is the persistent power of the myth of himself Akutagawa created through them—the portrait of himself as a tragic artist who flew too high on man-made wings—to shape the very criticism that condemns it. Even the severest critics of these works seem to recognize an uncanny affective power in them. One of his best biographers, Sekiguchi Yasuyoshi, reads Akutagawa's last works as a desperate turn against the literary identity that the author had created for himself. In his 1995 *Akutagawa Ryūnosuke* Sekiguchi suggests that the author purposefully deconstructs the artistic ideals in which he had taken refuge in an anxious effort to work out a new relationship between himself and a rapidly eroding sense of reality.[19] While this certainly does not break the pattern of binarism in Akutagawa scholarship, it does attribute more artistic intention to the shift in Akutagawa's methodology. Despite the promising premise, however, Sekiguchi ultimately concludes that the gripping emotional power of these works emerges chiefly as—you might have guessed by now—a failure to bridge the gap between life and art.

In the argument that follows, I consider what examination of Akutagawa's late *shōsetsu* might yield if we ignore received narratives concerning the author's state of mind and refuse to assume that novels must work principally through mimesis to engage ethics effectively. In this, I follow two main leads. First and foremost, I consider those late novels in terms that the author himself advanced in his writing on novel value, which will be the subject of the rest of this chapter. Then, in the following chapter, with those terms in mind, I will adopt the approach recommended by Kirsten Cather in her recent essay on Akutagawa, "Noting Suicide with a Vague Sense of Anxiety." Cather refreshingly "insist[s] on proximity to [Akutagawa's late] texts" and "resist[s] offering retrospective, selective readings colored by hindsight from the safe reader position of transcendent outsider," recommending that we "consider how these texts offered authors an embodied experience."[20] Read not as a record of personal shortcomings and deterioration but rather as a reflexive exploration of what Akutagawa envisioned as the commitments, limitations, and possibilities of self-other relations available in what he called "life within literature," *A Fool's Life* and *Cogwheels* confront boldly the very problems of novel representation and ethics that supposedly condition their failure.

A Novel Theory of Literary Affect: Akutagawa's Late Writing on *Shōsetsu*

The nervous, scattered, and sometimes flailing efforts of Akutagawa's late prose to achieve coherence become, in most critical accounts, reflections of personal despair. Yet just months before his death the author espoused a view of what he called the *hanashi-rashii hanashi no nai shōsetsu*, a "plotless novel," or, more directly, a "novel without a story-like story." This notion offers insight into an uncommon vision of novel form in which coherence, mimesis, and carefully architected stories do not serve as the most significant measures of novel value. Instead, Akutagawa counterintuitively champions the potential of novel language to convey a *shiteki seishin* (poetic spirit) as the defining achievement of the genre. By parsing some of the ideals adumbrated in this essay and then reading the themes and techniques of his late writing on these terms, we discover a powerful methodology at work—one that directly addresses core concerns about the ethical potential of the novel form through its very disjointed portraiture.

Akutagawa's contemporary and renowned author Tanizaki Junichirō (1886–1965) argued in 1926 that the novel as a genre depended on artfully crafted plots. He proposed looking at novels on architectural terms, emphasizing the careful arrangement of story-material to create a *kōsei-teki bikan* (structural beauty).[21] According to Akutagawa, Tanizaki claimed that "if you remove the interest of the storyline, you throw away the authority (*tokken*) of the form we call *shōsetsu*."²² Akutagawa took a contrary view. He argues in "Literary, All-Too Literary" that the "pure" (*junsui*) novel might be one that had little semblance of a story but rather moved readers through its embodiment of a poetic spirit.²³ He was thought to have lost this debate at the time (and in much scholarship since then), in part because he fails to produce a rational defense of his position. As with Akutagawa's late fiction, his writing in the essay meanders away from sequential logic into moments of suggestive imagery or digressive anecdote rather than providing a cogent argument. Yet this impressionistically conveyed theory offers a provocative account of the capacity of the novel to produce ethically moving experiences, one that builds quite consistently on his earlier work on the relation of ethics and literary affect.

Critics typically contrast Akutagawa's theory of the "plotless novel" with the vibrant plots of his early fiction to conclude that the late essay contradicts his earlier views and represents a crisis of faith in the genre. However, even in his earlier writing, Akutagawa consistently emphasized the affective force that *shōsetsu* could produce over the convincing, persuasive stories they could tell. He does so perhaps most explicitly in a short and largely neglected essay called "Art and Other Matters" (*Geijutsu sono ta*; 1920), wherein he argues against overemphasizing the mimetic function of the novel in discussions of its value. Art matters, he contends, not for its depiction of reality but rather for its capacity to move readers to perceive the world differently. Contemporaneous debates about whether "art either exists for its own sake or for the sake of real life," he claims, obfuscate *geijutsu-teki kangeki* (artistic affect) by reducing it to what can be measured in terms of value systems already in place.²⁴ The essay warns against relegating the deep emotional effects of art to entertainment or utilitarianism. Instead, Akutagawa claims a more vital role for readers' emotions in art, although he is vague about just what kind of value artistic affect produces. The essay concludes by suggesting that the affect created by the experience of powerful novel aesthetics opens the door for audiences to discover new ways of valuing rather than endorsing any particular values.²⁵ In other words, successful art makes room for socially productive emotions by moving readers to adopt new *modes* of perception rather than by providing new *objects* of perception.²⁶

Akutagawa makes a further case for the role of affect, rather than mimesis, as the ideal measure of artistic efficacy in an unfinished essay called "The Paradox of Japanese Literary Art" (*Nihon bungei no paradokkusu*). In this piece, he explains the paradox of the title as the fact that we need a general concept to understand and appreciate the particular but must have visceral experience of the particular to form a general concept.[27] He then argues that art and life serve as provisional epistemological constructions that exist only by virtue of one another. Each needs to be revised continually by experiences in the other domain. Neither art nor life has priority over the other; without representation we have no framework for making sense of experience, and without the experience of reality there is nothing to represent. What is critical for Akutagawa is the fact that each mode of experiencing moves us to new insight by stimulating our emotions, desires, and interpretations of what we experience.[28] While this formulation is at best vague and philosophically suspect—perhaps the reasons the essay never saw publication—it crucially identifies affect as the mobilizing force that shuttles subjects between life and representation to experience each in deeper, more moving ways. Mimetic representation and the "modeling" of real life here play minimal roles in comparison with the power of aesthetic form to absorb attention and to command different states of response.

Akutagawa consistently emphasizes the power of art and literature to move readers over any potential to represent life accurately or serve as an ethical guide for living (contra Shōyō and Ōgai). However, of all his writing, only "Literary, All-Too Literary" develops those general ideas about literature into an integrative theory of the novel as a genre. In this almost paradoxical effort to define the novel by its poetic spirit, Akutagawa abandons rational argument. He makes his case through disjunctive meanderings into anecdotes about literary texts, brief invocations of theories of literary value by other writers, memories, suggestive metaphors, and sentences that trail off into ellipses and leave their sense to the imagination of readers. The apparent disjointedness and roundaboutness in this writing has been read, of course, as symptomatic of diminishing cognitive ability. Yet it works astonishingly well to articulate what he suggests might be an ineffable value of the novel: its capacity to convey to readers a moving affect that cannot be achieved through careful plotting (of novels or argument).

"Literary, All-Too Literary" sets itself against norms of sense-making and logic, blurring the lines between conventions of biography, narrative fiction, and literary criticism in both form and subject matter. The essay explicitly identifies its own genre, *bungei hyōron* (literary criticism), on terms quite contrary to the critical standards according to which it has been judged. He explains that on his view such writing is not rational analysis but rather "a form of literary art ... and self-expression," one that examines the *bungei no naka no jinsei* (life within literary art).[29] We will discover that "life within literary art" is precisely the subject of his late fiction as well, although the notion there takes on dizzying metafictional overtones when his narrators recognize themselves as fictional constructs created through the stories they tell about themselves. For now, however, I want to examine how and why Akutagawa breaks down conventions of writing and self-representation to argue for the value of novel affect.

Rather than persuading through rational argument, Akutagawa's essay catches readers up in tentative turns of phrase that convey their sense holistically, through the accumulation of fleeting figures and partial gestures. Only once does the author offer something like a definition of the "poetic spirit" so central to his theme: he argues that novels can afford a *shiteki sōgon* (poetic sublime) achieved through a *jojō* (lyricism) capable of expressing and engaging us in *kyō no kanjō* (the feelings of the present).[30] In this key moment of explanation, Akutagawa tellingly departs from what we might call the structuralism of Tanizaki but also from the romanticism of the sublime conceived as an aesthetic experience of the individual in isolation. He instead figures the poetic spirit of the novel as what transports individual readers into communal experience of shared affect, the "feelings of the present" uniting contemporary readers.

The aesthetic argument here grounds itself in the social realm. This directly ties his theory of the novel as a genre to an early essay on the ethical function of the novel. In "The Morals of Tomorrow" (1925), Akutagawa discusses the novel as a catalyst for moving readers into a shared cultural ethos that provides a new vantage for developing revolutionary modes of imagining ethical values more relevant to the demands of emergent cultural moments.[31] Seen in relation to the central claim of this earlier essay, "Literary, All-Too Literary" does not break from previous theories of novel value so much as it adopts a new critical language for conveying what Akutagawa had conceived all along: that the value of the novel depends on its capacity to move readers to comport themselves adaptively with respect to the unpredictable demands of the present. For Akutagawa, the novel could achieve this more by disrupting its own conventions of representation, unsettling or surprising readers and requiring new modes of sense-making, than through transparently verisimilar representation, however compelling or nuanced the story it told.

The ethical basis of his late theory of novel aesthetics becomes clearer once we consider the way Akutagawa imagines novels to transmit affect. Scholarship on these debates with Tanizaki has generally held that Tanizaki emphasizes the concreteness of stories, whereas Akutagawa advocates a potentially art-for-art's-sake interest in the abstraction of "poetic spirit." Yet from Akutagawa's point of view, we might think of their positions as reversed. The story-material that Tanizaki favors—however "concretely" it may be specified, however vivid it appears, and with whatever architectural solidity it may be wrought through its telling—is essentially insubstantial and imaginary, an abstraction, a fictional image of unreal beings whose supposed actions and relations have no real-world presence. On the other hand, the affective experience of reading takes tangible real-world form as physiological response and felt emotion on the parts of readers. The supposedly abstract "poetic spirit" of the novel tethers solitary readers to shared social affect or *kyō no kanjō*, the real feelings of actual others in the present moment, rather than merely painting an image of the make-believe feelings of fictional beings.

By transmitting an affect that allows readers to share the experiences of others not vicariously but directly and physiologically, because they participate in the same affective response, the novel in Akutagawa's view harbors the potential not merely for achieving a compelling aesthetic form, as it does for different reasons in Tanizaki's view, but for immediate ethical effect—even if there is no particular directive or principle conveyed. As discussed in analysis of "Rashōmon" in Chapter 5, Akutagawa throughout his career explored how tensions between emotional investment and ethical judgment could serve their own meta-ethical purpose in calling for reflexive awareness of the way that our attitudes form in response to feelings and aesthetic experience. After all, Akutagawa was more interested in the new configurations of identity that intense aesthetic experiences could occasion than in advocating for any particular precepts of behavior; ethics was for him more constituted by affect than by cognitive orientation.

Even in moments where his prose seems most self-involved and abstracted from this supposed "debate" over novel value, Akutagawa continually returns to what proves an ethical vision of the capacity of the novel to bring readers into communal experiences of shared affect. In "Literary, All-Too Literary" he digresses from arguments about the novel form to comment on the disorganization of his own writing. He wonders if its *zappaku* (patchwork, confused, or disorganized) manner might really be an index of its *junsui* quality, its purity.[32] And just a few passages earlier he had argued that the purest novel may be that which has no clear *suji* (plotline).[33] The apparent digression not only pertains to but embodies the theme of the essay after all.

Akutagawa continues in what appears to be an act of free association: he recalls that he happened to have used the word "purity" in defining the poetic spirit of the novel earlier and uses the fortuitous recurrence of the term to make a jarring (meta-narrative) transition into sudden analysis of Shiga Nayoa (1883–1971), whom he claims is known for being the "purest" author. This leads to a surprising turn: Shiga's purity, Akutagawa opines, is anchored in the "moral cleanliness of his life" (*dōtokuteki ni seiketsu*). He then links this moral cleanliness to readerly affect, concluding that the *dōtoku kōki* (moral breath) and *dōtokuteki tamashi* (moral soul) of the author become *kanji-yasui* (easy to feel) when reading the *seishin-teki kutsū* (painful emotions) conveyed by Shiga's "pure" work.[34] The aesthetics that make these novels so powerful turn out to be their capacity to convey moral qualities of the authorial self.

The essay shifts from self-reflection on the absence of a clear line of reasoning in his own theory to the moral vision that produces the compelling affect at work in one of Japan's most famous contemporary writers—after establishing that criticism itself is a kind of novelistic means of expressing "life in literature." The reflexive, *zuihitsu*-like ("following the brush") manner of Akutagawa's writing, which seems constantly to trail away from arguments at hand, obscures the efficacy of its construction. He continually makes assertions about literature or literary value that "devolve" into discussion of the sensibilities of authors or the feelings that their work evokes—digressions that uncannily embody, through their refusal of conventional form, exactly what he has been arguing about the poetic spirit of the novel. Rather than supporting his conceptual claims with rigorous argument, Akutagawa makes palpable their roots in the lives and experiences of authors who transmit them.

What ties together the essay's digressions and dissolutions of logic is a focus on the collective ethos that can be generated through the aggregate experience of fragmentary moments in which the expression of morality and emotion reflexively disrupt conventions of writing and sense-making in efforts to convey impressions and sensibilities rather than meanings. This is not merely consistent with but really a culminating expression of the artful methodology we have seen developing in Akutagawa's earlier prose fiction, wherein tensions between reflexive narrative ethos and compelling story-level pathos involve readers in oscillation between states of feeling, valuing, and imagining, on the one hand, and those of self-reflective judgment and repositioning, on the other.

Akutagawa's vision of the novel in these essays could not be farther from those on which critics of his late writing base their critiques. "Literary, All-too Literary" suggests that the true essence of the novel consists in its ability to share the experiences, sensibilities, and "life" of the author, refracted through the aesthetics of writing. The goal on his view is not to communicate any facts, ideas, or moral messages per se but rather for readers to experience the "life in literature" as a transformative affective force. Even amid this strong emphasis on aesthetics, however, Akutagawa very deliberately carves out a foundational role for morality and—less directly but no less substantially—ethics. As Akutagawa's invocation of Shiga suggests, the "poetic spirit" that defines the novel as such may in fact be produced by the translation of authorial morality into something like ethics, a shared transformative affect that conveys the beauty of morality itself through the medium of literary aesthetics.

In the next chapter we will consider how Akutagawa's late writing innovates to effectively embody the "poetic spirit" produced through its representation of the "life in literature." By reading his final *shōsetsu* not on the established terms of literary criticism but rather on the terms he himself modeled in his critical writing, we can discover formal intricacies and innovations that explore new possibilities for an ethics of self-consciousness. We will also find that their dramatic failures to establish coherent narratives and anything like authentic social worlds can themselves evocatively transmit to readers an experience of alterity that had always haunted Akutagawa's writing.

8

Haunting Failures: The Transmission of Alterity in Akutagawa's Late Writing

A Haunted Life within Literature

Like so much of Akutagawa's previous work, his final *shōsetsu* concern the experiences of alienated individuals struggling to position themselves within hostile social worlds. They undo core principles of mimetic representation through reflexive and metaliterary turns. Yet rather than providing epiphanies that reorganize the dissonance between story and narrative sensibilities into transformative experiences, these late works fail to marshal their effects in the service of an organizing telos. Instead, they explore the capacity of the novel to transmit the unsettling effects of encounters with alterity rather than to transform them into edifying experiences. Their devastating reflexivity undoes the epistemological assumptions that make novel alterity legible on familiar terms. The bold unraveling of the threads of plot (*suji*) that stitch together the novel form comes at the cost of coherence and anxiety, but it also unearths the potential of the genre to provide experiences of otherness that elude the cognitive frameworks we have for making sense of them, paving the way for much contemporary experimentation with the ethics of metafiction.

The "life within literature" discussed in "Literary, All-Too Literary" (see previous chapter) is the vexed subject of Akutagawa's uncannily reflexive final works of autobiographical fiction. These two texts, *A Fool's Life* and *Cogwheels*, comprise fragmented autobiographical tales wherein experiences of reality and relations with others unnervingly come to feel no less fictive than those that take place within the fictional stories the author had written. The author-narrators at different points seem to intuit the fact that they are themselves quite literally "life within literature," fictional selves composed by the act of autobiographical storytelling. This anxious realization precipitates existential, literary, and ethical crises concerning the capacity of the self to find cogent ground for establishing real or meaningful relationships with others. In the end, these final works of fiction follow to difficult conclusions the failures and consequences of the very reflexivity to which Akutagawa had turned in his previous literature as means of situating the (literary) self in relation to others. By exploring the limitations of ethical self-consciousness through evocatively haunting language, these texts offer to readers what their authorial personae fail to find for themselves—deeply moving affective experiences that afford the possibility of ethical transformation.

Throughout his career, Akutagawa painted portraits of worlds on the verge of physical and social collapse wherein subjects struggle to make sense of irretrievably fragmented experience. In his earlier work, he created tensions between the ethos of his storytellers' wry points of view and the pathos of his characters' situations. With the autobiographical fictions *A Fool's Life* and *Cogwheels*, however, ethos and pathos have collapsed into one another. No lofty vantage is possible for narrators subsumed in their own fictional worlds. The authorial personae of these last works try to assemble the experiences of their lives only to discover, distressingly, that real life harbors an alterity that resists their efforts to convert it into the *suji* of a meaningful life story.

A Fool's Life and *Cogwheels* each purposefully deconstruct conventions of novel representation, interrogating the relationship between literary subjectivity and real-world responsibilities. In both texts the figured author fails to respond to others. At times he is overwhelmed by what feels like an oppressive alterity or *nani mono ka* (someone or something unknown) that exceeds his faculties of comprehension. In the end, the inaccessible otherness that haunts the author and disrupts the coherence of his life story emerges as an affective force for readers as well. Rather than writing this off as the symptomatic effects of a nervous mind struggling to document its decline, I want to consider how the affects produced by the *shōsetsu* put pressure on the language and conceptual frameworks we have for imagining how novels might convey the experience of alterity.

A Fool's Life-within-Literature

A Fool's Life tells the story of the author's life in brief vignettes that jump from scene to scene, focusing largely on experiences of longing, guilt, introspection, failed communication, and alienation from others. The narrator seems always nervous and unsettled, casting about for some way to become more genuinely involved in the world around him but feeling always like a spectator observing himself and others. In the end, the narrator seems to give up trying to connect the episodes of his life into a coherent life story, just as the past authorial self whose story he relates gives up on authentically inhabiting his life and relationships with others. The *shōsetsu* was dated one month before the author's suicide and published posthumously; it is often considered a kind of novelistic companion to the real suicide note delivered to his friend Kume Masao.

According to Japanese literature scholar Carole Cavanaugh, the anxious self-absorption in this text is a psychological symptom of a more pervasive cultural anxiety that weighed on Akutagawa. Her argument in "Portrait of the Writer as a Young Reader" focuses on the opening scene in which the author portrays himself atop a Western-style ladder in a bookstore famous for its translations of foreign books, poised above the hubbub of a crowd of shoppers and surrounded by works of fiction. Cavanaugh reads this scene as an allegory for the situation of the author himself: "the creation of [his own] persona depended on his participation in other, usually foreign, texts. Akutagawa's subjective response to the writing of others was the process through which he achieved subjectivity in writing about himself."[1] The scene belies for her an anxiety of influence affecting not only Akutagawa himself, but also more broadly the literary, cultural, and political situation of Japan:

> The reader-to-writer relationship he constructs in *Aru ahō no isshō* is correlative to Japan's status vis-à-vis the West: Europe and America authored the modern era, Japan decoded its categories of discourse. His ambivalence is both cultural and personal: like Japan in the Taishô era, he is the insatiable reader of a foreign canon, anxiously on the verge of writing his own text.[2]

In her assumption that an "anxiety of influence" is at work on the mind of the author of the *shōsetsu*, and not an intentional field of inquiry within the text, Cavanaugh sets up a psychoanalytic interpretation based on the pervasive sense of incompleteness that each fragment of the text delivers. In this sense, Cavanaugh follows Miyamoto Kenji and others in conflating authorial, narrating, and written selves to find their failures symptomatic of a cultural moment. Throughout her study, she places the author at "the *verge* of writing his own text"—a scene directly portrayed in the story itself—but unable to achieve the mastery of his foreign influences.[3]

Of course, both the real author and the narrating authorial persona have already completed the acts of writing that only the dramatized past self may be considered on the "verge" of undertaking. In fact, it is a testament to the masterful, evocative power of the text in portraying the author's failure to write that many scholars have focused on this image of incompletion to indict the work in which it figures as such an effective symbol. Cavanaugh is of course astute in recognizing the anxiety that "literature" and "foreignness" produce within this text, especially the demands they make on the author to account for himself. However, these are concerns that the writing effectively and deliberately, if despairingly, frames and faces. The anxiety evinced in this work does not transparently reflect Akutagawa's apprehension about creating original literature good enough for the Western Other. Rather, it is the effect of his inquiry into the capacity of novels to engage otherness at all. *A Fool's Life* tells the story of a writer confronting the ineradicable fissure between himself as fictional construct and as real agent responsible for both narrative and real-life sociality.

The *shōsetsu* certainly reads like the product of a mind in crisis. It consists of a series of brief, disjointed vignettes, some no more than a few lines and others running on for a page or two before breaking into some new thought or experience that has come to mind. Sections frequently trail off in ellipses that suggest unspeakable ends to present trains of thought. At other times the narration shifts jarringly to new memories whose threads of association with previous thoughts are gossamer at best. The autobiographical piece constantly recollects itself only to fall apart. Yet the tremors in language and structure resonate all-too uncannily with its thematic concerns about coherence and meaning-making, as well as the views put forth in "Literary, All-Too Literary"—consistently enough to suggest some design at work after all. Moreover, the anxieties that the narrator expresses about the coherence of his identity, the authenticity of his relationships to others, and the aims and effects of literary art disconcertingly coincide with concerns raised for readers by formal shifts, fissures, and metafictional reflection. As I shall argue in the ensuing analysis, this *shōsetsu* provocatively conflates literary, ethical, and epistemological concerns about identity and representation.

From its opening passage in the bookstore, the author of *A Fool's Life* comes into being within, and through the description of, a thoroughly textual world in which questions about identity and self-other relations take shape within a distinctly literary context. This is expressed powerfully in the conclusion of the opening bookstore vignette by an inter-textual moment that has been translated by Jay Rubin as "life is not worth more than a single line of Baudelaire."[4] The suggestion here that literary experience is preferable to that of real life accords well with the text's strange inversion of the literary and the real: art and literature possess a vibrancy that contrasts painfully with the insubstantial, illusory experiences that real life offers. Yet in the context of the thoroughgoing reflexivity we shall discover in the text, this passage harbors further metaliterary connotations. The line, "jinsei wa ichigyō no Bōdoreiru ni mo shika nai," could be rendered in a more direct translation: "life is no more than a line of Baudelaire."[5] In other words, we might say that there is no life for him beyond—or perhaps life exists for him as nothing other than—a line of literature.

The faint suggestion is amplified in other moments of self-reflection that point to the author's recognition that he has quite literally composed himself through autobiographical narrative—that the speaking subject of the story is quite literally a "life within literature." In one scene, the author views a clown puppet in a Western clothing store window and compares himself to the figure. The rumination about his lack of autonomy in real life quickly becomes overwritten by literary self-consciousness about previous acts of literary self-representation: "But, the self outside of his consciousness—that is, his own second self—had long ago stuffed those feelings into a short story."[6]

The apparently simple scene harbors an imbricated metafictional complexity. The author who sees the puppet recalls a past moment in which he wrote a story about his sense of himself as a puppet on strings. Yet the point of view expressed is strange. The other, "second self" is tellingly *not* the self he wrote into a story. It is on the contrary the self-as-author who should simply be himself, but who is experienced here as a self *outside* the consciousness of the presently recollecting narrative persona. The vignette is layered with the metaliterary suggestion that the third-person author doing the recollecting here is no more an autonomous agent than the characters whom the author has represented in the past. That is, the author in this *shōsetsu* appears aware of himself as an authored being, a figure more akin to the past self-representation that had been stuffed into a story and for whom his own real authorial consciousness remains inaccessible, a second self. This motif recurs later when the author encounters a stuffed swan and considers it a symbol for his own self-representation in the very text we are reading, creating even more dizzying metaliterary connotations (a scene we will examine later).

The fragmentation of selfhood occasioned by literary reflexivity in such moments hauntingly conveys the feeling of being at the mercy of outside forces despite feeling trapped within authorial consciousness. The "puppet strings" are composed of the very literary lines whereby the author seeks purchase on his own identity, only to create himself as a character who becomes entangled within his own life story. In other words, the authorial self turns out to be composed of the dislocations that alienate him from himself. He is haunted by an alterity that reflects the literal truth of his existence as a fiction of himself—an alterity whose reverberations alienate him even from himself. We have explored such a haunting alterity in Akutagawa's works in previous chapters, almost always as an effect of characters' self-complacencies shattering in the face of encounters with others. Here, however, the *nani mono ka* emerges as a fundamental condition of the "life in literature" and the author's efforts to apprehend others through the epistemological prison of literary existence. It is a disturbing but artfully wrought reflection that inheres both in story and narration.

A Fool's Life chronicles the author's failures to connect to the people in his life, many of whom come to feel more like fictions and symbols in a story than autonomous characters.[7] Indeed, in accordance with those conventions wherein autobiographical fiction effaces the names of real others for the sake of privacy, the people in his life are often referred to through metonymic and metaphoric symbols like "butterfly wings."[8] Curiously, although he fails to feel connections with other people as authentic, the author does obsessively relate himself to fictional others. In the vignette "Man-Made Wings," for example, the narrator explains that he had always avoided Rousseau, the writer famous for his own self-consciously literary autobiography *Confessions*, from an instinctual sense of their similarity.[9] In "Lies," the narrator reflects on his own falsity and flaws ("he was aware of all of his faults and weak points, every single one of them") and then notes how the autobiographical personae in Rousseau's *Confessions* and Shimazaki Tōson's (1872–1943) *New Life* (Shinsei) likewise seem to exist as lies.[10] He goes on to compare himself to the persona of the wastrel poet Francois Villon (1431–?) before concluding the passage by likening himself to a partially withered tree that Jonathan Swift (1667–1745) had used to describe the mental confusion that would precede his death—a reference that brings full circle the narrator's earlier discovery of an image of himself in a tree in the landscape (a scene to which we will briefly return).[11] And in yet another intertextual moment, the author reads *The Confessions of a Fool* by Strindberg and finds that the lies of the protagonist hardly differ from his own.[12] In sum, the author fails to identify with real others but feels strong connections to literary figures—especially representations of authors who, in autobiographical works, confront questions about authenticity in self-representation. The patterning here is far too carefully orchestrated for such occurrences merely to be happenstances clutched at by a distressed mind; the novel systematically thematizes the very kinds of crises of literary representation and real-life meaning for which it has been critiqued.

In *A Fool's Life* the real world becomes accessible only through and as literary experience; perhaps this is why literary identifications come so much more naturally to the author than interpersonal ones. Even in the earliest vignettes, we find a disturbing resonance between the feelings and states of mind of the author and the ostensibly real environments in which he finds himself. The physical world around him unnervingly reflects his mental landscape. The author continually finds images of himself in his surroundings that leave him feeling unreal, dislocated from some original but inaccessible self, and even further isolated from others. As mentioned, in one early scene he tries to forget himself in the view of a ragged landscape but cannot help "discovering himself in the cherry trees," catching his own image superimposed through a partially reflective window, as though even the natural world in this story exists as nothing more than a theater of self-reflection.[13] In other moments, also briefly noted already, the author finds created figures (a puppet and a stuffed swan) in shops that spur self-reflection about his past personae and his own fictional selfhood. In yet another scene, entitled "Mirrors" (*Kagami*), the author reflects on his failures to live up to the promises of his social commitments during a conversation. In that moment he notices how the café mirrors throw back "countless images" of himself reflected "coldly" and "threateningly."[14] The vignette cuts off abruptly in this moment that casts his internal dissociation into external reality, as though the mirror reflections have broken apart the compositional unity of his self-representation.

The author of *A Fool's Life* cannot escape the horizon of his own self-consciousness. The world he inhabits, even when it brings other people or places into view, exists as nothing more than authorial self-projection, a metaliterary fact that is quite literally and tragically the case for this character of autobiographical fiction. The world of the story purposefully echoes—indeed, is constituted by—the state of mind of the author of a work of autobiographical fiction anxious about his place in the world. That world is falling apart: the dreariness of trees in which he discovers himself, the enveloping spray of heavy rain catalyzing the noxious rubber smell of his coat, the shabby towns above which he tries to imagine himself soaring as Icarus, the stink of cow manure, and the odor of decomposing bodies among charred ruins after the earthquake all viscerally embody the representational and psychological decomposition of the landscape of the self.

This is much more than the pathetic fallacy whereby interior states are projected onto external ones. Indeed, within the metafictional self-consciousness of the text, the physical reality of the story-world exists as an extrusion of the mind of the author who inhabits it. An early vignette illustrates this imbrication of consciousness and reality with a potent literalness. The author visits an asylum and becomes profoundly disturbed by the image of a kind of white substance, presumably brain matter, spied on the skull of a corpse. The all-too-real image drives home for him the base physicality of all mental phenomenon and leaves him contemplating the nature of human faculties and perceptions of reality. A short while thereafter the section ends with narrator gazing out of a window to the wider world, where a thin layer of moss whitens the top of a brick fence—an uncanny iteration of organic whiteness seeping on a skeletal boundary separating the self from the external world.[15] This is hardly an accidental observation or literary image on which to end the vignette and seems unlikely to have been a faithfully recorded happenstance from years ago. The scene leaves us with the vertiginous suggestion that the entire external world quite literally reduces to mere projection in the mind of the narrator, a leakage of brain matter that has spilled into autobiographical recollection rather than an objectively material world. The physical environment disturbingly echoes the image in his head, which is an image of a head leaking the matter that composes its thoughts and, hence, the reality of the world. The vignette ends with this discovery.

If nothing else, the uncanny repetition of the image and the selection of the subject matter of the asylum visit reflect deliberate orchestration. The metaliterary truth of course is that the author *has* composed this world out of his own mental image, and the patterning of symbolism here and elsewhere alerts us to the author's recognition of this situation. Akutagawa is not just haphazardly stringing together memories in a failing effort to make sense of past experiences; he carefully composes and transmits to readers the unsettling, haphazard disarray of an all-too-self-conscious mind coming to terms with its own literary composition and the implications of that situation for his grounding his sense of selfhood in something real. The failures of the diegetic world to offer any stable external environment for the authorial self are a direct consequence of the narrative failures of the embedded author to sustain his composition—failures we will soon find directly tied to moral failings in the character of the author.

The Author as Icarus

A Fool's Life inverts the relationship between representation and reality so often painted by the mimesis of realist fiction, wherein authors must find language and methods that convey the reality of experiences. The embedded author in this text appears haunted by the truth that he inhabits a world he is in fact composing through narrative acts of recollection—a motif that comes to fuller and more dizzying fruition in recollections of past acts of authorial self-creation that we will soon examine. His private cogitations reverberate into the external world, unsettling any effort to read the text as straightforward autobiographical fiction.

Critics claim that such effects are symptoms of a mind incapable of grounding itself in reality, let alone composing a coherent novel (see previous chapter). Yet the careful architecture of patterning that signals the confluence of narrative and story-world breakdowns should give us pause. The failure of the autobiographical project and ultimate fall of the author is repeatedly and powerfully foreshadowed and underscored throughout the text. In one moment, after the author reflects on his identity as an author and the selves he had created through writing, a nebulous but implacable *unmei* (fate) gathers in the darkening street waiting to consume him. Another vignette ends with the sky unable to sustain itself and about to drop the burdensome rain it carries. Yet another ends with a coconut palm "soaring" on high across the ocean, destined to fall. Such patterned symbolism, combined with the echo effect between the embedded author's deteriorating state of mind and the supposedly external environment of the (fictional) world he occupies, quite consciously composes the portrait of the failure of the artist that critics have adopted as their own explanations rather than an internally crafted exploration.

A Fool's Life even offers an archetype that brings together these disparate moments of literary, existential, and (we shall see) ethical failure: the figure of Icarus.

> For the twenty-nine-year-old, life held not even the faintest light any more. And yet, Voltaire supplied him with artificial wings.
>
> He spread those artificially wings and soared effortlessly into the sky. The joys and sorrows of a life bathed in the light of the intellect fell away together before his eyes. Dropping ironies and smiles upon the miserable towns below, he surged upward through a sky without obstacle, climbing straight toward the sun. As though he had forgotten the ancient Greek who plunged to his death in the sea precisely because his artificial wings had been burnt by the sun.[16]

So compelling is this portrait that critics have much less self-consciously invoked it to discuss the fate of the implied author as an artist whose aesthetics could not sustain his flight from the real world. The efficacy of the image and wry self-knowledge it evinces, however, suggest more thoughtful artistry than has been assumed.

The man-made wings that reading provides the narrator bring to culmination a motif seeded by numerous passages using images of wings to mark moments of contact between imaginings and real experience—part of a pattern that belies the careful arrangement of this portrait of failure.[17] Tellingly, the author soars above the fallen world only "as though" he had forgotten the Icarus myth. The language implies the impossibility of the delusion or self-deception imputed to him. Even in his imagination, the tragically self-conscious author realizes that he can only project himself through the counterfactual modality offered by fiction, an unsustainable posture from which nothing but "ironies and smiles" can serve as outward-reaching, nonreciprocal points of intellectual and emotional connection to the world. The irony that proved so effective at creating energies through the tension between ethos and pathos in earlier work here becomes the habitual but ineffectual gesture of the author's doomed flight. The literary self-consciousness that holds the author aloft also tragically distances him from others, diminishing his immersion in the kinds of intense affects ("the joys and sorrows of the world, bathed in the light of reason, disappeared beneath his eyes") that acted as a socially grounding force in the author's earlier work. Having taken metaliterary flight into his own artistic creation, his return to the world becomes a deathward fall induced by the metaphysical vertigo of literary self-consciousness. Akutagawa thus prefigures, in highly evocative and concentrated literary form, the very paradigms that scholarship over the ensuing century has more laboriously drawn out in prosaic critique, believing them to be their own insights.

Not despite but through its broken portrait of ethical and artistic failure, *A Fool's Life* puts into practice the vision of novel representation for which Akutagawa had argued in "Literary, All-Too Literary." True, the *shōsetsu* never represents characters or the world with anything like authenticity or compelling realism; it never "satisfyingly represents even a single dog," as Miyamoto Kenji asserted.[18] However, the experience of those very failures powerfully conveys to readers the felt alienation of the author and the strain of his efforts to find existential and social purchase through literary reflection. Like the meandering illogic of "Literary, All-Too Literary," the disjointed stitching together and breaking apart of narrative *suji* work to compose not a realistic life story but rather powerful feelings of alienation, anxiety about otherness, and the failure of both reflexivity and literary retrospection to secure any kind of transcendental perspective or socially grounded identity that justifies or makes sense of experience. With the orchestration and purposefulness rather than merely symptomatic quality of this text's disorienting failures of coherence now established, as well as the intentional intertwining of questions of novel representation, ethics, and aesthetics, we are now prepared to examine the aims and effects of these methods as they merge more clearly tied to literary affect in *Cogwheels*. Through analysis of an intertextual turn, we will discover how the text explores the ethical fault lines beneath the ruptures in its own narrative, as well as how it endeavors to accomplish, by its own formal dissolution, the interpersonal transmission of affect and "poetic spirit" that the author could not achieve in his own relationships.

A-Sensei and the Transmission of Affect

A Fool's Life consists principally of the efforts of the author to recollect his life-in-literature through a series of vignettes strung together to compose a portrait of selfhood. Its counterpart *Cogwheels* consists of more temporally continuous vignettes in which the weary author experiences alienating dissociations while struggling with both his sanity and his personal tragedies. *Cogwheels* also attends closely to the experiences and effects of an alterity beyond the self, and to language as the material of lived relations through which such effects make themselves manifest.

Like *A Fool's Life*, *Cogwheels* brings up a number of the moral failings of the author—in particular his distance from family and friends and the way he disappoints relations seeking his intimacy. Part of what detaches the author from others is an oppressive awareness of the forms of mediation—particularly fiction and language—that entrap and even physically oppress him. Language becomes a palpable, alien, and physiological force in this *shōsetsu*. Even the familiar feels strange; at one point, the author finds himself unable to pronounce the name of a historical scholar and is "distressed by the thought that this was a Japanese word."[19] The unnerving effects of language constantly intrude upon and break apart the author's sense of himself and his connections to the world. In one moment, for example, he notices a foreign woman at a nearby table and suddenly "hears the words 'Mrs. Townshead' whispered to me by an invisible something (*me ni mienai mono*) that I could not see. 'Mrs. Townshead' was of course a name I did not know."[20] He experiences the otherness of the woman as foreign and disembodied language; she exists only as a name detached from any secure ground of reference to an authentic person.

The alterity of others in *Cogwheels* takes shape as speech that haunts the author from without but also burrows deep into the language of his own self-consciousness—and, of course, the narrative which represents it. In another moment, for example, "some kind of vague word just kept repeating on the phone …. I could not get the English word 'mole' out of my consciousness …. It transformed from 'mole' to 'la mort.'"[21] The phone connects him to something foreign which then intrudes upon his thoughts and alters them. The unsettling image of a rodent becomes transformed into death, which notion then prompts the author to self-reflection. He considers his own strange reaction to the word in the mirror, where he confronts a "second self" and then reminisces about the number of times others had mistaken someone else for him, claiming to have seen his doppelgänger, a self which is not the self. Alterity becomes self-alienation in the mind of the author, and then becomes part of the reality described in the story.

Foreignness in this text invades the sanctity of the self from without, permeating the language that composes the author's self-reflections and calling into question the authenticity of both his experience and its representation. He feels dislocated even from himself, especially when he considers matters of ethical responsibility. The figure that most powerfully represents this self-alienation in *Cogwheels* turns out, by now unsurprisingly, to be another fictional representation of a literati who writes an autobiographical work—that of Natsume Soseki's (1867–1916) famous character "Sensei."

In one critical and telling moment, Akutagawa's narrating persona directly links his experience of a haunting otherness to questions about the ethics of his identity. He describes how feelings of guilt alienate him from the role of "Sensei" conferred upon him by others:

> "A Sensei"—that was for me at this time the unhappiest phrase. I believed that I had committed every kind of sin. And yet on any occasion they kept calling me "Sensei." I could not help but feel in this a *nani mono ka* laughing at me. *Nani mono ka*? And yet my materialism could only refuse such mysticism. Just three months earlier I had published these words in a small literary journal: "I have nothing like an artistic conscience, or any kind of conscience at all. What I have is only nerves."[22]

The *nani mono ka* here appears only as a mocking rather than the transformative or potentially salutary force found in his earlier works. It amplifies his sense of alienation and drives home the impossibility of situating the self in any ethically meaningful (bearing relevance to his "conscience") orientation toward others. The experience of otherness leads directly to contemplation on his moral character as it is comprised by his activities in both art and life. As we might expect given the pervasive conflation of art and life we have discovered in his late work, his lack of an "artistic conscience" proves commensurate with lacking "any kind of conscience at all."

Of all the examples that might describe his alienation from young writers and intellectuals in the literary world of Japan, Akutagawa focuses on the feeling that he could not live up to the expectations inherent in the term "Sensei." He finds both himself and the world morally bankrupt, and wells with self-disgust at the misidentification. The circumstances and his response establish a clear parallel between himself and the protagonist of Natsume Sōseki's most celebrated *shōsetsu*, *Kokoro*, a character addressed throughout the text as "Sensei" despite his conviction of moral unworthiness. Sensei also commits suicide after penning his autobiographical story, as does Akutagawa himself and, by implication, his authorial persona. Sōseki in fact features importantly in both *A Fool's Life* and *Cogwheels*, both through direct reference and literary homage. But it is in the invocation of *Kokoro* here that persistent existential and ethical concerns coincide most powerfully with the metaliterary.

Like Akutagawa's own work, *Kokoro* also deals with the relation between ethics and writing through a carefully wrought and complex formal structure vitally important to the themes of the work. It grapples with the problems of communication and intimacy between self and others. *Kokoro* indeed makes an ideal intertextual touchstone for encapsulating the themes of Akutagawa's late fiction. Both *shōsetsu* focus on the affects produced within readers—indeed Soseki wrote a powerful treatise and a rather famous formula explaining literary affect.[23] Moreover, the figures who write their own autobiographies within these texts both remark upon their own struggles to achieve genuine, "living communication" in contrast to the "soulless dolls" of abstract ideas or empty expressions.[24] Sensei and Akutagawa's narrator both express core feelings of moral disgust and alienation from others. Both are desperate to find genuine forms of contact. Both write with the hope that by transmitting the story of their failures to come to terms with themselves and find true intimacy with others, some form of true intersubjective understanding can take place, even if that proves their literal undoing. And indeed, both turn to visceral, graphic images of pulling apart their own physical bodies to achieve living, transformative communication of the sort Akutagawa theorized in "Literary, All-Too Literary."[25]

Each self-conscious writer attempts to strip away the surface structures of communication and self-image. They strive to convey with authenticity their experiences of alienation and otherness in ways that will move readers as they themselves have been moved without reducing that otherness to the familiar terms of their own narratives. Their disturbing autobiographies limn solipsistic worlds haunted by a living presence that threatens their very existences. In both cases, what their desires for authentic communion with others seem to require, tragically, is the sacrificial opening of textual and real bodies for the sake of transmission to readers.

In Sōseki, it is reception of Sensei's testament by the narrator, and by extension the reader, that brings the spirit of Sensei's narrative to life and bridges the gap between self and other. Through its haunting structure the reader of *Kokoro* is ultimately folded into the positions of both the narrator and Sensei at once. In the last section of the *shōsetsu*, narrative time and story time become conflated; we read Sensei's letter as we presume the narrator to be reading it, with no intervening narration or final remarks beyond Sensei's own words. We become the medium through which Sensei's testament speaks just as the narrator occupies that same position, so that our subjectivities turn out to be mutually constitutive in their apprehension of Sensei. This overlaying of perspectives of course resonates with the real situation of reading in which the author speaks through the narrator's reproduction of Sensei's tale and his own (reflexive) act of reading to convey something real and meaningful to his readers.

The truncated narrative structure of *Kokoro*, which never returns to the position of the narrator after sharing Sensei's testament in its final third, becomes its means of rendering that text a living word, one that unsettles and moves readers rather than being reduced to mere information or meaning. The portrait of ethical failure, as well as the failure of Sensei's own introspective consciousness to save him from that failure, memorializes Sensei not by summing up his life or drawing conclusions but by leaving the narrator, and by extension readers, with the haunting experience of a perspective never represented as fully apprehended by its recipient.

Only by rereading with the "incompleteness" of the story in mind can we recognize that Sensei's life takes living shape for us not through any denouement, conclusion, or visible impact on future decisions of the narrator. Rather, we have been haunted by its presence all along in the narrator's manner of telling the tale itself. It is the form of the *shōsetsu*, rather any particular element of the story told or judgment rendered, that harbors the ethical effects of the testament. The traces of its continuing agency in moving the narrator are visible in the writing through which Sensei's story is told.

The Haunting Alterity of Akutagawa's Final *Shōsetsu*

With its metaliterary structure now firmly in view, and by recalling Akutagawa's own theory of literary affect in "Literary, All-Too Literary," we can see how Akutagawa's late works tragically echo both the sentiments and the methods of Sōseki's famous *shōsetsu*. At the heart of *Kokoro*, we find a story of ethical failure that impels narrative acts by both Sensei and the narrator in a dialogically layered text that provides the "living spirit" of Sensei with his own "life in literature" through the formal incompleteness of its representation of his failure. In the same way, a moving "poetic spirit" comes into effect through the portrait of the failure of the narrative effort of the author to come to terms with his own guilt and alienation in *Cogwheels* and *A Fool's Life*. Just as *Kokoro* positions readers to *experience* the act of communication and reception that it *represents*, Akutagawa's late texts, by their very refusal of realist and autobiographical conventions of novel closure, create for readers the disorientation and anxiety that plagues the author's own decohering experiences of self and otherness. What they convey are the failures of narrative to confer meaning and order upon the discrete and disjointed experiences that novels present as social subjects. In doing so, this failure gives living presence to the otherness that disrupts its own narrative.

In both of Akutagawa's texts, the author is barely strung together as the subject of his tale. Through the brokenness of language, disjointedness, and carefully arrayed glimpses and reflections which promise meanings never quite actualized, these final *shōsetsu* convey feelings and experiences that elude the capacity of the authorial self to recognize or describe. They boldly step beyond the method and structure of *Kokoro* by sacrificing themselves entirely, rather than by representing an act of self-sacrifice. By sharing anecdote after anecdote wherein the author comes across writing, speech, and sounds that should feel familiar but which exude a foreignness that alienates him—by delivering in quoted fragments the real utterances that obliterate his sense of selfhood—Akutagawa provides a novel means of passing on to readers experiences of otherness foreclosed to his authorial personae.

As critics have asserted, Akutagawa's late *shōsetsu* render the world beyond the self insubstantial; others appear as mere characters in the story of the life of the author. Akutagawa refers even to real family and friends through descriptions that attach their identities to symbolic terms like madness, moonlight, and butterfly wings. They do not appear as full beings in their own right; they are brief sketches whose words become detached and reverberate in the mind of the narrator far more powerfully than the impact made by their own presences, intentions, or relations to the author. The speech of others, however, harbors a kind of mythopoeic power. As embodied in the strangeness of the appellation *Sensei* that reduces the author to a bundle of nerves, language contains within itself a tantalizing foreignness that threatens the sanctity of the authorial self but which proves itself essential for interpersonal understanding.

In one moment of *A Fool's Life*, the words spoken by an elder writer, presumably Tanizaki Junichirō, blot out the existence of their speaker from the narrative entirely. As soon as this character speaks, the narration shifts from describing the interaction to conveying the disorienting effect of the speaker's language on the protagonist's world: "the words released him into a world of which he knew nothing."[26] The vignette breaks off thus lost in the affective experience of the utterance. Likewise, a scene entitled "Marriage" organizes itself not around his wife as a person or even their relationship, but around a "scolding," a set piece of dialogue uttered by his aunt and then delivered by him to his wife as though it were a material object.[27] His very family members here serve as mere conduits for the transmission of received utterances on social identity that act as binding forces defining the narrator's obligations in relation to them.

Cogwheels similarly focuses our attention on the formal features of its own language by having its first-person author continually interrupt the flow of his narrative to linger on linguistic associations. At one moment, a phrase someone had recently used, "really tantalizing," returns to mind suddenly in the middle of a description of his journey to a mental hospital: "'Irritating,—tantalizing—Tantalus—Inferno.' Tantalus was in fact my own self staring through the glass door."[28] The words of another taken on symbolic life and identify the author with yet another doomed fictional being—by now a powerful motif in these works. In another moment, the author is overcome with vertiginous unease when he hears a sound combination that feels foreign even though he knows it is his own Japanese tongue. Shortly thereafter, he hears the word on the phone that sound like "mole" and finds himself launched on an etymological chain of associations that "unsettles" and "attacks him"; words threaten the integrity of the self through their very unfamiliarity.[29] In one last and telling example, the author of *A Fool's Life* comes across the foreign words "*Talaria*," "*Tale*," and "*Tailpot*" in a dictionary and finds them so unsettling that an itch forms in his throat and he coughs up biological matter onto the dictionary.[30] Perhaps precisely because it originates beyond the authorial self, the speech of others and foreign words detach from their sources to take on uncanny life, one that supersedes the author's recognition of the feelings, identities, and intentions of others. Language conveys an alterity that does more than merely threaten symbolically the integrity of the authorial personae; within the metaliterary structure of these late texts, it has the potential to disturb and even refigure the body of the author.

In these and more passages, something reaches through language to affect the author on a physical level, reducing him to nerves. He finds himself deeply unsettled by designs and intentions that did not originate with him but directly affect his composure. In the case of the dictionary, for example, the unbidden words turn out to have several threads of connection with other images and events in his late *shōsetsu*.[31] As language laden with significances in excess of what can make sense for the represented author, but which nevertheless bear relevance for the recasting of his situation in the narrative of the autobiographical fiction in which he appears, these printed words threaten the author's sense of control over his own life—which in this metafictional world cannot be disentangled from its telling. Words are the nerves that thread together his literary self; as we witness the unravelling of that self we feel the pain that such words inflict precisely because they partake in a reality that the fictional subject of the narrative cannot attain.

In metaliterary moments that reflect on the power of language to obliterate the "life within literature" of the authorial personae, the unnerving otherness of language intrudes upon the narrator's own thinking and breaks apart the *suji* of this *shōsetsu*, which dissolves into ellipses and broken sentences. Readers of such scenes experience not the illusion of a realistic character empathizing or feeling alienated from fictional others but rather the emanation of represented affects into the language of the writing itself. These *shōsetsu* thematize the unraveling of the entrapping narratives to which their authorial personae desperately, and failingly, cling to hold themselves together. Alterity presents itself as the effects on the forms of representation through which the very ideas of self and other become legible for the self-conscious authors.

Conclusion

A Fool's Life and *Cogwheels* disturbingly resist the kinds of closures that autobiographical fiction typically invites us to confer upon it. What they convey is not a coherent life story but rather the unsettling failures of literary representation to make sense of perception, to create comprehensible and identifiable subjects, and to confer meaning upon their experiences. One cannot read these texts merely for the stories they tell; the stories are recursively fabricated by the form of their telling. And what one finds in both story and language is a haunting strangeness that alienates.

Not coincidentally, it is precisely the refusal of the speech of others to assimilate into the author's own sensibilities that proves so discomfiting to the author-protagonists. And as we have seen, their failures of sense-making are systematically linked with the social, familial, and ethical within the story insofar as they coincide with descriptions of the author's sense of guilt, responsibilities, and connections with people. What alienates him from others in these metafictional works is not simply his oppressive, self-conscious knowledge that "life in literature" is fictitious. It is almost the contrary problem. Others are too real, have too much inaccessible life of their own, for the author to convert into the story of himself. All that the author can convey is the sensory effects of encounters with their appearances and speech. In this regard, the work certainly fails as a piece of realist autobiographical fiction. Yet that failure itself evocatively conveys an otherness that refuses to be reduced to the subjective terms of authorial self-representation.

The aporia and dissolution that critics have assumed betoken failures in artistry and moral vision prove powerful methods of addressing the very systemic failures of novel representation that Akutagawa confronts in these works. Can *anyone* satisfactorily represent "a single dog," let alone other human beings, with authenticity? Or is it the best that novels can do merely to compose portraits that will be received as lifelike within established conventions and imaginary schema of recognition—the very implication of his reflection on the "puppet" who stands for the protagonist of the author's earlier fiction in *A Fool's Life*? The answer that Akutagawa adumbrates in "Literary, All-Too Literary" finds fuller realization in his late *shōsetsu*. It is by undoing the tidy symbolic structures, the telos of meaningful arrangement, and the self-consistency of literary subjects that have long been considered the hallmark of novel aesthetics that novels might more fully engage readers in moving experiences of otherness.

Alterity haunts these late accounts from without, disturbing the fragile and solipsistic self-identifications of an all-too-literary author through the very narrative form that represents them. Intertextual allusions populate these *shōsetsu* with literary ghosts, characters, and the self-representations of other authors, who feel more substantial in this metaliterary world than supposedly real others. Indeed, they have a material existence defined on terms other than those the author projects—they have been written into being by other authors— and so in that sense truly bring an otherwise unrepresentable otherness into the text that the author cannot achieve in his own representations of real people. The otherness that haunts the author without ever making itself available for understanding becomes manifest for readers through the very language that conveys the breakdown of the author's capacity to represent others.

Only metafiction can literalize and embody the alterity of language in this way. These texts conflate the means of representation with the experiences of the subjects composed by the narrative acts of recollection, subjecting readers to dramatized experiences not vicariously, through empathy, but directly through unsettling formal effects. What in the diegetic world the represented authors experience as dislocation from both self and others reverberates in our world through the very language whereby they attempt to compose themselves in autobiographical self-portraits of their own failure to create themselves as subjects. *A Fool's Life* and *Cogwheels* put readers into direct contact with the effects of an alterity that threatens the integrity of the very medium of its experience, speaking through and beyond the author's own account to disturb its entrapping solipsism.

As a genre partially defined by its creation of a sustained framework for representing characters and human interaction—its mimesis—the novel inscribes in the very language and structure of narration implicit standards of judgment and norms of recognition that predetermine and delimit what counts as a subject. Novels ossify perspective in narrative and therefore struggle to achieve authenticity in the presentation of an otherness that does not appropriate, reduce to the familiar, or exoticize. Akutagawa's turn to metaliterary self-consciousness, however, precludes the kind of immersive experience in novel mimesis that conventionally affords empathetic identification. He explores instead the possibility that real alterity exudes through the fictional *apprehended as such*—a point we shall find more overtly explored by contemporary author Murakami Haruki.

In sum, the plots and coherence of Akutagawa's stories and narrative identities "break down" in his later works, as many critics point out, but not the effectiveness of his writing. *Cogwheels* and *A Fool's Life* powerfully explore the capacities and limits of literary affect to breach the "enamel" of self-consciousness separating us from others, and to move us beyond the codified different versions of ourselves—the socially recognized "sensei," the alienated paranoiac, the guilty lover, the caring husband, and so on—through which we attempt to understand ourselves in our relationships to others. Authorial personae are stimulated, reduced to nerves, and rewritten by the otherness that reverberates through speech acts in the text. By conflating narrative and real bodies in the metaliterary milieu of his late fiction, literalizing what Bakhtin would later say about speech acts embodying subjectivities, Akutagawa demonstrates the reach of literary representation into physiological affect, the domain of ethical impact imagined in the "shared feelings" and "poetic spirit" of his theorizing.

The inward turn in modern Japanese literary ethics that this book has begun to trace, the effort to arrive at ethics through rather than in opposition to self-consciousness—and even self-absorption—in novel representation inaugurates a prescient exploration of the ethical positioning intrinsic to the narrative form of the genre that continues today. In the decade following Akutagawa's death, the Japanese writers and critical thinkers who most closely pursued the relationship between ethics and self-consciousness, such as Yokomitsu Riichi and Kobyashi Hideo, would attempt to work through reflection on the abstraction of literary language to arrive at some more concrete and tangible theory of literary ethics. They attempt to bring full circle the work begun by Ōgai and Akutagawa in exploring self-consciousness by working through it to arrive at something un-self-conscious, more rooted in real life and experience than in the abstractions of literary and theoretical writing.[32]

Akutagawa's distressing portrait of the narrator's failure to escape modern self-consciousness need not itself be cast as an ethical or artistic failure. On the contrary, by making the worlds of his final *shōsetsu* so clearly solipsistic and so consciously fictional, and yet having something beyond the self speak through the work anyway while powerfully tying this final message both to literary fiction (*Kokoro* and others) and his own all-too-real death, Akutagawa makes a powerful case for the capacity of metafiction rather than mimetic fiction to engage real-life ethics.

9

Imaginary Worlds and Real Ethics: The Case of Murakami Haruki

The Immanent Ethics of Murakami

The twenty-first century has seen the rise of an international industry of popular and critical publication dedicated to the work of Japanese author Murakami Haruki (1949–). His novels represent for many a coded guide for life, whereby everyday *kodawari*, or "careful discrimination," in personal habits from choosing music to preparing sandwiches promises meaningful shifts in moral character and social relationships. Japan's mainstream literary world, however, has registered serious doubts about the ethics of Murakami's writing—particularly the notion that an inward turn can, in the manner of Foucauldian self-stylization, produce real interpersonal growth. Internationally distinguished scholar Karatani Kōjin declared in the late 1980s that Murakami merely plays "empty formal games," a claim repeated by well-known critic Masao Miyoshi in 1991.[1] In the mid-1990s, Nobel Prize winner Ōe Kenzaburo protested, "Murakami doesn't take an active attitude toward society, or even toward the immediate environment of daily life. He works by passively absorbing influences from various genres, as if he were listening to background music. He just goes on spinning within his interior fantasy world."[2] And in his 2006 monograph, the eminent scholar Komori Yōichi accused Murakami of both ethical reductionism and relativism and of constantly murdering women in his novels.[3]

Counter to most criticism, I argue that the reflexive formal structures, the thematic and generic interest in fantasy, and even the apparent relativism of Murakami's writing all serve ethical ends occluded by conventional assumptions about the relationship between novel representation and reality. Scholars have dismissed his work, I find, because they so often theorize novel ethics as becoming effective through oscillation between immersive experience in mimetic worlds and subsequent reflection on the value of that experience for real life. Against such models, Murakami insists on the intrinsic value of our experience of novel alterity. His characters cross diegetic and ontological planes to enter verisimilar worlds of fantasy and fiction while maintaining a shadow life that operates simultaneously within an originary reality. They find themselves responsible for both real and manifestly fictional others who inhabit different worlds—some in separate spheres of social life, and some quite literally on different planes of existence. Readers, therefore, directly confront questions about how we regard *fictional* alterity as part of their immersive experience, rather than through subsequent reflection. This recursive, reflexive quality of his ethical inquiry—among others—has proven a blind spot for critics of his work.

Much ethical criticism of the novel, not just in Japan and not just on Murakami, conceives its task as transposing ethical principles from the field of novel representation into the political domain of real life. Murakami's novels complicate this critical gesture by making the process of ethical transpositioning, across value systems and between fiction and real life, the subject of their inquiry. Rather than encoding guides for real life in the ethos of verisimilar worlds, Murakami speaks to global theories of novel ethics by calling attention not to the ethics found in novels but to those of our experiences of fiction itself. Through analysis of a novel notorious for its turn toward solipsistic fantasy, I conclude that what I will identify as the author's "fractal realism" develops an immanent ethics of reading that directs readers to reconsider the role that the imaginary plays in our processes of encountering and caring for others.

Murakami Criticism and the Fantasy of Realism

Modern Japanese literature scholar Kiyoshi Mahito sums up the persistent ethical theme of Murakami's fiction as attempting to move from the prison house of subjectivity into genuinely free and interactive social relationships: "How can someone captured in private worlds implode (*naiha*) them and break free? In other words, how can individuals escape and move toward a world full of the potential to meet and interact with others?"[4] The association of acts of ethically oriented self-construction with restriction and violence here brings to light the fraught nature of Murakami's work. The term "implosion" in this account describes the destruction of those calcified terms through which the self has come to apprehend itself as an alienated social agent—as we find in a character's effort to expose and thereby nullify the power of magical lore used to control cult members in the 2009–10 novel *1Q84*, for example. Yet such an implosion also implies a kind of narrative terrorism, a violent resistance that may adversely affect the lives of others (not just tyrants and manipulators) who depend on such calcified terms for their livelihoods and social identities—including, for example, those who live within that cult and find themselves disempowered as a result.

Murakami's explorations of self-empowerment through narrative acts have drawn much hostile criticism from ethicists, which for the sake of expediency I will summarize as divisible on three primary grounds: solipsism, misogyny, and detachment from socio-historical reality. The solipsistic critique faults Murakami for promoting a kind of tyrannical subjectivity in which the production of autonomous selfhood supersedes responsibility to others. Matsunaga Miho's argument in a special issue of the journal *Gunzō* dedicated to Murakami eloquently typifies charges laid on this ground: she contends that his focus on subjective perspective privileges the construction of a strong ego only by sacrificing the reality of others, so that all his protagonists achieve in the end are relationships with shadows, not genuine people—a critique resonant with the challenge Vogler makes to novel ethics more generally (see Chapter 6).[5] The misogynist critique typically focuses on what critic Tokō[6] Kōji describes as a "thinness of imagination" with respect to female characters, who seem constructed out of stereotypical fantasies. Finally, historical critiques like those of Japanese literature scholar Hasumi Shigehiko contend that Murakami's simplified, imaginary worlds grossly oversimplify the complexity of human embeddedness in historically produced positions of social, political, and economic power, reducing ethics to a false binary between self and other.

All of these approaches converge in seeing Murakami as privileging the development of a strong individual point of view at the expense of a sufficiently complex and "real" social vision. This paradigm is so pervasive that even the strongest defenses of Murakami's ethics reproduce it. For example, in his 2010 survey of Murakami criticism, Matthew Strecher sums up the now orthodox (among Murakami supporters) argument that the author attempts to deconstruct the mechanisms by which our "controlled society" (*kanri shakai*) exerts power over its subjects. On this view, externally produced ideologies weaken individuals' holds on what Strecher calls "internal narratives," the story-form in which our sense of selfhood takes mental shape for us. In essence, powerful hegemonic forces (in the form of capitalism or cults) create strong narratives of individual identity and purpose that replace internal accounts of the self with prefabricated ones, subordinating personal will to what are cast as larger social goods.[7] Murakami, according to many proponents, resists such controlling narratives by empowering his narrators to rewrite these terms themselves through an inward turn. This is essentially the same argument that Murakami's detractors make.

The defense that Strecher outlines rightly emphasizes narrative as the essential field of ethics in Murakami. But the body of Japanese scholarship Strecher discusses overwhelmingly ignores the reflexive and literary dimensions of his writing. Even US scholar Marc Yamada, who explicitly focuses on "Murakami's Post-AUM Metafiction," looks at the reflexive impulses in Murakami entirely in terms of the way represented narrative acts by character-authors and narrators *parallel* the assertions of power made by authority figures in real life. In other words, ethical analyses of Murakami remain anchored in a mimetic tradition of criticism that seeks to posit analogies between a self-consistent fictive microcosm and an external reality. "Narrative" matters in these accounts not insofar as it gives shape to novel representation through or against genre conventions, nor insofar as it positions or engages readers, nor again because of its heteroglossic orchestration of real language. Rather, it matters insofar as its occurrences *within* the text are taken symbolically to represent "real" formations of discursive power outside the text. Yamada draws attention to "metafiction" principally to clarify an analogy: in Murakami's novels we see that represented characters exercise narrative power *like real* authors or politicians. This is why Yamada makes the blanket claim that Murakami's characters want to become "*surrogate* narrators," despite the fact that the very first character he analyzes is the actual narrator of that novel.[8] Narrative acts in Murakami's fiction become surrogates for the personal and public "narratives" embracing real people in the real world outside the novel. Their essential difference from such narratives, the fact that represented narrative acts are mere fictions, must be posited for critics to assume the requisite distance that makes insight and analysis possible. The metafictional qualities of Murakami's writing disappear in the turn to ethics.

Ethical critics of Murakami tend to divorce novel representation from reality and then translate its symbolic values into terms relevant for real life. Yet as Michael Seats has argued effectively in his monograph on the simulacrum in Murakami's fiction, it is the hallmark of Murakami's work to dispel polarizing distinctions between the real and the symbolic.[9] The author defuses efforts to translate novel ethos into real-life ethics by insisting on the fundamental inseparability and even sameness of these domains, as when the worlds of embedded novels and the "real world" of 1984 become inextricably fused in *1Q84*. Considering the level of formal interest in this author's unique brand of magical or anti-realism, and the widespread concern with the ethics of his writing, it is surprising how few scholars have sought to reconcile these dimensions of his work, or even consider their relation. Once the relationship between ethics and formal reflexivity comes into focus, the apparent thinness in his representations of others, who do indeed often feel more like imagined characters than real people, may appear not an ethical failing but a self-conscious inquiry into the way we imagine and respond to a distinctly *novel* alterity.

Alterity and Oscillation in New Ethical Theories of the Novel

As we have seen in previous chapters, contemporary theories of novel alterity generally fall along a continuum defined by two major poles: theories of identification, which emphasize the recognition or empathy that mimetic representation can foster, and what Robert Eaglestone and Dorothy Hale have called "new ethical theories" influenced by postmodern thought, which emphasize the ethical implications of the formal qualities of representation itself. Do novels immerse us productively in characters' lives to promote understanding of other points of view, as Martha Nussbaum, Suzanne Keen, and Blakey Vermeule all variously assert? Or do they instantiate restrictive (narrative) paradigms that reproduce or remind us of the possible violence done to subjects by prevailing norms of recognition, as Judith Butler, Michael Wood, and Lynne Huffer each very differently maintain?

In my discussion of Mori Ōgai, I argued that his stereoscopic vision might help us recast the question of alterity as conceived in contemporary ethical theories of the novel by questioning a premise fundamental to both points of view. The vast majority of ethical theories of the novel today, including ostensibly oppositional theories like those mentioned above, assume that novel ethics take hold through oscillation between immersion in fiction, on the one hand, and reflection on that experience, on the other.[10] Empathy produced by immersion and caring for fictional characters becomes ethical when it translates into real-world habits of perception and reflection according to theorists like Nussbaum. On the other hand, for Butler and other "new ethical theorists," ethical reflection on the restrictive force of discursive paradigms crystalized in novel representation can also develop only after the immersive experience of characters as human beings. Both camps posit oscillation between immersion and reflection; they just differ on whether the immersive part or the reflective part performs the real ethical work.

Oscillation holds such a privileged place in current ethical theories because it promises a solution to philosophical and epistemological problems of subjectivity and solipsism, and to the practical critical problem of theorizing the relationship between literature and real life. Oscillation provides a model of departing from an entrenched point of view and returning to it enriched by an immersive experience of otherness. It allows us to theorize the ethical value of solitary work: the forms of imagination, self-reflection, and philosophical contemplation that reading can entail. Yet what if, following the line of self-conscious inquiry that we have traced in the work of Ōgai and Akutagawa, Murakami does not seek to immerse us in models of reality from which we might return with ethical lessons, but rather in what are already self-conscious explorations of the ethics of dwelling in fiction? His writing presents us with characters who cannot distinguish between real and imagined encounters with others—not due to the flaw of solipsism but due to the nature of the manifestly fictional reality in which they find themselves. His novels do not present microcosms of any straightforwardly "real" experience, but rather confront us directly and recursively with questions about characters' and our own complicity in the kinds of imaginative projections that fiction invites us to undertake. To theorize the ethical value of his work, we cannot simply translate the morality that operates within his novel worlds into real-life ethical principles. On the contrary, we must first trace Murakami's theory of ethical transpositioning itself.

Fractal Realism and the Ethics of Transpositioning

No single authentic field of human interaction, not even a stable ontological ground, exists in Murakami's long fiction. What I call the fractal realism of his writing comprises multiple contingent worlds, each of which produces its own unique (and often restrictive) value system. The term "fractal" refers to the repetition of similar patterning in the boundaries of figures at progressively larger or smaller scales; whether you zoom in or out, you encounter the same configurations of borders. Just so, in Murakami's novels we constantly face ambiguous boundaries between real life and fiction, whether we immerse ourselves in the experiences of characters or pull back to reflect on the structure of the novel itself. Worlds that seem real turn out to be set within or composed by fictions, as when a protagonist in *1Q84* finds that she inhabits the world of a novel written by the other protagonist, whose own reality may similarly have been authored. Even within any single ontological or diegetic plane, "reality" always proves constituted by multiple social or ideological worlds, such as those of cults and clandestine organizations, that lay claim to objective truth through largely fictional but nevertheless reality-shaping narratives. One thus finds in Murakami's work not a single shared universe but the blend and clash of embedded immersive *realisms* whose borders with one another become sites of dramatic action and ethical transformation.

Murakami works through a simple, matter-of-fact tone and dwells on the concrete details of his environments in the manner that Roland Barthes described as producing "reality effects."[11] But unlike authors committed to conventions of realism, he does not attempt to render seamless, monolithic realities in the bad faith to which Barthes was so hostile. On the contrary, he paints with realist brushstrokes a heterogeneous reality formed by patterns of mutual interference among embedded worlds, each of which, upon inspection, proves at least partially constituted by fiction. Immersion in this fractal realism does not produce a naïve reality-effect but rather immanently involves reflection on its unreal nature. For example, Murakami's novel *Colorless Tsukuru Tazaki and His Years of Pilgrimage* (2013) directly invites readers to visualize its world as comprising wholly embedded but sealed-off, self-contained spheres of experience—spheres shaped by a simpler version of what Derrida has called the "heteronomic dissymmetrical curvature of social space," the totalizing surface of difference that envelops subjects in given discursive and value systems.[12] "He woke in a dream," Murakami writes. "Strictly speaking, it might not be a dream. It was reality, but a reality imbued with all the qualities of a dream. A different sphere of reality."[13]

In this chapter I refer to such "spheres of reality" as "world systems," a term I use for its combination of the immersive, totalizing connotations of "world" and the suggestions of process and contingency implied by "systems." World systems in Murakami have strong affinities with what James Paul Gee has called "semiotic domains," or "any set of practices that recruits one or more modalities (oral or written language, images, equations, symbols, sounds, gestures, graphs, artifacts, etc.) to communicate distinctive types of meanings."[14] Murakami, however, is more interested in how the different semiotic domains that we inhabit can knit together to form entrapping cultural, ideological, literary, and ontological spheres of experience. I use "world systems" to suggest supersets of semiotic domains (genres, ideologies, religious narratives, etc., all of which contain their own sets of semiotic practices) that exert normative force and feel comprehensive and totalizing from within, despite their internal pluralities and relative contingencies.

The fractal realism of Murakami's fiction essentially effaces ontological distinctions. Manifestly imaginary world systems make ethical demands no less urgent or real than those made by the social and ideological world systems commonly taken for reality. Actions in dreams often have frighteningly real effects, including actual impregnation or murder. World systems in his fiction are almost always defined by taboos and ethical rules; they are reified *ethoses* that have accrued cultural or psychological power over the individuals who inhabit them.

In every one of his novels we find characters isolated within totalizing structures of discursive and disciplinary power: both real-world systems, such as religious or political groups, and sometimes fictional or imaginary world systems, like those of novels, alternative realities, and dreams.

"Parallel worlds" and "other worlds" in Murakami are not quite the imaginary physical spaces of speculative fiction. Rather, they are embodiments of the totalizing effects of containment within (discursively constituted) world systems. These often appear wholly disconnected from other domains of experience (such as life within a cult compound) even though they may border or inhere within them. Whether totalizing or not, however, social, political, psychological, and fantastic world systems in Murakami all impose normative standards of conduct and recognition that wind up isolating protagonists from others. In order to realize themselves as social and ethical beings, and to achieve some kind of genuine relationship with others who inhabit different worlds, protagonists must escape into new world systems by transitioning through semiotic domains that different world systems have in common—as when a protagonist in *1Q84* transitions from the world of a cult to a position with a sports club by retaining an inner language of prayer and healing but applying it to physical rather than spiritual bodies. Usually, what makes growth and interpersonal connections possible is not the particular values fostered by new experiences, nor the greater authenticity or reality of any given world system; rather, it is the flexible and responsive manner in which characters learn to traverse world systems themselves. This focus on movement across fictively constructed ideological and social worlds makes it difficult to extract particular ethical principles from his novels.

Murakami thus appears to accept an extreme relativism. Indeed, as a sage antagonist in *1Q84* observes, "Good and evil (*zenaku*) do not exist in some kind of fixed relationship. They continually change position (*basho*) and perspective (*tachiba*). What is good one moment might be evil the next …. What matters is the balance of the movement."[15] I will return to the way that Murakami links ethical to physical orientation when I expand on the emphasis on "kinetic ethics" in his 1985 *Hard-Boiled Wonderland and the End of the World* (*Sekai no owari to hādo-boirudo wandārando*). For now, I want to suggest that "balance" here implies an imperative to respond attentively to the shifting relations among divergent perspectives and value systems without overly privileging one or the other. "The difficult thing," this religious figure continues, "is maintaining balance between these constantly circulating values of good and evil."[16]

While specific values might change, the need to adapt to shifting systems of value transcends that relativity. All knowledge claims, from the social to the epistemic or ethical, prove equally suspect in Murakami's worlds. Once made by authoritative sources such as politicians, cult leaders, or authors, however, such claims form real avenues of interrelation (political affiliations, religious factions, etc.) that characters must navigate with responsiveness to their particularities and the power they exert over subjects. As my analysis will demonstrate, such responsiveness requires holistic apprehension that incorporates within itself a balance between involvement and detachment. That is, to maintain ethical orientation toward others, characters must willingly immerse themselves in different world systems so as to apprehend them, and those within them, as much on their own terms as possible (as when an author enters a fictional world to find the woman trapped within it in *1Q84*). Yet they must simultaneously remain vigilantly self-conscious about the provisional qualities of both that immersion and those new terms themselves (versus simply exchanging one set of delimiting values for another). For Murakami, such balance is necessary to achieve relationships with alterity not predicated on either assimilation (an engulfing proximity) or objectification (a reductive detachment).

The relationship to persons, regardless of their status as real or fictional subjects, proves the absolute axis around which the shifting value systems in his novels revolve. But Murakami argues that to apprehend persons as such requires first the difficult work of developing a balanced approach to the alterity of world systems themselves. In a 2010 interview, he opposes the notion that we should directly bring given values to bear in cross-cultural encounters. Instead, he claims, we must first undertake what I call ethical transpositioning, and what

Murakami refers to in this interview as "soft landing" (*sofuto-randingu*): flexible adaptation and partial translation of principles into those of other value systems through a shift in self-positioning.[17] This is a tentative process whereby both original and potentially new values are held in suspension, as points of difference and commensurability among semiotic domains and value systems themselves are explored in a progressive exchange.[18] In short, Murakami intimates that we should approach others holistically and even circuitously, through provisional immersion in the world systems that produced them as subjects—and that fiction can help us do this.[19]

His novels foster dispositions required for ethical transpositioning in part by creating resonances between represented world systems that characters must navigate, and the real systems of representation that readers encounter in the language, genre, and worldviews embodied by novel narration. For example, the narrator of *Hard-Boiled Wonderland and the End of the World* has been produced as a calculating and nonempathetic agent by a powerful corporate world system—but the novel invites us to see him equally as product of its own self-conscious and at times parodic reliance on the conventions of detective fiction. This character at first approaches everything as a cognitive puzzle to be mastered, precluding his acceptance or even recognition of alterity as such. Yet in part through his mental entrapment in a fantasy world, he begins to fathom the fantastic and unknowable possibilities of sharing love with a librarian, a woman who tellingly brings him a fantasy text by Borges on what becomes their first date. In the process of conveying this story, the novel alternates between chapters saturated with the conventions of hard-boiled detective fashion and those imbued with the dreamlike qualities of the fantasy genre. The novel thus both represents efforts at transpositioning and helps readers to build proficiency in it by accustoming them to continual shifts in perspectives and systems of valuation. By making ethical relations the goal of represented transpositioning, showing characters who must adapt themselves to form relationships with others in different (often manifestly literary) world systems, and then embroiling readers in not just analogous but very much the same processes of adaptation, Murakami tethers reading to ethics.

His characters face urgent questions we might ask of real political and interpersonal situations. How can they know and treat justly others who inhabit different worlds and live by different codes of conduct? Can they avoid subordinating others to terms of recognition that do violence to their freedom and difference? For readers, however, such questions come embedded in further questions that reflect the fictional, literary natures of Murakami's realities. How do the forms of responsiveness solicited by novel representation differ from those required of real-life interaction? How can reading about others in fiction require real ethical work, and what might this work accomplish?

Murakami's protagonists cross into what even for them are unreal or expressly novel worlds and must take responsibility for dispositions and actions toward fictional beings. In *1Q84,* for example, characters in dreams or dreamlike states of paralysis witness sexual crimes that they themselves commit against young girls—girls who may be physically embodied fictions created by supernatural narrative power, and not real people. Can we absolve these dreamers of their imaginary participation in fictional crimes when physical damage results? Complicated situations like this confound the tendency in ethical criticism to privilege a self-consistent mimetic world as the essential domain of novel ethics. They force readers to attend to the ways that real emotions, values, and responsibilities may take shape through imaginary or fictional experiences not easily transposable into or even comparable against real-life situations. Murakami thus asks us to consider how our manner of experiencing novel worlds may enmesh us in responsibilities that must be undertaken and regarded for their immanent effects and values, despite an apparent disconnect from reality and outright refusal of any clear-cut, take-home ethical imperative.

Unlike Ōgai and Akutagawa, for whom ethical concerns with novel narration and its manipulative potential spurred experimentation with reflexivity to undo the powerful telos of realist narrative forms, Murakami returns to metafiction because reflexive forms of consciousness have become constitutive of contemporary experience. He infuses metafictional self-consciousness into essentially realist modes of narration to focus on the ethical dilemmas that emerge from experiences of both real and represented alterity. Such methods differ from the postmodern forms of metafiction that Linda Hutcheon has famously deemed "narcissistic narratives."[20] Although he draws on metafictional devices (e.g., referencing the textual nature of represented realities), Murakami refuses the tendency of iconic postmodern metafiction to reduce ethics and politics to language games. He does not disrupt mimesis simply to deconstruct the fabricated value structures informing it; on the contrary, real ethical imperatives make themselves felt through the very fictional narrative structures whose unreality, contingency, and oppressive force their writing exposes. Of the author's work, *Hard-Boiled Wonderland and the End of the World* most clearly exemplifies this approach by making the persistence of ethics in and through fictional experience the direct premise of its story: the narrator's brain has been wired to perceive a manifestly fictional world, but his actions within it have real ethical valence and consequences.

This novel ties its story-level exploration of ethics to reader response by reflexively identifying its own narrative-level genre systems among the immersive world systems that characters and readers alike must navigate. The alternating chapters, each written in a different style, foreground the extent to which its realities are generically constructed and therefore make competing interpretive and, I will argue, ethical demands. Although scholarship has tended to critique Murakami's awkward use of "genre fiction," I suggest that this move complements perfectly his aims in both the story (to represent the different forms of navigation required by different world systems) and reader response (requiring readers to adjust their own interpretive postures). In other words, genre fiction makes the social conventions and norms that inform representation more vivid, because they become more predictable and obvious. Genres can make palpable, as Fredric Jameson argues, the reified ethos of culture jealous to maintain its power structures in the face of shifting contemporary values.[21] But even such real ethos is simultaneously fictional for Jameson and Murakami in the sense that it falsely presents as universal what is in fact a historically provisional, constructed value system inadequate or irrelevant to the diversity and complexity of social life in the present moment.

By adopting rhetorical methodologies linked to genre conventions, and then self-consciously exposing the contingencies of those conventions through juxtaposition with each other, Murakami involves readers in the very problems of ethical transpositioning (across worlds established by ethos) that his characters face. We confront the way that genre shapes values as we shuttle between these very different modes of experience. In Murakami's fiction, the existence of multiple world systems, each of which develops its own relative value structures, destabilizes the analogical structure between mimetic representation and reality so often assumed by ethical criticism.

Into Wonderland: Models of Reading

My goal in examining *Hard-Boiled Wonderland and the End of the World* is first to flesh out the roles that fiction and acts of reading play in constituting the ethical relations that take shape within the complicated stories told by Murakami's novels, and then to demonstrate how his fractal realism implicates reader response in the ethics played out within those story-level scenarios. The stories told by this novel directly concern how the knitting together of linguistic and cultural codes in different genres conditions our interpretive habits and hence our capacities for recognition and response. The text departs from conventions of realism in both form and content while thematizing the relevance of those departures for the ethical growth of its protagonist—a largely unrecognized pattern that continues in all of Murakami's subsequent novels.

In *Hard-Boiled Wonderland and the End of the World*, the neurological tampering of an auteur-scientist plunges the narrating protagonist into his own unconscious mind. In odd chapters, we follow him in what we suppose to be reality as he navigates hidden spaces beneath a futuristic, cyberpunk Tokyo to find out what has been done to his brain. In even chapters, however, we experience what initially appears to be another narrator's point of view on a fantasy world. This world features an amnesiac narrator who explores an eerily perfect town populated by only a handful of subdued residents, roaming unicorns, and a giant Gatekeeper who guards the only point of access. The town is embedded in a pastoral environment surrounded in every direction by impassable walls. This bizarre setting turns out to be the psychic space of the Tokyo-narrator's own mind, populated only by personified psychological mechanisms and the images of real people that he has formed in his unconscious.

The parallel storylines converge insofar as the narrator's journeys through each world help him to transcend an objectifying approach to relationships that he has internalized through his occupation as an information-processing agent working for "The System" in Tokyo. Both plots concern an evolving love story directly connected to acts of reading. The woman he comes to love is in each storyline a librarian to whom he first turns for information, but then eventually begins to regard and respect for innate qualities that he does not fully understand. This shift happens concomitantly with a shift in his reading practices themselves, especially those undertaken in the immersive (totalizing to the extent that he has no memory of the "real" world of Tokyo) "fantasy" world. To tie his transformation as a reader in and of this manifestly fictional environment to the ethical change in his ostensibly real Tokyo life, and then finally to readers' experience of the novel as a whole, we must first work out the experiences and allegories of reading that each world presents.

The overly rational and pragmatic detective-like narrator of the odd chapters functions as a classically conceived critical reader. He reads and interprets clues—maps, enigmatic messages, and so on—to discern the meaning and structure of the immersive "world" (*sekai*), which turns out to be an image of his unconscious mind that has been extracted, edited, and placed into a walled-off part of his brain. The narrator's role as a data-processing agent has inculcated in him a habit of expecting real, valuable information to be hidden—literally encoded—beneath the surfaces of things, just as it also conditions him to regard human relationships as exchanges of information, services, and currency. His only intimate relations just before the novel begins are with prostitutes. This man approaches the world in the manner Isobel Armstrong describes in her article on textual harassment, as though it conceals pleasure and value that await his discovery through professional deciphering.[22]

Within the symbolic realm of the even-numbered fantasy chapters, however, a different logic prevails. That storyline begins with a narrator at the gateway of an enclosed world. Unlike the Tokyo narrator, he speaks in the present tense, without the benefit of retrospection and its implied conversion of experience into codified narrative stories. His shadow, later identified as his conscious mind, is cut from him and imprisoned as a condition of entry, and his eyes are pierced by a magical blade that violently inscribes upon his body a new identity as a "dreamreader." This operation leaves him partially blinded and pained by direct light, but now capable of "reading" unicorn skulls kept in a dimly lit library—a process that involves running his fingers over the surfaces of the skulls and thereby releasing trapped, fragmentary images into the ether. The narrator himself has no idea what dreamreading means and cannot understand the fleeting images he glimpses. In other words, ordinary ways of making sense are foreclosed in this reading process, and the narrator must learn to experience the forms of representation provided by The Town and its environs on their own terms, literally for their surface qualities. Like readers of the novel, he can only try to follow along with the unfolding logic of the text as he encounters it; this world stands, in mise-en-abyme fashion, for the novel itself.

The narrator's response to his surroundings embodies the same kind of disposition required of the dreamreading he must perform within The Town. He simply wanders, following the contours of the landscape with no aim other than to experience it and make a map of its terrain (at the enigmatic direction of his shadow, and without any personal motivation for that activity). This uncritical reader takes in stride violence done to himself, inexplicable restrictions on his conduct, the impending loss of his shadow, the presence of unicorns, and even his lack of memory about what has happened before. Instead of attempting to grasp the meaning of his situation, the narrator simply immerses himself in its rhythms. He takes long walks, gazes at the unicorns (which he only knows as "beasts"), and watches the landscape undergo subtle transformations each season without ever hypothesizing what these experiences might mean for a "real life" from which he has become disconnected.

His approach stands in marked contrast to the literal and figurative spelunking undertaken by the Tokyo narrator in the odd chapters, who insists on digging into his surroundings to unearth the truth about the system of power hidden beneath. The fantasy world invites reception rather than perception, immersion rather than critical detachment. It resists the transactional logic, the will to power through the transfer of information from one to another set of terms, that conditions social intercourse in the other (Tokyo) world, as embodied by the large-scale information wars that have taken over all of Japan. The fantasy world cannot be deciphered into clear correspondences with extrinsic elements. In this sense, it is truly "The End of the World" (the title of the even chapters and the name of the edited consciousness implanted in the Tokyo-narrator's brain) because it demands that its experience be treated noninstrumentally, as an end in itself.

The difficult work that the narrator (and readers) must perform here involves not cognitive mastery but rather acclimation to the rhythms and workings of this environs while letting go of the need for rational understanding that drives the narrator in the "real" world of hard-boiled Tokyo. He reflects, meditates, and muses on the librarian and the symbolic environment, but without the aggressive pursuit of conclusions. This activity embodies the manner of reading advocated by the argument against critical oscillation (between immersive experience of the literary object and the detached reflection of abstract theorization) made by James A. Knapp and Jeffrey Pence in "Between Thing and Theory":

> Missing at both poles of our heuristic dichotomy is something like non-instrumental reflection: pausing over difficulties, lingering at the point of judgment, resisting categorical but not evaluative judgments, revising, combining, and second-guessing choices. The kind of reflection we are suggesting is ... open-ended attentiveness to the object of critical scrutiny—here understood as the traces of another subjectivity's interests and aspirations.[23]

By attuning himself to the overall tone and ethos of the fictional world, often lingering near the unicorns just for the sake of observing them and taking walks without any clearly planned direction, the narrator achieves a kind of balance between cognitive and kinetic modalities. He pays the kind of diffuse but no less close attention to the "complexity of literary surfaces ... rendered invisible by symptomatic reading" that Stephen Best and Sharon Marcus advocate in their endorsement of "Surface Reading," and which embodies the kind of holistic and receptive adaptability that Murakami finds requisite for ethical transpositioning.[24]

The narrator's exploration of the contours of what is even for him a fictional world does not just symbolize an ethical mode of nonappropriative encounter with representations of alterity. His efforts quite literally serve for him as real means of approaching the "traces" of the librarian's "subjectivity" that have proven otherwise inaccessible. He seems to intuit the limits of normal conversation as a means of getting to know her. To imagine that she could speak "on her own terms" in this fictional environment would recapitulate the solipsistic logic of The Town that produced the norms of recognition that stripped her of autonomy and subjectivity in the first place. After all, the woman he encounters is merely his own introjected image of a real person. The otherness she represents for him is no more than his own imagination woven around a kernel of real alterity to which he has no access, since the actual woman exists outside the psychic reality of The Town. This is, of course, what many alterity theorists fear may be the case with our apprehension of all literary representations of others.

Murakami, however, insists that the potentially solipsistic work done in this fictional world has immanent value regardless of what reason leads us to conclude about the ontological status of the other. Furthermore, he invites us to see how a shift in the manner of apprehension may help avoid the bad faith of appropriative understanding. Rather than projecting an identity for the woman or soliciting her own account of herself, the narrator chooses a more kinetic and holistic, if apparently circuitous, approach. By taking solitary walks and adjusting himself to the climate and patterns of life and movement, especially those of the unicorns, he becomes actively familiar with the entire system of representation in which the woman has become ensconced, even if he cannot say what that system means. The "soft landing" of such attunement to this environment actually proves to be the most effective means of approaching the librarian possible: we learn from the Tokyo chapters that the unicorns he spends so much time observing embody mechanisms of his own unconscious mind that absorb the unassimilable aspects of others' selfhood, including those of the librarian. By spending time out among the unicorns, becoming a more proficient surface reader of this imaginary world system, the narrator has in fact been drawing closer to the "real" librarian as literally and directly as possible—without consciously realizing it—because these impossible, fictional beasts harbor living traces of her alterity.

What he cannot know, but readers do, is that his conscious self, the hard-boiled data-processing agent of interwoven odd-numbered chapters, undergoes changes in his own life while the fantasy narrator performs this inner work. The physical traversal of paths in "The End of the World" literally maps out the reformation of the pathways of neural reception in the brain of the Tokyo narrator—a fact readers are directed to surmise when the map the fantasy narrator finally completes reveals the entire enclosure to be shaped like his brain. The narrator's attentive and responsive manner of immersing himself in fantasy, then, corresponds with simultaneous changes in his mindset and orientation toward others in Tokyo. We can see this correspondence most clearly in the climactic sequence begun when the fantasy narrator enters a borderland near woods populated by unassimilated and presently inaccessible, unseen others. He finds a musical instrument, which he brings back and plays for the librarian. In contrast to the solitary practice of dreamreading through touch, this other-oriented, shared acoustic performance sets all of the unicorn skulls aglow at once. The calcified fragments of consciousness stored within each skull spontaneously come to life and coalesce, restoring her mind and autonomy without his ever deciphering them.

In a parallel moment of the subsequent chapter, the Tokyo narrator has his first genuinely interpersonal, mutually satisfying and intimate encounter with the "real" librarian. To signal the simultaneity of these events, and also the conflation of fiction and reality, the same song plays on the radio and the mere model of a unicorn skull in the Tokyo apartment impossibly begins to glow after they have intercourse. Efforts undertaken in a fictive world, with regard to a nonreal being, thus correspond with real interpersonal shifts in the life of the conscious narrator. This transformation does not result from subsequent reflection and conscious decision, or even from the adoption of an attitude that is then later deployed toward real beings. Instead, the effects of immersion in the fictional world are produced simultaneously, contiguously with real life. Rather than existing in separate, analogous relationships, fiction and reality prove inextricable: the fantasy world is quite literally and materially connected to the Tokyo narrator's brain, so that its experience is directly constitutive of the ongoing life of the conscious narrator at the same time it symbolically represents that life and cognitively mirrors it.

Out of Wonderland: Modes of Reading

Murakami does not just model ethical practices of surface reading. Nor is he content merely to represent the kinds of simultaneity whereby the literary event effaces distinctions between the real and the fictional, engaging his protagonist in a clearly unreal and yet immanently ethical experience. On the contrary, his texts work thematically, structurally, and rhetorically to involve readers in the transformations that his characters undergo, as they experience them. If we follow the allegories of reading discovered in the preceding section, we can begin to surmise consequences for our own cognitively dissonant experience of the novel.

Tokyo at first establishes itself as a baseline model of reality. The Town, by contrast, appears a mere fantasy world that the narrator enters to learn something about himself. This dual structure seems to provide a conventionally ideal model for imagining how novel experience (the fantasy world) might translate to real-life ethics (the world of Tokyo)—but such a model quickly proves inadequate to the complex imbrication of the novel's fractal realism. First, the ostensibly real world of Tokyo proves, in itself, structured by genre conventions that increasingly draw attention to their fictional quality. For example, the narrator casually drinks whiskey and observes with wry detachment while stereotypical underworld goons destroy his apartment and then knife him, apologetically because this violence is apparently required, in an over-the-top parody of hard-boiled fiction. Second, the apparently divergent genres of each set of chapters bleed into one another with increasing obviousness, blurring their boundaries: at first, paper clips from the hard-boiled world show up in the fantasy library, while later on, fantastic beasts appear under Tokyo, and so on. Third, it becomes an explicit plot point that in the narrator's mind linear chronology and "cause and effect" have become confused, so that mirrored actions and events in either world cannot clearly be said to have either originated or resulted from one sphere of reality or the other. Fourth, each storyline produces a version of something like ordinary realism in the end, despite the contrastive promises of their different genres. The detective leaves behind the intrigue of information wars, enters a fantastic underground labyrinth populated with mythical creatures, and emerges just to do laundry, get a haircut, and buy nail clippers in the final hours of his life. Similarly, the fantasy hero gives up his life as a dreamreader, pulls off a prison break, and then ultimately decides on a simple, agrarian existence in what he comes to realize is nothing more than a mental impression of the world.

Even *within* each world, the narrator effectively shifts into different genre systems, arriving at something like an authentic relationship with the librarian only by first modulating himself to very different means of pursuing meaning and encountering others.

Whatever binary thinking the dual structure seems to invite, the complexity of the relationship between and within worlds precludes us from imagining that fiction simply "models" reality, or even that events in the Tokyo world are somehow more important or real. By crossing genre signals, and by reflexively calling attention to unreal nature of both diegetic worlds, *Hard-Boiled Wonderland and the End of the World* renders the mimetic premise of much ethical criticism untenable. Neither world offers itself as an analog or predicate for ethical actions in the other because they are not separate realities but modalities of the same, irreducibly fractal experience of life.

In the end, the fantasy narrator discovers for himself what has already become apparent to readers and the narrator's other self: that the entire world exists in his own brain as a fictionalized version of his unconscious mind. He becomes aware of the unreality of this world even as he remains immersed and continues to experience it as reality. This state of simultaneous immersion and self-conscious reflection leads to his incredible and, for most critics, deeply troubling final decision. He refuses to return to the "reality" of Tokyo with his shadow, solely out of a sense of commitment to what he has realized is nothing more than an internalized image of the world. In a move roundly condemned by critics, he sends his shadow (again, possibly his "conscious self") through the whirlpool and presumably back into real life, while he himself remains trapped with the librarian to spend the rest of their days as outcasts from The Town. Since both still possess autonomous, unassimilable minds, they will be confined to the liminal space between The Town and the unknowable outside, a space whose rules and value structures are as yet unknown to both narrator and librarian.

Murakami marks this as an expressly ethical choice. The narrator remains not to enjoy and exercise authorial control over a fantasy world, as many have interpreted the move, but to become beholden to what that world has failed to represent adequately (and which has therefore been relegated to a marginal space). He even repeats terms for "responsibility" four times when explaining his decision:

> I know very well what it means for me to stay here. I know that the right thing is for me to return with you to the former world. That is, for me, the true reality

(hontō no genjitsu), and I know that running from that is the wrong thing. But I can't leave ….

I discovered just what it means that I made this place. And so I have a duty (gimu) to remain here, a responsibility (sekinin) ….

I have my own responsibility. I can't just abandon these people or this world I've made just to suit myself. This is my own world. But I have to take responsibility for what I've done.[25]

By risking his own autonomy to restore that of the librarian, and then by resigning himself to a marginalized life in the woods at the outermost border of his own mind, the narrator chooses to undertake the difficult work of fostering a sense of commitment to the alterity of another from within a potentially foreclosed horizon of subjectivity. From a point of view insistent on binary distinctions between fiction and reality, the narrator has simply chosen fantasy and "detachment" from the real world, rendering him susceptible to ethical accusation. But such an insistence, convenient and perhaps necessary for some forms of ethical criticism, makes little sense when applied to the fractal realism of Murakami's literary worlds. *Both* worlds in this novel are unreal, mutually dependent "alternative" realities as far as we (and the narrator) experience them. The apparently "real" world of Tokyo proves no less underwritten by genre conventions than the fantasy world.[26] For Murakami, responsive participation in fictional worlds is no less an ethical comportment toward others than participation in the real systems of representation operative in political or social spheres. Both fiction and reality confront subjects with responsibility for responding to the alterity of world systems that shape our apprehension of others. Fiction like Murakami's can therefore provide a more effective, if circuitous, means of ethically encountering alterity, because it directly calls for states of self-conscious immersion and apprehension that facilitate nonappropriative transpositioning. Our ongoing, active responses to fractal realism can orient us ethically because, as the fantasy narrator discovers, the alterity may be real whether or not the represented subjects are.

The Fantasy of Realism

For most theorists we either read immersively or reflectively, apprehending characters as human beings or elements of fiction, but never both in any given moment—much as we can only see either a duck or a rabbit in the famous optical illusion.²⁷ The ethics of reading thus appears to require oscillation between immersion and detachment; the reader must move back and forth between representation and reality to better ascertain the relationship between the values we adopt as immersed readers and those adduced by ethical theories of literature. This approach meshes conveniently with the proclivity of ethical criticism to view novel alterity through hermeneutic models, imagining that readers acquisitively expand their fields of knowledge in a cycle of tentative appropriation and then reflective reconsideration of otherness that eventually "gets it right."

As an alternative to the model of oscillation at the core of most ethical criticism today, Murakami both thematizes and invites readers to experience what Richard Wollheim has theorized as a fuller model of how we apprehend human figures in art: through the "twofoldness" of holistic attention that simultaneously comprehends both the imputed reality and the aesthetic dimensions of represented figures.²⁸ For Wollheim, even while imagining the reality of figures, we are always aware of compositional elements like paint or ink and formal qualities like style or tone. We may not see both duck and rabbit, but we can know that the duck is a drawing of loose and elegant lines even as we focus our attention on imagining it as an animal. Not just aesthetics but specifically a kind of aesthetic self-consciousness, or awareness of the unreal, artistic quality of the representation, shapes our cognitive and emotional responses to represented content even when we imagine its reality. Wolheim's model can help criticism avoid a strong mimetic bias and allow us to theorize novel ethics as taking immanent shape through our dispositions toward the representation of alterity as such, rather than through self-forgetful experience merely *analogous* to real-life attitudes and interactions with others.

By not permitting even the illusion of self-forgetting immersive experience, Murakami's fractal realism does not allow us to hold in tension two very different sets of values, one for our real lives, in which we know the novel to be mere fiction, and one imputed to an immersed and credulous reader whose position we provisionally occupy. Instead, it insists on holistic engagement with the reflexive narrative structures that produce the manifestly fictional world systems in which it nevertheless invites us to become invested. The narrator of *Hard-Boiled Wonderland and the End of the World* becomes capable of ethically transformative action only once he becomes cognizant of the unreality of his experience and assumes responsibility for it anyway, as if it were real. His interactions with an image of the woman he loves turn out to matter in themselves, precisely because of his awareness of their imaginary qualities, and not because they prepare him for a relationship any less mediated by fiction or imagination in real life. By endorsing the narrator's commitment to a fantasy world, one that stands in mise-en-abyme fashion for the text itself, the provocative ending suggests that the experience of fractal realism can engage readers in ethical transpositioning even more effectively than real life.[29]

Murakami's blend of the metafictional and the everyday resonates with readers, despite its oddness and complexity, because it reflects the hyper self-consciousness of a world that has internalized and even popularized many of the lessons of post-structuralism and deconstructionism. Fractal realism is a realism for an age in which reflexive awareness of the narratively constructed dimensions of experience has been built into the social conventions and especially the media through which we encounter others.[30] Murakami's writing does not pretend to simulate some kind of transparent, authentic experience via the production of fictional characters presumed to be like real autonomous beings. Instead, it produces real experiences of alterity through structural and rhetorical demands for ethical transpositioning across the kinds of semiotic domains and world systems that interfere with our efforts to apprehend others as subjects in their own right. By rejecting the fantasy of realism, Murakami's writing paradoxically establishes new conditions of possibility for real ethical engagement with novel alterity.

In *Hard-Boiled Wonderland and the End of the World* we encounter the interplay of juxtaposed realisms and points of view, none of which ever provides access to anything like genuine truth about his characters or novel worlds. There exists no singular reality beneath fictive appearance for judicious or empathetic investigation to get right. In order to remain ethically oriented toward others in such an epistemologically uncertain milieu, protagonists and readers alike must continually adapt their value systems and modes of response to accommodate the different forms of surface contact with alterity that novel experience makes available. The goal of such reading becomes not deep understanding nor even the acquisition of new knowledge about others but rather the immanent experience of more intuitive and kinetic forms of going along with the singularity of new encounters. Murakami thus manages to flesh out an ethics of surface reading that remains abstract in theoretical accounts and overlooked by criticism of his work, one that avoids the potential intellectual imperialism of hermeneutic approaches. By calling for reparative acts of holistic reception and self-directed transformation, rather than potentially appropriative acts of understanding or deciphering, *Hard-Boiled Wonderland and the End of the World* engages readers in the adaptive and dialogic processes of transpositioning required to make "soft landings" in other world systems.

Notes

Introduction

1 The term *shōsetsu* was adopted from the Chinese literary tradition and repurposed in the Meiji period (1868–1912) to describe foreign novels and prose fiction modeled after or inspired by them. The word combines *shō* (small) and *setsu* (theory) to designate the minor, more subjective or personal, generally more accessible, and often philosophically speculative aims of the prose, in contrast to the weightier kinds of national, political, or religious public work that more elite forms of prose writing performed. The term also implicitly distinguished the new Japanese novel from traditional forms of *monogatari* (storytelling) and from the popular entertainment of *gesaku* ("frivolous writings"). As a term borrowed from the distinguished tradition of Chinese literature, the word *shōsetsu* lent much-needed validity to the nascent Japanese genre. *Shōsetsu* was popularized as a translation of "novel" by Tsubouchi Shōyō in 1885–6 in an essay that will be treated in the first chapter of this book. See the excellent discussion of the term in Atsuko Ueda's 2007 *Concealment of Politics, Politics of Concealment* (8–13).

2 Many previous Japanese writers, including luminaries such as Murasaki Shikibu (973–1025?) and Ihara Saikaku (1642–93), had experimented masterfully with narrative point of view in prose fiction, to compelling effects. However, their work did not aim at systematic critique or exploration of (scarcely existent) genre conventions, nor did it consistently call attention to the narrative rendering of perspective as a central thematic concern. It is not until the advent of the modern novel that narrative point of view becomes a definitive and salient concern of prose fiction (see also Kamei Hideo's argument in his 1983 *Kansei no Henkaku* (Transformations in Sensibility) that the modern Japanese novel came into being and distinguished itself as a form through its creation of sustained narrative point of view (Kamei, 8–12).

3 Karatani, *Nihon kindai bungaku no kigen*, 61.
4 Powell, *Writers and Society*, 60; Karatani, *Nihon kindai bungaku no kigen*, 78.
5 Miyoshi, *Accomplices of Silence*, xiv–v.
6 Jacob, *Critical Insights*, x.
7 Jacob, *Critical Insights*, xii.
8 Said, *The World, the Text and the Critic*, 20–3.
9 Spandri, *Contact Zones*, Elena 20–4.

10   Damrosch, *Global Comparatism*, 622–4; Tsu, *Getting Ideas*, 290–1.
11   Claviez, "Done and Over With," 609.
12   Gerow, *Visions of Japanese Modernity*, 13.
13   Palumbo-Liu, *The Deliverance of Others*, 12–3.
14   Nussbaum, *Love's Knowledge*, 175.
15   Black, *Fiction Across Borders*, 4.
16   I refer readers interested in the range of provisional and flexible perspectives on ethics informing this study to work by Simon Blackburn, Judith Butler, Berys Gaut, Adam Zachary Newton, and Martha Nussbaum (in particular, Blackburn's challenging and much-challenged notion of quasi-realism, that is, ethical statements project emotional attitudes rather than expressing propositions, undergirds this study's interest in the ethics of novel narration and the performative constitution of fictional subjects).
17   Hearn, *Japanese Ghost Stories*, 167–170.
18   Kyōka, *The Holy Man*, 5:358.
19   Shiga, "Kozō no kamisama," 54:279–84; Shiga, "Shoji," 54:279–84.
20   Tansman, *The Aesthetics of Japanese Fascism*.
21   Kamei, *The History of Meiji Literature*, 83.

Chapter 1

1   Akutagawa, "Literary, All-Too Literary," 15:200.
2   As mentioned in the Introduction, the novel emerged in Meiji-period Japan as a polymorphous genre in the process of being both interpolated and invented by writers including Shōyō and Futabatei. Before the Meiji period, although the word we now translate from Japanese as "novel" (*shōsetsu*) existed, it was used to designate various styles of writing that can differ considerably from what we consider novels, including fables, tales of romance, and classics imported from neighboring nations, especially China. Again, I recommend the discussion of the term in Atsuko Ueda's 2007 *Concealment of Politics, Politics of Concealment* (8–13).
3   The term *I-novel* loosely signified a form of supposedly autobiographical writing in which the author recounted (and often sensationalized or fabricated) lived experiences and struggles to find meaning in life and work. The form was something of a cross between "confessional literature," modeled on Rousseau, and *zuihitsu*, a traditional form of Japanese essay-like writing in which the author "followed his pen" and was not concerned about having a closed plot structure. In essence, the I-novel was a form of "writing the self" influenced by Western literature that could nevertheless claim its roots in traditional Japanese

literature. See Tomi Suzuki's *Narrating the Self: Fictions of Japanese Modernity* for more on the genre.

4   Washburn, *The Dilemma*, 183–6.
5   Ueda, *Modern Japanese*, 123.
6   See Dorothy Hale's *Social Formalism*.
7   What came to be called *genbun'itchi* was a complex conglomerate of several movements that converged in mid-Meiji. Despite sharp divisions in ideological aims, reasoning, and proposed transformations, these movements were largely united in endeavoring to make literary language more commensurate with spoken Japanese. This shared goal problematically involved not only transforming literary writing itself but also consolidating the various provincial dialects into a standardized form of Japanese that would become the national norm. See Nanette Twine's 1991 book *Language and the Modern State—The Reform of Written Japanese* and Kamei Hideo's *Transformations of Sensibility* (*Kansei no henkaku*) for more on this phenomenon.
8   Yanagida, *Meiji shoki*, 35; According to Yanagida, Edo-period (1603–1868) men of letters contended that the highest function of prose writing, and the only justification for indulging in it, lay in its capacity to deliver a moral message that could reach a wide audience (a view modeled perhaps on *setsuwa*, exemplary or parabolic tales illustrating Buddhist principles). This accords with what we will soon see as Tanizawa Eiichi's view that moralism endemic to literary criticism precluded recognition of the value of the novel form through the beginning of the early Meiji period.
9   Kamei, *Kansei*, 9–14.
10 Tanizawa, *Kindai Nihon*, 23.
11 Tanizawa, *Kindai Nihon*, 23–4.
12 Tsubouchi, *Shōsetsu shinzui*, 185. After many pages defending the novel on aesthetic grounds, Shōyō returns almost verbatim to this formulation of the novel's power to "reveal obscure connections to the world," and cites the work of British scholar John Morley on the writing of George Eliot in a chapter entitled "The Aims of the Novel." It is immediately after citing this work on the renowned English defender of an ethically relevant empathy in the novel that Shōyō makes his own argument for the benefits of the novel: namely, that it stimulates self-reflection that can allow readers to recognize the complex *inga* (causal relations) with others that make up the social fabric of society.
13 Tsubouchi, *Shōsetsu shinzui*, 200.
14 Shōyō's move here both echoes the defense of fiction advanced by Tamakazura (and, ultimately, Genji himself) in Lady Murasaki's *The Tale of Genji* and presages contentions by Catharine Gallagher (2006) and Blakey Vermeule (2010) that novels

simulate social complexity to foster decision-making skills about trustworthiness and the consequences of actions.
15 Shōyō argues that it is precisely such "realism" at which the artistic novel aims through its fictional devices: "it attempts to handle its imaginary characters and their imaginary setting in as realistic a fashion as possible." Tsubouchi, Shōyō, *The Essence of the Novel*, 32.
16 Tsubouchi, *Shōsetsu shinzui*, 197.
17 Yoshida, *Kindai bungei hyōronshi*, 43.
18 Twine, *Language*, 26. I cite Twine's translation here and in the next long quotation because she captures expertly the sense of the responsibilities of the novelist that Shōyō means to convey. Elsewhere I use my own translation, largely to clarify the ethical overtones of his language.
19 Twine, *Language*, 28.
20 Itō, *Nihon kindai bungaku*, 36.
21 Hokubō, "The Responsibility of the Novelist," 84.
22 Hokubō, "The Responsibility of the Novelist," 84–5.
23 Nishinodō, "On Criticism," 77.
24 Nishinodō, "On Criticism," 78.
25 Nishinodō, "On Criticism," 78.
26 Nishinodō, "On Criticism," 79.

Chapter 2

1 Uchida, *Uchida Roan zenshū*, 83.
2 Fuminobu, *Ideology and Narrative*, 16.
3 Isogai, *Meiji Twenties*, 26.
4 Kabe, *Mori Ōgai: shoki bungei hyōron no riron to hōhō*, 43.
5 Frentiu, "Intellectual Conscience," 49.
6 Bowring, *Modernization*, 141–7.
7 Rimer, in Ōgai, 213. Ōgai, Mori, *Mori Ōgai: Youth and Other Stories*.
8 Marvin, "Biographical Quest," 237.
9 Frentiu, "Intellectual Conscience," 53.
10 Jacobs, "Between East and West," 13.
11 Hasegawa, *History of Modern Japanese Criticism*, 15.
12 Vincent, *Two-Timing*, 84.
13 O'Neill, *Portrait*, 296–7.
14 O'Neill, *Portrait*, 297.
15 Mori, "Shōsetsuron," 452.

16 Bowring, *Modernization*, 85–6; I quote Richard Bowring's translation here for its effective if loose rendering of the tone and sentiment.
17 Mori, "Tower of Silence," 275.
18 See Dennis Washburn's *Translating Mount Fuji: Modern Japanese Fiction and the Ethics of Identity* for excellent analysis of *Youth* (107–36).
19 His emphasis on reflexive detachment becomes even clearer in his later, signature emphases on "*akirame*" (resignation) and the role of the "*bōkansha*" (bystander) in literary representation. Both of these positions involve a kind of giving up and standing back from real-life moral work *as an ethical gesture* that provides the requisite distance for clear-sighted reflection on the proper attitudes and courses of engagement. For more on Ōgai's interest in the position of the bystander, see John Dower's excellent study "Mori *Ogai*: Meiji Japan's Eminent *Bystander*."
20 Bowring, *Modernization*, 84.
21 Snyder, "Limits of Fiction," 12–13.
22 The narrative of disillusionment is so strong in scholarship that although Steven Snyder notes a pervasive reflexivity at work in Ōgai's oeuvre, he dismisses it as a side-effect of an anxiety of influence rather than the method of a deliberate inquiry into the form of the novel: "From the outset, moreover, and in the same vein, the literary encounter with the West carried buried within it a kind of reflexive 'looking over the shoulder,' a repeated return to the reference point of traditional Japanese themes and narrative methods, if at times only as a way of measuring how far they had come" (Snyder, "Limits of Fiction," 9). He writes this despite elsewhere noting that "few writers were as concerned with questions of voice, privilege, point of view, and chronology" as Ōgai (Snyder, "Limits of Fiction," 31).
23 Ōgai made his critical debut on the literary scene the same year as the essays by Nishinodō and Hokubō, with his own arguments about novel value in an untitled manifesto and the essay "A Theory of the Novel Based on Medical Approaches" (*Igaku no setsu yori idetaru shōsetsu-ron*; 1889). In the latter, Ōgai appealed to European philosophical, rhetorical, and aesthetic standards in his contention that Japan must not adopt the kind of naturalism advocated by Emile Zola (whose work was virtually unknown in Japan at the time). Ōgai held that the scientific discipline of objective observation was incompatible with the artistic discipline of novel writing, which necessarily transformed the object of observation. The novelist could not hope to reproduce objective reality as (he believed) Zola suggested. On the contrary, he argued, novels need the guidance of the literary critic, who can work with one foot in each discipline, bringing the creative sensibilities of the artist and a scientific capacity for detached observation to novel representation. His conclusion in these early essays is that *kansatsu* (detached observation) and *bunseki* (analysis) are required for both criticism and *shōsetsu*, but that in *shōsetsu*

they must be tempered with individual *myōsō* (insight) and *kūsō* (imagination). The novel, he opined, should incorporate both detached objectivity and immersed subjectivity. Ōgai thus reverses Hokubō's claim, which privileged the critic as the more self-conscious figure. Ōgai claims the "stereoscopic" dual perspective, the extra helping of self-consciousness, for the accomplished novelist.

Increasingly, the stories told by Ōgai's *shōsetsu* become ciphers for discovering the ethical implications of the narration that frames them (and vice versa). Novel pathos in such texts stands in a near mise-an-abyme relation to novel ethos. This effort to work from within forms of novel representation to reflect on the nature and implications of narrative forms constitutes the practice of self-conscious critique I see at work in his "stereoscopic" vision of the novel. Nearly all of Ōgai's fiction works, at some level, to produce illusions of mimesis through refractions of points of view whose fictionality lies exposed for readers. Indeed, this process itself is sometimes even an explicit part of the stories his *shōsetsu* tell.

24. By "plot" here I mean the sense that Peter Brooks gives the term, as the interpretive activity solicited by the relationship between the story told and its narrative frame, or the invitation to find the arrangement and representation of story elements meaningful and evocative. This sense of plot combines the objective ("actual" events at the diegetic level) and the subjective (representation by a narrator) in the kind of synthetic amalgam that Ōgai singled out as constitutive of novel aesthetics. It also allows us to see that his concern with novels had more to do with the value of the affective and hermeneutic activity that this critical sense of "plot" foregrounds than with the proper subject matter of novels themselves, which was one of the main topics of literary debate around the turn of the century.

25. My sense of the assumed function of autobiography here is informed by James Olney's 1972 *Metaphors of Self* and Philippe Lejeune's 1989 *On Autobiography*. Of course, more recent critiques, and even older ones such as Georges Poulet's work on "criticism of consciousness" (in various publications from 1969 to 1977), problematize the notion that autobiographical writing can bestow coherence and linearity upon its subject by virtue of its telos. However, it seems to me that Ōgai is interrogating conventional expectations of genre, and that *The Dancing Girl* is the story of Ōta's invocation of autobiography in the service of precisely such aims.

26. Hill, "Resentful Narrator," 383.
27. Hill, "Resentful Narrator," 384.
28. Hill, "Resentful Narrator," 376.
29. Hill, "Resentful Narrator," 384.
30. Hill, "Resentful Narrator," 382.
31. Ningetsu, *Maihime*, 86; Ningetsu's *The Dancing Girl* is the article that sparked "The 'Dancing Girl' Debate" and was recognized by many Japanese scholars as still

one of the most relevant critiques of the story nearly a century later, as noted for example by Koizumi Kōichirō in his introduction to a collection of Ōgai's work (Mori, *Ōgai zenshū*, 28). In this exchange, Ōgai rather disingenuously sidestepped the real point of Ningetsu's criticism by answering in the form of a response by Ōta's friend Aizawa himself. This decision to write from the perspective of a fictional character naturally allowed Ōgai to take all of Ōta's actions as "real" and therefore "necessitated" or at least adequately motivated by circumstances, skirting the issue of the responsibility of the novelist. In this rhetorical move Ōgai once again deliberately invokes the power of narrative perspective to bring fictional and critical perspectives together while still maintaining an illusion of objective, rational argument. In this way, his critical strategy in this debate reveals itself as a kind of "prelude" to the way he will put competing perspectives in tension in the "stereoscopic" vision of his later work. It is also in the course of this debate that Ōgai "dismisses the question of the content of the author's ideas, on which Ningetsu had focused his argument, and instead turns his attention to their *form* as expressed in the novel" (Isogai, *Meiji Twenties*, 127). This, too, is consistent with the argument that I have made about Ōgai's enduring interest in the forms of the novel and literary criticism over against the "ideas" that he is typically taken as championing.

32 Mori, *Dancing Girl*, 157.
33 Yōda, "First-Person Voice," 283.
34 Yōda argues that the pronoun exists only as a rhetorical feature of written discourse, one that indicates the narrating self, and is not a part of spoken Japanese tradition.
35 Yōda, "First-Person Voice," 283.
36 Yōda, "First-Person Voice," 299.
37 Yōda, "First-Person Voice," 298.
38 Mori, *Dancing Girl*, 166.
39 Yōda, "First-Person Voice," 299.
40 Yōda, "First-Person Voice," 304.
41 It seems difficult to imagine that the final lament is retrospective projection attributed to an unspecified moment after the end of the action but before the time of writing. Nothing else refers to such a time period. Moreover, the phrase "to this day" implies the specific time provided by the present (actively writing) narrator who has told us when and where he is writing, and not the continuum of relational "past time" for which no particular moment is specified. There is also no indication anywhere that Ōta's decision, or his writing, has helped him come to terms with this dissonant aspect of himself and attain the sovereignty promised by the unification that autobiographical writing ostensibly produces. Only the fact of his journey, artificially abstracted from the account of it, and nothing in his thinking or outlook, could suggest anything other than a deliberately ambivalent ending. Ōta

42 Mori, *Dancing Girl*, 166. Even the grammatical form of the word works in tandem with Ōgai's reflexive attention to Ōta's narrative as such. The *-keri* ending is a classical form of verb conjugation that signals a "storytelling past"—that is, a tense that signals a past action narrated in the present. A translation could conceivably read "it is that it remained," or "it is written that it remained," although these overemphasize the largely implicit function of the verb ending. What is relevant is that the language includes attention to the fact of narration and to the story's concern with the relation of the present narrative perspective on the past.
43 Vincent, *Two-Timing Modernity*, 84.
44 We will consider the device of the stereoscope in more detail in Chapter 4.

Chapter 3

1   Masao, *Accomplices of Silence*, 38.
2   Bowring, *Modernization*, 194; Karatani, *Nihon kindai*, 80–1.
3   Snyder, *Fictions of Desire*, 13.
4   Hasegawa, *Ōgai bungaku*, 9.
5   Bowring, *Modernization*, 102.
6   Mori, "Who Is Ōgai Gyoshi," 305.
7   Mori, "Who Is Ōgai Gyoshi," 306.
8   Mori, "Who Is Ōgai Gyoshi," 306.
9   Mori, "Who Is Ōgai Gyoshi," 306.
10 If the "I" who wrote as Ōgai Gyoshi is mere abstraction and not the real Mori Ōgai (let us remember that Ōgai is also a pen name), how can we expect the critical "I" of the present narration to be anything but another fiction? Wayne Booth's concept of the "Implied Author" is useful for parsing both the rhetorical structure of the text and Ōgai's reflections on literary authority and authenticity. Booth argues in *The Rhetoric of Fiction* that artifice is inevitable in narrative representations of identity, and that narrative perspective is always mediated by what he calls the implied author, or the author's "second self." The implied author is the name he gives to the inferred creator of the text, a figure who stands somewhere between the text's narrative voice and the "real author," and whose perspective gives the novel its coherence and significance. We might think of the concept of the implied author as the real subject of the piece, even more so than the literary world upon which Ōgai reflects.
11 Mori, "Who Is Ōgai Gyoshi," 304.
12 Mori, "Who Is Ōgai Gyoshi," 304.

13 Mori, "Who Is Ōgai Gyoshi," 305.
14 Suzuki, *Narrating the Self*, 7.
15 Mori, *Vita Sexualis*, 211–2.
16 Mori, *Vita Sexualis*, 212.
17 Mori, *Vita Sexualis*, 212.
18 Mori, *Vita Sexualis*, 213.
19 The introduction elsewhere emphasizes the connection between sexuality and textuality through its direct references to the language whereby we apprehend sexuality. For example, we are told of the narrator's need to translate the Chinese word for sexuality into Japanese using the character for *yoku* (desire), and how the last name of the perpetrator of an act of sexual aberrance (the rape of a woman) became a slang term referring to that act.
20 Mori, *Vita Sexualis*, 238.
21 Mori, *Vita Sexualis*, 242.
22 Mori, *Vita Sexualis*, 242.
23 Mori, *Vita Sexualis*, 247.
24 Mori, *Vita Sexualis*, 227.
25 Mori, *Vita Sexualis*, 237.
26 Mori, *Vita Sexualis*, 248.
27 Mori, *Vita Sexualis*, 248.
28 Both Ōgai and Bakhtin also formulate this ethical problem in terms of *passivity*. We have seen that Kanai refused to aggressively pursue his desire, instead letting himself be led into situations from which he could maintain an emotional and intellectual distance, and how this attitude characterizes his writing. Apropos of this, Bakhtin writes:

> A passive understanding of linguistic meaning is no understanding at all ... insofar as the speaker operates with such a passive understanding, nothing new can be introduced into his discourse; there can be no new aspects in his discourse relating to concrete objects and emotional expressions. Indeed the purely negative demands ... leave the speaker in his own personal context, within his own boundaries; such negative demands are completely immanent in the speaker's own discourse and do not go beyond his semantic or expressive self-sufficiency. (Bakhtin, *The Dialogic Imagination*, 281)

Bakhtin's description applies to Kanai's speech with uncanny precision; although willing to relate situations that might embarrass him (but also attest to his bold honesty in confessing them), Kanai rarely if ever allows anything to modulate his "expressive self-sufficiency." He maintains the same cool, detached tone and never dares to let the discourse or even personalities of others emerge in ways that would demand its modification.

29 Holquist, "Introduction," xxviii.
30 *Vita Sexualis*, as a parody of the kinds of pseudo-psychological studies that attempt to isolate and understand particular behaviors or attitudes through narrative histories, points out a common problem of psychological approaches that Bakhtin elucidates in the following terms:

> Discourse lives, as it were, beyond itself, in a living impulse toward the object; if we detach ourselves completely from this impulse all we have left is the naked corpse of the word …. *To study the word as such, ignoring the impulse that reaches out beyond it, is just as senseless as to study psychological experience outside the context of that real life toward which it was directed and by which it is determined.* (Bakhtin, *The Dialogic Imagination*, 292; original emphasis)

Through Kanai's approach to both sexual and literary activities (remember especially the pleasure he took in reading "through" texts to contrast their effects with the desires of their authors), *Vita Sexualis* demonstrates the danger of believing one can apprehend the "truth" of human life or desires through interpretive engagements that fail to understand the context which give them significance. Of course, it differs significantly from Bakhtin insofar as it delivers its critique and constitutes itself as a novelistic form through the very structures whose delimiting power it exposes.
31 Bakhtin, *The Dialogic Imagination*, 280.

Chapter 4

1 In the final section of this chapter, I argue that the titular wild goose serves as a substitution for the heroine. I have therefore chosen the singular "goose" rather than plural "geese" for the title, against the original English translation by Sanford Goldstein and Kingo Ochiai and with the more recent (2014) translation by Meredith McKinney.
2 In the process of elucidating the ethics of Ōgai's formal experimentation, I draw on concepts and terminology made available by debates on alterity in contemporary ethical criticism. However, I do this only to the extent that these debates illuminate the relevance for contemporary criticism of what Ōgai frames as direct objects of his *own* investigation into novel ethics. My goal is to demonstrate the relation of formal patterning—the structure of plot, narrative reflexivity, and systematic experimentation with narrative perspective—to the ethics of the situations that *The Wild Goose* dramatizes, and not to apply terms of Anglo-European theory for the purpose of exegesis. My findings suggest that the methods of immanent critique employed by *The Wild Goose* can prove instructive

for contemporary ethical theories, rather than the reverse. By focusing on immanent acts of self-theorizing and comparing the results to the theorization in contemporary scholarship, rather than reading the *shōsetsu* as an object of analysis by means of the latter, I hope to keep the relationship between literary theories of novel ethics and Ōgai's text dynamic and mobile, without subordinating one to the terms made available by the other.

3 Ōgai appreciated but also mistrusted the tendency of Western novels to authorize the sensibilities of narrators by virtue of the implicit homology between the structural progression of novelistic narration and the development of the "character" of the narrator. In his creative writing, he often disrupted the illusions of credibility and objectivity achieved through novel conventions by staging reflexive scenes of reading and producing rhetorical dissonances that invite readers to reflect on both the sensibilities of his narrators and the aims of the novel in calling attention to its construction of narrative perspective. By tracing the ethics of Ōgai's increasingly experimental narrative frameworks through *The Wild Goose*, we discover a culmination in the trajectory over the course of a fiction-writing career hitherto characterized as a series of discontinuities. His subsequent "break" toward historical fiction may turn out to have been the natural extension of his method of putting competing narrative perspectives in tension in order to avoid the monologic, self-authorizing perspective that so often accompanies the "realism" of the Western novel. That is, in his historical fiction, Ōgai juxtaposes "objective" descriptions of events with author's notes. In those notes we find subjective, self-referential intrusions commenting on the process of composition. The composite effect is that of a "stereoscopic" experience resonant with rather than opposed to that of *The Wild Goose*.

4 Shiokawa, "*Nihon kaiki*," 115.
5 Washburn, *Translating Mount Fuji*, 185.
6 Washburn, *Translating Mount Fuji*, 186.
7 Ikeuchi, *Kindai Nihon*, 172.
8 Bowring, *Modernization*, 84; Miyoshi, *Accomplices of Silence*, 48.
9 Snyder, "Limits of Fiction," 17.
10 These questions haunt the protagonist's and the narrator's treatment of the heroine, as I argue later in this chapter.
11 Mori, *Wild Goose*, 304.
12 Mori, *Wild Goose*, 304.
13 Mori, *Wild Goose*, 305; In 1911, the narrator finds himself writing in what he terms the "age of the novel," on the cusp of a wave of enthusiasm for naturalist efforts to describe the world truthfully "as it is" (Mori, *Wild Goose*, 303). But he also notes that the events he describes took place decades earlier, before the modern novel

took root in Japan, in an age of romantic tales and frivolous fiction such as *gesaku*. To understand the mindset of his characters, he suggests, we must understand how banal and trite romances prevalent in Japan in the late nineteenth century informed their thinking (whereas, he implies, it is the sensibilities of modern literature that informs his own, more authentic representations). Thus the relationship between the frame of the writing (the circumstances of its composition) and its content (the consciousness of the characters represented) manifests the same oppositional relationship between realist and romantic text as we found inscribed in the formal dissonance of the first line.

14 The narrator injects a description of Okada's reading of Chinese romantic tales into the introduction of Okada's relationship with Otama. The one specific tale the narrator mentions concerns a woman who preserves her beautiful appearance throughout grave illness and even when facing death, which the narrator says represented the "ideal" image of feminine beauty for Okada (Mori, *Wild Goose*, 26). The narrator thus uses literature to establish the "character" of his characters, describing their attitudes through their reading habits, and then commenting on or illustrating how those reading habits determined their actions and interactions, as he also does with Otama's father (Mori, *Wild Goose*, 27).

15 The walk itself, though situated in the "real" space of Tokyo, serves as a metaliterary reminder that we are reading a deliberately crafted work of fiction: strolls through Tokyo localities were widely recognized as a staple trope of Meiji literary fiction, particularly the kind of first-person mode that would come to be known as the "I-novel." See Dan O'Neill's 2006 article "Portrait of a Writer in Tokyo, 1910: Mori Ogai's *Seinen*" for more on Ōgai and the convention of literary walks.

16 Washburn, *Translating Mount Fuji*, 189.

17 Vincent, *Two-Timing Modernity*, 52.

18 Girard, *Deceit*, 15.

19 I have argued in an article from which this chapter was adapted that *The Wild Goose* brings together a Bakhtinian emphasis on the discursive ethics of novel narration and a more Girardian insight into the relationship of desire and novel perspective, situating metaphysical desire not only at the level of the plot itself, where Girard principally locates it, but also at the level of narration (see "Triangulating an Ethos"). That is, the triangular structure Girard uncovers may register as such a powerful truth of the novels he examines less because of how accurately it represents a universal psychological condition of human desire than because it mirrors the dynamics in which particular kinds of reflexive, self-conscious novelistic narratives engage their readers. Reading Ōgai with Girard's theory in mind can help us discover its limitations as well as its broader narrative applicability. By considering triangular desire as it applies to the relationships

that *The Wild Goose*'s self-conscious narrator establishes with both characters and readers, we discover the utility of Girardian terms for discussing formal features of reflexive novels. We also discover the limitations of Girard's assumptions about the realist foundation of the novel.

20 Vincent, *Two-Timing Modernity*, 57.
21 Sakaki, *Recontextualizing Texts*, 144–6.
22 The narrator's diegetic desire to assert himself over Okada and his metadiegetic desire to assert control over the narrative itself amount to one and the same metaphysical desire to occupy the authoritative position of the author and exercise control over the story of another that threatens to leave him on the periphery. Through both the thematic illustration of the narrator's desire for Otama and the metatextual reflection on his narrative manipulations themselves, Ōgai points to the strong connection between mimetic desire and narrative mimesis, both of which operate to secure authoritative positions vis-à-vis the rendering of other points of view. The narrator's wresting of Okada's tale from its original teller (the narrator prefers reported speech to direct quotation) proves both an aesthetic and an ethical manipulation, one that the *shōsetsu* itself exposes by reflexively calling attention to the parallel between narrative methods and the story told.
23 Mori, *Wild Goose*, 348.
24 Mori, *Wild Goose*, 303.
25 Mori, *Wild Goose*, 318.
26 Manipulative acts of mind-reading are so pervasive as to become the perspectival norm in this text. For example, in intermittent scenes of interaction between the women and their maids, the narration focuses on the ways the characters attempt to gauge each other's moods and thereby manipulate each other's behavior. Similarly, in a scene with Otama and her father, the narration emphasizes to the point of tedium how each makes assumptions about the other's feelings and therefore fails to communicate in ways that might actually bring them both solace, further isolating them instead. And of course nearly all of the narrator's own interactions are predicated upon presumed access to the ulterior motives of others.
27 In the course of this imaginative projection, he believes that he has discovered the real feelings behind her disjointed accusations and strange fits of silence and productivity: that she wants him to hit her. The overt violence of this conclusion, and the fact that he assumes she wants Suezo to demonstrate his authority over her, exposes the self-serving nature of the apparently empathetic process by which he attempts to understand her.
28 Mori, *Wild Goose*, 321.
29 Butler, *Giving an Account*, 25.
30 Butler, *Giving an Account*, 26.
31 Butler, *Giving an Account*, 34.

32 Rather than offering itself wholly as an immersive experience, the novel induces a kind of shuttling between immersion and reflection. In this way we might say that it functions more like ethical criticism than a conventional novel. As Andrew Gibson observes, most ethical criticism operates under the tacit assumption that the ethical force of the novel arises from its realistic portrayals of human beings in particular situations (Gibson, *Postmodernity*, 8). It is our cognitive and emotional responses to the pathos of novel realism, our engagement with characters *as if* they were real human beings, that situate us in the realm of ethics for most novel theorists. Although critics today differ widely on how we should apprehend and value literary representations of others, most fall on a spectrum between what I have called (following Dorothy Hale) an "ethics of identification" and an "ethics of letting be" (Hale, "Aesthetics," 126). The former has a long critical history dating back to ancient Greece in the Western tradition and the "Fireflies" chapter in *The Tale of Genji* in Japanese literary history (Murasaki, *Genji*, 190). On this view, the novel presents a kind of neo-Aristotelian "model of life" that closely approximates the experience of human interactions. The latter, in contrast, suggests that identification may produce dangerously colonizing attitudes in readers, insofar as it might encourage appropriating rather than respecting the differences that mark others as such. In its most polarized form, this point of view radically mistrusts the possibility that one can ever truly "identify" with an "other," particularly through engagement with a genre whose language materializes those social, political, and cultural codes that delimit, often traumatically, the way we apprehend and recognize others as subjects. By shuttling readers between immersion and reflection—by inviting identification and then deconstructing its possibility by reminding readers of the illusory and possibly self-serving nature of the characters as fictions created by an embedded narrator-author—*The Wild Goose* holds these different views in tension and draws our attention to them as ethical effects of novel experience.
33 Mori, *Wild Goose*, 348.
34 Vermeule, *Why Do We Care*, 39–41.
35 Harpham, *Shadows of Ethics*, 27.
36 Harpham, *Shadows of Ethics*, 27.
37 Booth, "Ethical Criticism," 360.

Chapter 5

1 Ozawa, "Divergence of Theory," 48.
2 Külpe, et al., *Introduction to Philosophy*, 111.
3 We find similar emphases in other tales as well. For example, in "*Yabu no naka*" (In a Grove; 1922), the very idea of arriving logically at some just understanding of

criminal passions proves illusory and untenable, part of an oppressive system that produced those violent consequences in the first place. And in "Kappa" (1927), the experience of nonhuman creatures reveals the disturbing unfairness and cruelty in the supposedly rational world of humanity.

4 Marra, *Modern Japanese Aesthetics*, 94.
5 Akutagawa, "The Morals of Tomorrow," 7. Although Akutagawa addresses particular moral laws and social conventions here, the essay's overall attention to the processes whereby morals are formed, and whereby concepts of morality themselves take shape, points to its interest in ethics as I have distinguished it from morality. Intriguingly, the dialectic notion of history that plays out here also resonates with that espoused by Ōgai in "The Tower of Silence" (see Chapter 2).
6 Akutagawa, "Rashōmon," 1:145.
7 Akutagawa, "Rashōmon," 1:146.
8 Akutagawa, "Rashōmon," 1:146.
9 Descriptions of Rashōmon, the gate, apply equally to "Rashōmon," the story. Before the narration transitions to the servant's struggles, he explains, "The evening darkness brought the sky ever lower until the roof of the gate was supporting the dark, heavy clouds on the ridge of its jutting tiles" (Rubin, *Rashōmon*, 4). We face here an optical illusion; the material structure of the gate appears to support the dark, cloudy atmosphere that pervades it, just as the contours and disrepair of the gate produce much the same pervasive atmosphere for the servant and readers. The text thus sustains a haunting mood that envelops readers in its affective experience through its embodiment of images whereby material objects produce such effects. The principal subject of this story is, after all, the various ways that aesthetics produce and sustain ethically freighted moods.
10 Akutagawa, "Rashōmon," 1:149.
11 Akutagawa, "Rashōmon," 1:147.
12 Akutagawa, "Rashōmon," 1:147.
13 Akutagawa, "Rashōmon," 1:150.
14 Akutagawa, "Rashōmon," 1:153.
15 Akutagawa, "Rashōmon," 1:153.
16 Sako, *Ethical Explorations*, 133–57.
17 In *The Dancing Girl*, for example, we found that a final, resounding ambivalent note serves as a provocation to reflect on the complicities of authorial desire and the capacity of the novel form to naturalize sensibilities and instantiate worldviews through its formal production of ethos. Self-consciousness vis-à-vis the ideological commitments of novel narration was not only a method but an ethical end of much of Ōgai's work. The revelation of the manipulative power of novel ethos and the formative power of literary (and other narrative or linguistic) conventions to shape worldviews was a meta-narrative goal of much of his writing.

18 Harpham, *Shadow of Ethics*, 27.
19 Altieri, *Canons and Consequences*, 203.
20 Altieri, *Particulars of Rapture*, 16.
21 Altieri, *Particulars of Rapture*, 49.
22 Altieri, *Particulars of Rapture*, 118–19.
23 Altieri, *Particulars of Rapture*, 17.
24 This is another reason that ethical criticism tends to fail to account for the ethical value of literary affect for Altieri. "If art provides mostly knowledge of possibilities or exemplifications, why should these possibilities matter mostly in terms of what they offer as knowledge. That something is possible is often obvious on any general level. What matters then is the vitality by which the possibility is rendered so as to become desirable. We would need a different vocabulary from the cognitive domain to characterize what matters in what is exemplified" (Altieri, lecture notes, n.p.).
25 Altieri, *Particulars of Rapture*, 122–3.

Chapter 6

1   Gibson, *Postmodernity*, 8.
2   Altieri, *Painterly*, 3–9.
3   Phelan, "Rhetorical Literary Ethics," 629.
4   Akutagawa, "Green Onions," 5:237.
5   Akutagawa, "Green Onions," 5:239–40.
6   Akutagawa, "Green Onions," 5:241.
7   Rubin, "Green Onions," 120–1; Here and in two other instances I felt that Rubin's translation conveyed everything that I felt important about the passages I cite; all other translations are my own.
8   Akutagawa, "Green Onions," 5:234.
9   Akutagawa, "Green Onions," 5:238–9.
10 The irony in the passage above expands beyond the level of story of this writer to include metaliterary reference to Akutagawa's own literary reputation, raising the question of the relation of the literary representation of the narrative personae to the "real" Akutagawa. In attempting to discern the attitude of the narrator toward his represented character, we find ourselves forced to reflect on the analogous relation of the real author to his fictionalized narrative self. The narrator's ironic stance itself may even prove an object of authorial irony, insofar as the text invites us to consider the parallels between its narrator's ironic worldview and the sentimental worldview of the character he derides. Our efforts to apprehend the narrator's perspective on his story demand that we work through the very

questions about the relationship of fictionalized literary representations to real-life emotions, conditions, and identities that we shall see the story thematizes in the experiences of its protagonist.

11 Akutagawa, "Green Onions," 5:238.
12 Rubin, "Green Onions," 125.
13 Akutagawa, "Green Onions," 5:241.
14 Akutagawa, "Green Onions," 5:246.
15 Rubin, "Green Onions," 123.
16 Akutagawa, "Green Onions," 5:246–7.
17 Akutagawa, *Cogwheels*, 15:55.
18 Terada, *Feeling in Theory*, 21.
19 Terada, *Feeling in Theory*, 36.
20 This inversion of the real and fictional in the treatment of affect precipitates the devastating crisis in his final writing, as we shall see.
21 Terada, *Feeling in Theory*, 23.
22 Terada, *Feeling in Theory*, 48.
23 Terada, *Feeling in Theory*, 48.
24 De Man, "Criticism and Crisis," 76.
25 Nietzsche, *The Gay Science*, 317.
26 Perhaps in a manner reminiscent of de Man's suggestion that irony is the "reversed mirror-image" of allegory, the narrator's emotional stance toward his fiction inverts O-Kimi's own emotional stance toward literature. De Man's concluding remarks on irony in Schlegel capture the effects of the narrator's self-conscious exposure of the fictionality of "Green Onions" remarkably well:

> [Irony] is the permanent parabasis of allegory.... Irony is no longer a trope but the undoing of the deconstructive allegory of all tropological conditions.... As such, far from closing off the tropological system, irony enforces the repetition of its aberration. (De Man, "Criticism and Crisis" 301)

By suspending us between the allegory of the narrated story and the irony of its narrative frame, "Green Onions" functions ultimately as a "deconstructive" response to the epistemic crisis of literary self-consciousness.

27 De Man sees *Julie* as an "allegory of unreadability" in which

> the imperatives of truth and falsehood oppose the narrative syntax and manifest themselves at its expense. The concatenation of truth and falsehood within the values of right and wrong is disrupted, affecting the economy of narration in decisive ways. We can call this shift in economy *ethical*, since it indeed involves a displacement from *pathos* to *ethos*. Allegories are always ethical, the term ethical designating the structural interference of two distinct value systems. The ethical category is imperative to the extent that it is linguistic and not

subjective ... Ethics (or one should say, ethnicity) is one discursive mode among others. (De Man, "Criticism and Crisis," 206)

Here de Man argues that ethics emerges as a discursive practice generated by the self-conscious reference to authorship in the preface of the text. For him, literary ethics does not concern the will of a subject or the relationship between subjects so much as it represents a "linguistic category," or "one discursive mode among others." It manifests itself as a "shift in the economy of narration" that disrupts conventional associations of truth and falsehood with right and wrong, and instead confronts readers with the "linguistic aporia" that results from the displacement of conventional reading practices that the "allegory of unreadability" enacts (De Man, "Criticism and Crisis" 206).

Chapter 7

1   Sipos, "Akutagawa Ryūnosuke," 168.
2   Sipos, "Akutagawa Ryūnosuke," 168.
3   Sipos, "Akutagawa Ryūnosuke," 162.
4   Sipos, "Akutagawa Ryūnosuke," 163.
5   Lippit, *Topographies*, 50.
6   Lippet, *Topographies*, 51.
7   Miyamoto, "Haiboku no bungaku," 227.
8   Miyamoto, "The Literature of Defeat," 227.
9   Miyamoto, "The Literature of Defeat," 240.
10 Miyamoto, "The Literature of Defeat," 223.
11 Miyamoto, "The Literature of Defeat," 244.
12 Fukuda, "Akutagawa Ryûnosuke," 44–78.
13 Fukuda, "Akutagawa Ryûnosuke," 46.
14 Akutagawa, "Literary, All-Too Literary," 15:208.
15 Yoshida, "Akutagawa Ryūnosuke," 26.
16 Yoshida, "Akutagawa Ryūnosuke," 73.
17 Ueda. *Modern Japanese Writers*, 111–44.
18 Sako, *Ethical Explorations*, 73.
19 Sekiguchi, *Akutagawa*, 173–9.
20 Cather, "Noting Suicide," 28.
21 Tanizaki, "Jyōzetsu roku," 145.
22 Akutagawa, "Literary, All-Too Literary," 15:121.
23 Akutagawa, "Literary, All-Too Literary," 15:154.
24 Akutagawa, "Art and Other Matters," 5:164.

25 Akutagawa, "Art and Other Matters," 5:164.
26 Akutagawa, "Art and Other Matters," 5:165.
27 Akutagawa, "Paradox of Japanese Literature," 22:419.
28 Akutagawa, "Paradox of Japanese Literature," 22:418.
29 Akutagawa, "Literary, All-Too Literary," 15:173.
30 Akutagawa, "Literary, All-Too Literary," 15:200.
31 Akutagawa, "The Morals of Tomorrow," 3–21.
32 Akutagawa, "Literary, All-Too Literary," 15:154.
33 Akutagawa, "Literary, All-Too Literary," 15:153.
34 Akutagawa, "Literary, All-Too Literary," 15:154.

Chapter 8

1 Cavanaugh, "Portrait of the Writer," 152.
2 Cavanaugh, "Portrait of the Writer," 153.
3 Cavanaugh, "Portrait of the Writer," 153.
4 Rubin, "Rashōmon," 187.
5 Akutagawa, *A Fool's Life*, 16:38.
6 Akutagawa, *A Fool's Life*, 16:56–7; The passage refers readers to Akutagawa's *shōsetsu*, "Noroma Puppets" (*Noroma Ningyō*; 1916), about how a fictional persona's encounter with a puppet prompts meditation on the degree to which art reflects free, independent thought or can only take forms that are predetermined by cultural values. The allusion here conflates the narrated self's nervous existential sense of himself as a mere puppet of biological and cultural forces with metaliterary consciousness of the fact he exists as an act of self-performance in the theatre of a projected, fictional world created by an author—that second self—who writes him into this epistemological prison.
7 The unnamed protagonist of this text is an autobiographical self written in the third person. I will refer to this figure as the "author" rather than narrator because he is indeed an author, and because the text purposefully conflates Akutagawa himself, his narrator, and the persona who inhabits the text. I will still use the term "narrator" when the need arises to distinguish the writing self of the authorial personae from his representation of himself in the past.
8 Akutagawa, *A Fool's Life*, 16:47.
9 Akutagawa, *A Fool's Life*, 16:49.
10 Akutagawa, *A Fool's Life*, 16:63.
11 Akutagawa, *A Fool's Life*, 16:63.
12 Akutagawa, *A Fool's Life*, 16:51; In one moment of *A Fool's Life*, the author reads a work by "Sensei," referring to Natsume Sōseki, and becomes lost in the stillness of

uncanny affect solicited by the encounter with this textual invocation (Akutagawa, *A Fool's Life*, 44). In *Cogwheels*, the resonance between the authorial persona and the figure of "Sensei" from Sōseki's own *shōsetsu Kokoro* (1914) becomes clearer, as does the ethical relevance of the intertextual identification.

13 Akutagawa, *A Fool's Life*, 16:40.
14 Akutagawa, *A Fool's Life*, 16:60.
15 Akutagawa, *A Fool's Life*, 16:39.
16 Akutagawa, *A Fool's Life*, 16:48.
17 The narrating author uses the faint impression of a butterfly's "wing dust" lingering on his lips as an image for the woman with whom he once stole a fleeting moment of intimacy, describes his dialogue about the evils of capitalism and ethical problems of his own participation in that system as a "conversation with an angel—an angel in an impeccable top hat," and meditates on the yellowness of the wings of a stuffed swan that symbolizes himself as author (Akutagawa, *A Fool's Life*, 16:47, 60). Images of wings consistently recur and serve as indices differentiating the authorial persona who employs this symbolic motif and the narrated self who has not yet converted such experiences into meaningful literary symbolism. The text in fact consistently puts on display the experience of a kind of supplementary consciousness that interposes between writing and written selves, divorcing the writer from the authenticity of experience his narrative attempts to recollect—as we have seen with the puppet behind the pane of glass and will shortly revisit one last time in the image of the stuffed swan.
18 Miyamoto. "The Literature of Defeat," 244. (See previous chapter.)
19 Akutagawa, *Cogwheels*, 15:67.
20 Akutagawa, *Cogwheels*, 15:77.
21 Akutagawa, *Cogwheels*, 15:68-9.
22 Akutagawa, *Cogwheels*, 15:52-3.
23 Sōseki, "Theory of literature (Bungakuron, 1907)," 17-24.
24 Sōseki, Kokoro, 43.
25 The Japanese character for "peeling" (*haku*) appears five times in *A Fool's Life* and once in what could serve as a prefatory note, Akutagawa's brief message to Kume Masao, wherein he refers to the work as peeling away the "skin" of Akutagawa's urbane identity (Akutagawa, *A Fool's Life*, 16:4). In peeling away the mimetic structure of the novel, Akutagawa also peels away the protective mechanisms of the self.
26 Akutagawa, *A Fool's Life*, 16:41.
27 Akutagawa, *A Fool's Life*, 16:46.
28 Akutagawa, *Cogwheels*, 15:55.
29 Akutagawa, *Cogwheels*, 15:69.
30 Akutagawa, *A Fool's Life*, 16:41.

31 The winged sandals recall myths and gods, artificial wings and Icarus, the figure with whom he most directly identifies. The English word for "story" bears an obviously critical relation to this self-reflexive *shōsetsu* echoed back to the author in foreign form. "*Tailpot*," the word for an enormous tree with umbrella-like leaves, as rendered in Japanese incorporates the word "tale." Moreover, the narrator "sees himself" in a tree and related the self-figuration to a tree discussed by Jonathan Swift. Additionally, umbrellas catch the narrator's attention repeatedly throughout *Cogwheels*, as manufactured boundaries that thinly protect the self from dissolute and dissolving surroundings. The fine web of associations spun throughout the text belies the artistry of its entrapping affect.

32 Yokomitsu's work, especially his long novel *Shanhai*, establishes parallels between physical and national bodies and seeks to destroy what he saw as stultification in the language through which we apprehend those bodies to allow us to position ourselves in more open-ended relationships that break down received narratives of personal and national identity (see Yokomitsi, *Shanhai*). Kobayashi, in works like "Multiple Designs" and "The Face of the Author," opposes flesh-and-blood subjectivity to literary representations of bodies and subjects in an effort to work against the regressive self-absorption he found endemic to literary language, while at the same time deliberately employing reflexive literary self-consciousness as a means of immanent critique (Kobayashi, "Multiple Designs," 202–9; "The Face of the Author," 226–9). Kobayashi's ethical project, while far too complex and fraught with real and apparent contradiction to begin to explain here, involved bringing about recognition of the obfuscating force of the language both constitutive and representative of human relationships. His revolutionary and self-consciously meta-critical writing might be said to have culminated a transition from tentatively reflexive literary and academic writing to something more like full-blown metaliterary theory, a fitting memorialization for the testament that Akutagawa's fiction provides.

Chapter 9

1 Kurihara, "Murakami," 20.1.
2 Quoted in Roquet, "Ambient," 106.
3 Komori, *Murakami*, 11–20.
4 Kiyoshi, "Jiga to sono kage," 8.
5 Matsunaga, "Zadankai," 145–7.
6 Tokō, "Sōzō ryoku wo kaita kyōryōsa." 100.
7 Strecher, "At the Critical Stage," 863.

8   Yamada, "Exposing," 2.
9   Seats, *Murakami*, 176.
10 Hale, "Aesthetics and the New Ethics," 900.
11 Barthes, "The Reality Effect," 143.
12 Derrida, *The Politics of Friendship*, 231.
13 Murakami, *Colorless*, 122.
14 Gee, *Unified Discourse Analysis*, 17–8.
15 Murakami, *1Q84* vol. II, 245.
16 Murakami, *1Q84* vol. II, 245.
17 Murakami, "Tamashi." 10.
18 Murakami's "soft landing" strategy closely aligns with the idea of transcultural conversation advocated by Kwame Appiah as the ethical requirement of contemporary cosmopolitanism, although no scholars have yet viewed his writing on these post- and de-colonial terms (Appiah 97–9).
19 Murakami, "Tamashi," 11.
20 Hutcheon, *Narcissistic Narrative*, 1–6.
21 Jameson, *The Political Unconscious*, 141.
22 Armstrong, "Textual Harassment," 405.
23 Knapp, "Between Thing and Theory," 662.
24 Best and Marcus, "Surface Reading," 10–11.
25 Murakami, *Sekai no owari*, 589–90.
26 *Hard-Boiled Wonderland and the End of the World* insists that aesthetic consciousness gives shape to ethics both within and without novel worlds. It is an explicit plot point that reading fiction like Dostoevsky's shaped the landscape of the narrator's psychic world by providing him models of self-other relationships. One of the very few moments in which the alternate realities of the two sets of chapters briefly adjoin occurs when the Tokyo narrator meditates on Russian literature and then briefly imagines "high walls" surrounding its characters—the same high walls that enclose the fantasy world. Thus the fantasy world, which provides the conceptual framework for his interpersonal encounters, has been and continues to be constructed by not just fictional but explicitly *literary* experience.
27 Brooks, "Persons and Optics."
28 As Paul Crowther writes in an edited volume on Wollheim's work, "Wollheim's position … is that the elements of twofoldness do, indeed, must, permit *simultaneous* perception" (emphasis added) (91).
29 The status that the narrator finally achieves as a self-conscious and yet immersed reader allows him to perform ethical work that is simultaneously both self- and other-oriented. His reflexive awareness of the unreality of his world confronts him with the fact that he has loved but an image of the real librarian. Yet his persistence

in valuing her presence as if it were real, even knowing otherwise, inspires him to seek out some mutual ground on which they might meet more authentically. This self-transpositioning work takes kinetic form in the novel through the attentive and tentative traversal of what the narrator has recognized as a contingent, imaginary world system for which he can now take responsibility. Armed with this self-awareness, he learns to "read" this fictional world with new purpose: to seek out places of potential overlap in the different world systems he and the woman inhabit, such as the space between The Town and the unassimilated Woods where he finds the musical instrument. In the end, by self-consciously tracing over the surfaces of a fictional world he literally overwrites the neural pathways that constitute his apperceptive habits, reshaping his actual relationship with the librarian in ways that he could not have accomplished without his kinetic deployment of this reflexive consciousness.

30 Palumbo-Liu, *The Deliverance of Others*, 19–21.

Bibliography

Akutagawa, Ryūnosuke. *Akutagawa Ryūnosuke zenshū*. 24 vols. Tokyo: Iwanami Shoten, 1997.

Akutagawa, Ryūnosuke. *Haguruma* [Cogwheels]. In *Akutagawa Ryūnosuke zenshū* [The Complete Works of Ryūnosuke Akutagawa], vol. 15. Tokyo: Iwanami Shoten, 1997, 40–86.

Akutagawa, Ryūnosuke. "Negi" [Green Onions]. In *Akutagawa Ryūnosuke zenshū* [The Complete Works of Ryūnosuke Akutagawa], vol. 5. Tokyo: Iwanami Shoten, 1997, 234–48.

Akutagawa, Ryūnosuke. "Bungeiteki na, amari ni bungeiteki na" [Literary, All-Too Literary]. In *Akutagawa Ryūnosuke zenshū*, vol. 15. Tokyo: Iwanami Shoten, 1997, 147–230.

Akutagawa, Ryūnosuke. "Ashita no dōtoku" [The Morals of Tomorrow]. In *Akutagawa Ryūnosuke zenshū*, vol. 12. Tokyo: Iwanami Shoten, 1997, 3–21.

Akutagawa, Ryūnosuke. "Rashōmon." In *Akutagawa Ryūnosuke zenshū*, vol. 1. Tokyo: Iwanami Shoten, 1997, 145–55.

Akutagawa, Ryūnosuke. "Aru ahō no isshō" [A Fool's Life]. In *Akutagawa Ryūnosuke zenshū*, vol. 16. Tokyo: Iwanami Shoten, 1997, 37–68.

Akutagawa, Ryūnosuke. "Ashita no dōtoku" [The Morals of Tomorrow]. In *Akutagawa Ryūnosuke zenshū*, vol. 12. Tokyo: Iwanami Shoten, 1997, 3–21.

Akutagawa, Ryūnosuke. "Bungeiteki na, amari ni bungeiteki na" [Literary, All-Too Literary]. In *Akutagawa Ryūnosuke zenshū*, vol. 15. Tokyo: Iwanami Shoten, 1997, 147–230.

Akutagawa, Ryūnosuke. "Geijutsu sono ta" [Art and Other Matters]. In *Akutagawa Ryūnosuke zenshū*, vol. 5. Tokyo: Iwanami Shoten, 1997, 164–72.

Akutagawa, Ryūnosuke. "Nihonbungei no paradokkusu" [The Paradox of Japanese Literature]. In *Akutagawa Ryūnosuke zenshū*, vol. 22. Tokyo: Iwanami Shoten, 1997, 417–23.

Akutagawa, Ryūnosuke. "Noroma Ningyō" [Noroma Puppet]. In *Akutagawa Ryūnosuke zenshū*, vol. 1. Tokyo: Iwanami Shoten, 1997, 217–21.

Altieri, Charles. *Painterly Abstraction in Modernist American Poetry: The Contemporaneity of Modernism*. Cambridge: Cambridge University Press, 1989.

Altieri, Charles. *Canons and Consequences: Reflections on the Ethical Force of Imaginative Ideals*. Evanston: Northwestern University Press, 1991.

Altieri, Charles. "Lyrical Ethics and Literary Experience." *Style* 32 (1998): 272–97.

Altieri, Charles. *The Particulars of Rapture: An Aesthetics of the Affects*. Ithaca: Cornell University Press, 2003.

Altieri, Charles. "Untitled Lecture, Research Seminar." *Philosophy and the Arts* (Spring 2009).

Andō, Reiji, Miho Matsunaga, et al. "Zadankai: Murakami Haruki 『1Q84』 wo tokoton yomu." *Gunzō* 64, no. 8 (2009): 142–59.

Appiah, Kwame. *Cosmopolitanism: Ethics in a World of Strangers*. New York: W. W. Norton, 2006.

Armstrong, Isobel. "Textual Harassment: The Ideology of Close Reading, or How Close Is Close?" *Textual Practice* 9, no. 3 (1995): 401–20.

Attridge, Derek. *J. M. Coetzee and the Ethics of Reading: Literature in the Event*. Chicago: University of Chicago Press, 2004.

Bakhtin, Mikhail. *The Dialogic Imagination: Four Essays*. Translated by Caryl Emerson and Michael Holquist. Austin: University of Texas Press, 1981.

Bakhtin, Mikhail. "Discourse in the Novel." Translated by M. Holquist and C. Emerson. In *The Dialogic Imagination*, edited by M. Holquist. Austin: University of Texas Press, 1981, 259–422.

Barthes, Roland. "The Reality Effect." In *The Rustle of Language*, translated by Richard Howard. Oxford: Blackwell, 1986, 141–8.

Best, Stephen and Sharon Marcus. "Surface Reading: An Introduction." *Representations* 108 (2009): 1–21.

Black, Shameem. *Fiction Across Borders: Imagining the Lives of Others in Late Twentieth-Century Novels*. New York: Columbia University Press, 2010.

Blackburn, Simon, Robert Brandom, Paul & Williams Horwich and Michael Price. *Expressivism, Pragmatism and Representationalism*. Cambridge: Cambridge University Press, 2013.

Booth, Wayne. *The Company We Keep: An Ethics of Fiction*. Berkeley: University of California Press, 1988.

Booth, Wayne C. "Why Ethical Criticism Can Never Be Simple." *Style* (University Park, PA) 32, no. 2 (1998): 351–64.

Bowring, Richard. *Mori Ōgai and the Modernization of Japanese Culture*. Cambridge: Cambridge University Press, 1979.

Brooks, Peter. "Persons and Optics." *What Is the Nature of Literary Being?* Center for the Study of the Novel Annual Conference. Stanford, CA. 12 April 2013. Conference Presentation.

Butler, Judith. *Giving an Account of Oneself*. Fordham: Fordham University Press, 2005.

Butler, Judith. "Values of Difficulty." In *Just Being Difficult? Academic Writing in the Public Arena*, edited by Jonathan Culler and Kevin Lamb. Stanford: Stanford University Press, 2003.

Cather, Kirsten. "Noting Suicide with a Vague Sense of Anxiety." *The Journal of Japanese Studies* 46, no. 1 (2020): 1–29. doi:10.1353/jjs.2020.0002.

Cavanaugh, Carole. "Portrait of the Writer as a Young Reader: Akutagawa Ryūnosuke in Maruzen Bookstore." In *Studies in Modern Japanese Literature: Essays and Translations in Honor of Edwin McClellan*, edited by Dennis Washburn and Alan Tansman, vol. 20. Ann Arbor, MI: Center for Japanese Studies, University of Michigan, 1997, 151–74.

Claviez, Thomas. "Done and Over With—Finally? Otherness, Metonymy, and the Ethics of Comparison." *PMLA* 128, no. 3 (2013): 608–14.

Crowther, Paul. "Twofoldness: From Transcendental Imagination to Pictorial Art." In *Richard Wollheim on the Art of Painting: Art as Representation and Expression*, edited by Rob Van Gerwen. Cambridge: Cambridge University Press, 2001, 85–100.

Damrosch, David. "Global Comparatism and the Question of Language." *PMLA* 128, no. 3 (2013): 622–8.

De Man, Paul. "Criticism and Crisis." In *Blindness and Insight: Essays in the Rhetoric of Contemporary Criticism*. Minneapolis: University of Minnesota Press, 1983.

Derrida, Jacques. *The Politics of Friendship*. Translated by George Collins. London: Verso, 1997.

Dower, John. "Mori Ogai: Meiji Japan's Eminent Bystander." *Harvard Papers on Japan* 2 (1963): 57–101.

Duara, Prasenjit. "Nationalism in East Asia." *History Compass* 4, no. 3 (2006): 407–27.

Foucault, Michel. *Ethics: Subjectivity and Truth*. Edited by Paul Rainbow. New York: The New Press, 1998.

Frentiu, Rodica. "Intellectual Conscience and Self-Cultivation (*shūyō*) as Imperatives in Japan's Modernization: Mori Ōgai, *Youth* (*Seinen*, 1910–11)." *Review of European Studies* 5, no. 2 (2013): 48–59.

Fukuda, Tsuneari. "Akutagawa Ryūnosuke." In *Akutagawa Ryūnosuke Kenkyû*, edited by Yoshida Seiichi. Tokyo: Shinshô shuppan, 1957.

Futabatei, Shimei. "*Ukigumo*" [Floating Clouds]. 2 vols. In *Kindai Nihon bungakukan*. Tokyo: Kinkōdō, 1973.

Gallagher, Catherine. "The Rise of Fictionality." In *The Novel, Volume 1: History, Geography and Culture*, edited by Franco Moretti. Princeton: Princeton University Press, 2006, 336–63.

Gaut, Berys. *Art, Emotion, and Ethics*. New York: Oxford University Press, 2009.

Gee, James Paul. *Unified Discourse Analysis: Language, Reality, Virtual Worlds, and Video Games*. London: Routledge, 2015.

Gerow, Aaron. *Visions of Japanese Modernity: Articulations of Cinema, Nation, and Spectatorship, 1895–1925*. Berkeley: University of California Press, 2010.

Gibson, Andrew. *Postmodernity, Ethics and the Novel*. London: Routledge, 1999.

Girard, René. *Deceit, Desire and the Novel: Self and Other in Literary Structure*. Baltimore: Johns Hopkins University Press, 1965.

Guillory, John. "The Ethical Practice of Modernity: The Example of Reading." In *The Turn to Ethics*, edited by Marjorie B. Garber, Beatrice Hanssen and Rebecca L. Walkowitz. New York: Routledge, 2000, 29–46.

Hale, Dorothy J. "Fiction as Restriction: Self-Binding in New Ethical Theories of the Novel." *Narrative* 15, no. 2 (2007): 187–206.

Hale, Dorothy. *Social Formalism: The Novel in Theory from Henry James to the Present.* Stanford: Stanford University Press, 1998.

Hale, Dorothy. "Aesthetics and the New Ethics: Theorizing the Novel in the Twenty-First Century." *PMLA* 124, no. 3 (May 2009): 896–905.

Harootunian, Harold. *Overcome by Modernity: History, Culture and Commodity in Interwar Japan.* Princeton: Princeton University Press, 2000.

Harpham, Geoffrey. *Shadows of Ethics.* Durham: Duke University Press, 1999.

Hasegawa, Izumi. *Ōgai bungaku no kikō.* Tokyo: Meiji Shoin, 1979.

Hasegawa, Izumi. *Kinda Nihon bungaku hyōronshi* [History of Modern Japanese Literary Criticism]. Tokyo: Imura Printing Co., 1965.

Hasumi, Shigehiko, *Shōsetsu kara tōku hanarete.* Tokyo: Nihonbungeisha, 1989.

Hearn, Lafcadio and Murray Paul. *Japanese Ghost Stories.* London: Penguin Books. 2019.

Hill, Christopher. "Mori Ōgai's Resentful Narrator: Trauma and the National Subject in 'The Dancing Girl.'" *Positions: East Asia Cultures Critique* 10, no. 2 (2002): 365–97.

Hokubō, Sanji, "Shōsetsuka no sekinin" [The Responsibility of the Novelist]. In *Nihon kindai bungaku hyōron taikei* [Survey of Modern Japanese Literary Criticism], edited by Sei Itō. Tokyo: Kadokawa Shoten, 1969, 83–6.

Holquist, Michael. "Introduction." In *The Dialogic Imagination*, edited by M. Holquist. Austin: University of Texas Press, 1981, xxiv–xxxiv.

Huffer, Lynne. "'There Is No Gomorrah': Narrative Ethics in Feminist and Queer Theory." *Differences: A Journal of Feminist Cultural Studies* 12, no. 3 (2001): 1–32.

Hutcheon, Linda. *Narcissistic Narrative. The Metafictional Paradox.* London: Methuen & Co., Ltd., 1980.

Ikeuchi, Kenji. *Mori Ōgai to kindai nihon* [Mori Ōgai and Modern Japan]. Kyoto: Mineruva Shobo, 2001.

Isogai, Hideo. *Mori Ōgai–Meiji nijūnendai o chūshin ni* [Mori Ōgai—Focusing on the Meiji 20s]. Tokyo: Meiji Shoin, 1979.

Itō, Sei. *Nihon kindai bungaku hyōron taikei* [Survey of Modern Japanese Literary Criticism]. Tokyo: Kadokawa Shoten, 1969.

Jacob, Frank, ed. *Critical Insights: Modern Japanese Literature.* Ipswich, Massachusetts: Salem Press, 2017. https://search-ebscohost-com.jpllnet.sfsu.edu/login.aspx?direct=true&AuthType=ip,cookie,url,uid&db=nlebk&AN=1510456&site=ehost-live.

Jameson, Fredric. *The Political Unconscious: Narrative as a Socially Symbolic Act.* Ithaca, N.Y.: Cornell University Press. 1981.

Kabe, Yoshitaka. *Mori Ōgai: shoki bungei hyōron no riron to hōhō.* Tokyo: Ōfūsha, 1980.

Kamei, Hideo. *Kansei no henkaku* [Transformations of Sensibility]. Tokyo: Kōdansha, 1983.

Kamei, Hideo. *Meiji bungakushi* [The History of Meiji Literature]. Tokyo: Iwanami Shoten, 2000.

Kaneko, Akio. "Shinbun no naka no dokusha to shōsetsuka—Meiji 40 nen zengo no 'Kokumin no tomo' wo megutte." *Bungakukai* 53 (1993): 73–86.

Karatani, Kojin. *Nihon kindai bungaku no kigen*. Tokyo: Iwanami Shoten, 2004.

Keen, Suzanne. *Empathy and the Novel*. Oxford: Oxford University Press, 2007.

Kiyoshi, Mahito. "Jiga to sono kage: Murakami Haruki • Neumann • Nietzsche." *Bungaku • Geijutsu • Bunka* 24, no. 1 (2012): 1–15.

Knapp, James A. and Jeffrey Pence, "Between Thing and Theory." Introduction to a special issue of *Poetics Today* 24, no. 4 (2003): 641–71.

Kobayashi, Hideo. "Watakushi shōsetsu-ron" [Discourse on I-Novels]. In *Kobayashi Hideo zenshū*, vol. 3. Tokyo: Shinchōsha, 2001, 119–45.

Kobayashi, Hideo. "Samazama naru isho" [Multiple Designs]. In *Kobayashi Hideo shū*, vol. 60 of *Gendai Nihon bungaku taikei*. Tokyo: Chikuma Shobō, 1969, 202–9.

Kobayashi, Hideo. "Sakka no kao" [The Face of the Author]. In *Kobayashi Hideo shū*, vol. 60 of *Gendai Nihon bungaku taikei*. Tokyo: Chikuma Shobō, 1969, 226–9.

Koizumi, Kōichirō. *Mori Ōgai ron jisshō to hihyō*. Tokyo: Meiji Shoin, 1981.

Komori, Yōichi. *Murakami Haruki ron: "Umibe no Kafuka" o seidoku-suru*. Tokyo: Heibonsha, 2006.

Külpe, Oswald, Walter Bowers Pillsbury and Edward Bradford Titchener. *Introduction to Philosophy: a Handbook for Students of Psychology, Logic, Ethics, Aesthetics and General Philosophy*. Germany: S. Sonnenschein & Co., Ltd., 1897.

Kurihara, Yūichirō. "Murakami Haruki-ron no shūten." *Yuriika* 42, no. 15 (2011): 197–211.

Kyōka, Izumi. "Kōya hijiri" [The Saint of Mt. Kōya]. In *Gendai Nihon bungaku taikei*, vol. 5. Tokyo: Chikuma Shobō, 1979, 336–61.

Lawall, Sarah N. *Critics of Consciousness: The Existential Structures of Literature*. Cambridge: Harvard University Press, 1968.

Lejeune, Philippe, Paul John Eakin and Katherine Margaret Leary. *On Autobiography*. Minneapolis: University of Minnesota Press, 1989.

Lippit, Seiji. *Topographies of Japanese Modernism*. New York: Columbia University Press, 2002.

Love, Heather. "Close but Not Deep: Literary Ethics and the Descriptive Turn." *New Literary History* 41 (2010): 371–91.

Maeda, Ai. *Toshikūkan no naka no bungaku* [The Text in the City-Space]. Tokyo: Takuma Gakkei Bunko, 2008.

Marra, Michele. *Modern Japanese Aesthetics: A Reader*. Honolulu: University of Hawaii Press, 2001.

Marvin, Marcus. "Mori Ōgai and the Biographical Quest." *Harvard Journal of Asiatic Studies* 51, no. 1 (1991): 233–62.

Masao, Miyoshi. *Accomplices of Silence*. Michigan: University of Michigan Press, 1996.

Miyamoto, Kenji. "Haiboku no bungaku" [The Literature of Defeat]. In *Akutagawa Ryunosuke kenkyu shiryo shusei*, edited by Sekiguchi Yasuyoshi, 4:2 22–46. Tokyo: Nihon Tosho senta, 1993.

Miyoshi, Masao. *Accomplices of Silence*. Michigan: University of Michigan Press, 1996.

Mori, Ōgai. *The Wild Geese*. Translated by Kingo Ochiai and Sanford Goldstein. Rutland: Charles E. Tuttle Co., 1959.

Mori, Ōgai. "*Chinmoku no tō*" [The Tower of Silence]. In *Gendai Nihon bungaku taikei*, vol. 7. Tokyo: Chikuma Shobō, 1968, 272–6.

Mori, Ōgai. "Jōshi no genkai wo ronjite waisetsu no teigi wo oyobu." In *Gendai Nihon bungaku taikei*, vol. 1. Tokyo: Chikuma Shobō, 1968.

Mori, Ōgai. "*Maihime*" [The Dancing Girl]. In *Gendai Nihon bungaku taikei*, vol. 7. Tokyo: Chikuma Shobō, 1968, 157–66.

Mori, Ōgai. *Mori Ōgai shū*. Edited by Takenouchi Shizuo, vol. 1. Tokyo: Chikuma Shobō, 1969.

Mori, Ōgai. "Vita Sexualis." In *Mori Ōgai shū*, edited by Takenouchi Shizuo, vol. 1. Tokyo: Iwanami Shoten, 1969, 211–49.

Mori, Ōgai, "*Maihime*" [The Dancing Girl] in *Nihon kindai bungaku taikei*, vol. 11. Tokyo: Kadokawa Shoten, 1974, 336–61.

Mori, Ōgai. "Shōsetsuron" [On the Novel]. In *Ōgai zenshū* [*Ōgai Collection*], edited by Koizumi Kōichiro, vol. 38. Tokyo: Iwanami Shoten, 1975, 451–3.

Mori, Ōgai. "Ōgai Gyoshi to wa dare zo" [Who Is Ōgai Gyoshi]. In *Gendai Nihon bungaku taikei*, vol. 8. Tokyo: Chikuma Shobō, 1979, 304–7.

Mori, Ōgai. "Vita Sexualis." In *Gendai Nihon bungaku taikei*, vol. 7. Tokyo: Chikuma Shobō, 1979, 211–48.

Mori, Ōgai. *Mori Ōgai shū* [*Mori Ōgai Collection*]. Edited by Koizumi Kōichiro, vol. 1. Tokyo: Iwanami Shoten, 2004.

Mori, Ōgai. *Vita Sexualis. Nihon gendai bungaku taikei shū*. Edited by Koizumi Kōichiro, vol. 7. Tokyo: Iwanami Shoten, 2004, 211–49.

Mori, Ōgai. *The Wild Goose*. Translated by Meredith McKinney. Braidwood, New South Wales: Finlay Lloyd Publishers, 2014.

Murakami, Fuminobu. *Ideology and Narrative in Modern Japanese Literature*. Assen: Uitgeverij Van Gorcum, 1996.

Murakami, Haruki. *Sekai no owari to hādo-boirudo wandālando* [*Hard-Boiled Wonderland and the End of the World*]. Tokyo: Shinchōsha, 1985.

Murakami, Haruki. *1Q84* (I-III). Tokyo: Shinchōsha, 2009–10.

Murakami, Haruki. "Tamashi no sofuto • randingu no tame ni: nijūisseiki no 'monogatari' no yakuwari" ["For a 'Soft Landing' of the Soul: The Role of 'Stories' in the 21st Century"]. By Ozawa Eimi. *Yuriika* 42, no. 15 (2011): 9–21.

Murakami, Haruki. *Shikisai wo motanai Tazaki Tsukuru to Kare no Junrei no Toshi* [*Colorless Tazaki Tsukuru and His Years of Pilgrimage*]. Tokyo: Shinchōsha, 2013.

Murasaki, Shikibu. *The Tale of Genji: Abridged*. Translated by Royall Tyler. New York, N.Y.: Penguin Books, 2006.
Murasaki, Shikibu and Royall Tyler. *The Tale of Genji: Abridged*. New York, N.Y.: Penguin Books, 2006.
Nancy, Jean-Luc. *The Pleasure in Drawing*. New York: Fordham University Press, 2013.
Natsume, Sōseki, "Kokoro." In *Sōseki zenshū*, vol. 6. Tokyo: Iwanami Shoten, 1966, 39–41.
Natsume, Sōseki. "Theory of Literature (*Bungakuron*, 1907)." *Japan Forum* 20, no. 1 (2008): 17–24. doi:10.1080/09555800701796834
Newton, Adam Zachary. *Narrative Ethics*. Cambridge: Harvard University Press, 1995.
Nietzsche, Friedrich. *The Gay Science*. Translated by Walter Kaufmann. New York: Vintage, 1974, 317.
Ningetsu, Ishibashi. "Maihime." In *Kindai bungaku hyōron taikei*, vol. 1. Tokyo: Kadokawa Shoten, 1971, 84–8.
Nishinodō, Koji. "On Criticism" [Hihyōron]. In *Nihon kindai bungaku hyōron taikei* [Survey of Modern Japanese Literary Criticism], edited by Sei Itō. Tokyo: Kadokawa Shoten, 1969, 76–83.
Nussbaum, Martha C. *Love's Knowledge: Essays on Philosophy and Literature*. New York: Oxford University Press, 1990.
O'Neill, Daniel C. "Portrait of an Artist in Tokyo circa 1910: Mori Ōgai's *Seinen*." *Japan Forum* 18 (2006): 295–314.
Ōgai, Mori. *Mori Ōgai: Youth and Other Stories*. Translated by J. Thomas Rimer. Honolulu: University of Hawaii Press, 1994.
Olney, James. *Metaphors of Self: The Meaning of Autobiography*. Princeton: Princeton University Press, 1972. http://www.jstor.org/stable/j.ctt1m3nz3x.
O'Neill, D. Cuong. "Portrait of an Artist in Tokyo circa 1910: Mori Ōgai's *Seinen*." *Japan Forum* 18, no. 3 (November 2006): 295–314.
Ozawa, Yasuhiro. "Akutagawa Ryūnosuke 'Geijitsu sono ta' to 'Bungeiteki na, amari ni bungeiteki na' - riron to jissaku no kairi." ["Akutagawa Ryūnosuke's 'Art and Other Matters' and 'Literary, All-Too Literary': the Divergence of Theory and Actual Text"]. *Bulletin of Faculty of Education* 26 (1983): 48.
Palumbo-Liu, David. *The Deliverance of Others*. Durham: Duke University Press, 2012.
Phelan, James. "Rhetorical Literary Ethics and Lyric Narrative: Robert Frost's 'Home Burial.'" *Poetics Today* 25, no. 4 (December 2004): 627–51.
Powell, Irena. *Writers and Society in Modern Japan*. London: Palgrave Macmillan, 1983.
Ricoeur, Paul. *Time and Narrative*. Translated by David Pellauer and Kathleen McLaughlin. Chicago: University of Chicago Press, 1990.
Roquet, Paul. "Ambient Literature and the Aesthetics of Calm: Mood Regulation in Contemporary Japanese Fiction." *The Journal of Japanese Studies* 35, no. 1 (2009): 87–111.
Rubin, Jay, trans. "Rashōmon." In *Rashōmon and Seventeen Other Stories*. By Ryūnosuke Akutagawa. New York: Penguin Books, 2006.

Rubin, Jay, trans. "Green Onions." In *Rashōmon and Seventeen Other Stories*. By Ryūnosuke Akutagawa. New York: Penguin Books, 2006.

Said, Edward. *The World, the Text and the Critic*. Cambridge: Harvard University Press, 1983.

Sakaki, Atsuko. *Recontextualizing Texts: Narrative Performance in Modern Japanese Fiction*. Massachusetts: Harvard University Asia Center, 1999.

Sako, Junichirō. *Kindai nihon bungaku no rinriteki tankyū* [Ethical Explorations in Modern Japanese Literature]. Tokyo: Shunjūsha, 1966.

Schwarz, Daniel. "A Humanist Ethics of Reading." In *Mapping the Ethical Turn: A Reader in Ethics, Culture, and Literary Theory*, edited by Todd F. Davis and Kenneth Womack. Charlottesville: University of Virginia Press, 2001, 3–16.

Seats, Michael. *Murakami Haruki: The Simulacrum in Contemporary Japanese Culture*. New York: Lexington Books, 2009.

Sekiguchi, Yasuyoshi. *Akutagawa Ryūnosuke to sono jidai* [Akutagawa Ryūnosuke and his Era]. Tokyo: Chikuma Shobō, 1999.

Serpell, C. Namwali. "Mutual Exclusion, Oscillation, and Ethical Projection in the Crying of Lot 49 and the Turn of the Screw." *Narrative* 16, no. 3 (2008): 223–55.

Shiga, Naoya. "Kozō no kamisama" [The Shop-Boy's God]. In *Gendai Nihon bungaku taikei*, vol. 34. Tokyo: Kadokawa Shoten, 1964, 279–84.

Shiga, Naoya. "Shoji" [The Paper Door]. In *Shiga Naoya zenshū*, vol. 3. Tokyo: Iwanami Shoten, 1973, 59–77.

Shiokawa, Tetsuya. "*Ōgai 'Nihon kaiki' no kidō*" [The Orbit of Ōgai's "Return to Japan"]. *Bungaku* 1, no. 3 (May 2000): 115.

Shōyō, Tsubouchi. *Shōsetsu shinzui*. Tokyo: Shōgetsudō, 1972.

Sipos, George T. "Akutagawa Ryūnosuke: The Modernist Temptation." In *Critical Insights: Modern Japanese Literature*, edited by Frank Jacob. Salem Press, 2017, 154–70.

Snyder, Stephen. "Ōgai, Kafū, and the Limits of Fiction." In *Fictions of Desire: Narrative Forms in the Novels of Nagai Kafū*. United States: University of Hawai'i Press, 2000, 8–33.

Snyder, Steven. "Ogai and the Problem of Fiction: *Gan* and Its Antecedents." *Monumenta Nipponica* 49, no. 3 (Autumn 1994): 353–73.

Spandri, Elena. "*Contact Zones:*" *Rewriting Genre Across the East–West Border*. Naples: Liguori, 2003.

Spivak, Gayatri. "Can the Subaltern Speak?" In *Colonial Discourse and Postcolonial Theory: A Reader*, edited by Patrick Williams and Laura Chrisman. Hemel Hempstead: Harvester Wheatsheaf, 1993, 196–220.

Strecher, Matthew. "At the Critical Stage: A Report on the State of Murakami Haruki Studies." *Literature Compass* 8, no. 11 (2011): 856–69.

Suzuki, Tomi. *Narrating the Self: Fictions of Japanese Modernity*. Stanford: Stanford University Press, 1996.

Tanizaki, Junichirō. "Jyōzetsu roku" [A Garrulous Note]. In *Gendai Nihon bungaku ronsōshi*, edited by Hirano Ken, 1:145. Tokyo: Miraisha Co., 1956, 144–7.

Tanizawa, Eiichi. *Kindai Nihon bungakushi no kōsō* [The Concept of Modern Japanese Literary History]. Tokyo: Shōbunsha, 1964.

Tansman, Alan. *The Aesthetics of Japanese Fascism*. Berkeley: University of California Press, 2009.

Terada, Rei. *Feeling in Theory: Emotion after the "Death of the Subject."* Cambridge, Massachusetts: Harvard University Press, 2001.

Toker, Leona. *Nabokov: The Mystery of Literary Structures*. Ithaca: Cornell University Press, 1989.

Tokō, Kōji. "Sōzō ryoku wo kaita kyōryōsa - 『1Q84』 ni okeru jendā hyōshō." *Yuriika* 42, no. 15 (2011): 93–101.

Treat, John. "Yoshimoto Banana Writes Home: Shojo Culture and the Nostalgic Subject." *Journal of Japanese Studies* 19, no. 2 (1993): 353–87.

Tsu, Jing. "Getting Ideas about World Literature." *Comparative Literature Studies* 47, no. 3 (2010): 290–317.

Tsubouchi, Shōyō. "*Shōsetsu shinzui*" [The Essence of the Novel]. In *Gendai Nihon bungaku taikei*, vol. 1. Tokyo: Chikuma Shobō, 1968, 182–235.

Tsubouchi, Shōyō. *Tosei shosei katagi*. Tokyo: Iwanami Shoten, 1937.

Twine, Nanette. *Language and the Modern State: The Reform of Written Japanese*. New York: Routledge, 1991.

Uchida, Roan. *Uchida Roan zenshū*, vol. 1. Tokyo: Yumani Shobō, 1984.

Ueda, Atsuko. *Concealment of Politics, Politics of Concealment: The Production of "Literature" in Meiji Japan*. Stanford: Stanford University Press, 2007, xi–237.

Ueda, Makoto. *Modern Japanese Writers and the Nature of Literature*. Stanford: Stanford University Press, 1996.

Vermeule, Blakey. *Why Do We Care about Literary Characters?* Baltimore: Johns Hopkins University Press, 2010.

Vincent, Keith. *Two-Timing Modernity: Homosocial Narrative in Modern Japanese Fiction*. Cambridge: Harvard University Press, 2012.

Vogler, Candace. "The Moral of the Story." *Critical Inquiry* 34, no. 1 (2007): 5–35.

Vogler, Candace. "The Moral of the Story." *Critical Inquiry* 34, no. 1 (Autumn 2007): 12–15.

Warner, Michael. "Uncritical Reading." In *Polemic: Critical or Uncritical*, edited by Jane Gallop. New York and London: Routledge, 2004, 13–38.

Washburn, Dennis. *The Dilemma of the Modern in Japanese Fiction*. Connecticut: Yale University Press, 1995.

Washburn, Dennis. *Translating Mount Fuji: Modern Japanese Fiction and the Ethics of Identity*. New York Chichester: Columbia University Press, 2006.

Weinberger, Christopher. Triangulating an Ethos: Ethical Criticism, Novel Alterity, and Mori Ōgai's "Stereoscopic Vision." *Positions* 1, no. 23 (May 2015): 259–85. doi: https://doi.org/10.1215/10679847-2860990

Wollheim, Richard. *Painting as an Art*. London: Thames and Hudson, 1987.

Wood, Michael. *The Magician's Doubts: Nabokov and the Risks of Fiction*. London: Chatto and Windus, 1994.

Yamada, Marc. "Exposing the Private Origins of Public Stories: Narrative Perspective and the Appropriation of Selfhood in Murakami Haruki's Post-AUM Metafiction." *Japanese Language and Literature* 43, no. 1 (2009): 1–26.

Yanagida, Izumi. *Meiji shoki no bungaku shisō* [Ideas of Literature in Early Meiji]. Tokyo: Shunjūsha, 1965.

Yōda, Tomiko. "First-Person Voice and Citizen-Subject: The Modernity of Ōgai's *Maihime*." *Journal of Asian Studies* 65, no. 25 (2006): 43–65.

Yōda, Tomiko. "First-Person Voice and Citizen-Subject: The Modernity of Ōgai's 'The Dancing Girl'" *Journal of Asian Studies* 65, no. 2 (2006): 277–306.

Yokomitsi, Riichi, *Shanhai*. Tokyo: Iwanami Shoten, 2008.

Yoshida, Seiichi. *Kindai bungei hyōronshi* [A History of Modern Literary Criticism]. Tokyo: Shibundō, 1971.

Yoshida, Seiichi. "Akutagawa Ryunosuke no shôgai to geijitsu." In *Akutagawa Ryūnosuke Kenkyû*. Tokyo: Shinshô Shuppan, 1957, 8–43.

Index

abstraction 15, 33, 57, 136, 138–9, 144–5, 166, 168
aesthetics/aestheticism 7, 14–17, 20–2, 24–7, 32–5, 37–41, 53, 55, 57, 59, 65, 71–2, 74, 77, 81–2, 84, 93, 96, 98–100, 103–6, 108–9, 111, 114, 118, 121–2, 126, 130, 135–6, 136, 138, 140, 142–3, 145–7, 158, 166, 189
   aesthetic experience of Akutagawa 96
   ethical aesthetics of Ōgai 87–92
affect 7, 18–19, 21, 27, 94–8, 103–5, 108–9, 115, 124, 128, 130–1, 144–5, 147, 159, 165
   affective ethics 94, 106–12
   artistic affect (*geijutsu-teki kangeki*) 142
   fictional affect 127–30
   literary (*see* literary affect)
   and narrative positioning 117
   transmission of 159–63
Akutagawa Ryūnosuke 1, 7, 15–17, 93–5, 108, 114, 125–7, 129–31, 133–4, 168, 174, 179, 207 n.10
   aesthetic experience of 96–104
   alterity of final *shōsetsu* 163–5
   "Art and Other Matters" (Geijutsu sono ta) 142
   biteki seikatsu (beautiful living) 95
   Cogwheels (Haguruma) 18, 132, 141, 149–50, 159–61, 163–4, 166–7, 211 n.12, 212 n.31
   critical orthodoxy on late fiction 134–41
   A Fool's Life (*see A Fool's Life* (Aru ahō no isshō))
   "Green Onions" (*see* "Green Onions" (Negi))
   "Handkerchief" (Hankechi) 96–7
   late writing on *shōsetsu* 141–7
   life within literature 141, 149–50, 153–4, 165
   "Literary, All-Too Literary" (Bungeiteki na, amari ni bungeiteki na) 134, 138, 142–6, 149, 152, 158, 162–3, 166
   "The Morals of Tomorrow" (Ashita no dōtoku) 144, 206 n.5
   vs. Murakami 174, 179
   "Noroma Puppets" (Noroma Ningyō) 210 n.6
   vs. Ōgai 15–16, 19–22, 93–6, 106, 111, 114, 126, 143
   "The Paradox of Japanese Literary Art" (Nihon bungei no paradokkusu) 142
   plotless novel 141–2
   "Portrait of the Writer as a Young Reader" 151
   "Rashōmon" 17, 93–4, 96, 98–106, 108–11, 114, 116, 118, 120, 124, 145, 206 n.9
   shiteki seishin (poetic spirit) 19
   suicide of 133, 140–1, 161
   "Suspicion" (Giwaku) 96–7
   "The Morals of Tomorrow" (Ashita no dōtoku) 95, 108
   "Yam Gruel" (Imogayu) 96, 99, 112, 114, 118
alterity 4, 7–8, 19, 66, 71, 91–2, 97–8, 100, 107, 110, 113, 134, 147, 149–50, 154, 160, 167, 170, 173, 179, 184, 188–90, 201 n.2
   of Akutagawa's final *shōsetsu* 163–5
   in new ethical theories 173–4
Altieri, Charles
   on literary affect 109, 115, 127
   lyrical ethics 98, 110, 115–17
   The Particulars of Rapture: An Aesthetics of the Affects 107
anecdotes 53, 142–3, 163
Anglo-European 6, 8, 91, 201 n.2
artistic novels 24–8, 195 n.15

Index

artistic representation 21, 27, 37
authenticity 40, 51, 59–60, 64, 67, 71–5, 77, 84, 96–7, 117, 129, 131, 136–7, 147, 152, 154, 160, 166–7, 174, 176, 187, 190, 211 n.17
authorial persona(s) 20, 51, 55–9, 67, 136, 150–1, 160, 163, 165, 168, 210 n.7, 211 n.12
authorial self 55–9, 65, 67, 146, 151, 154, 156–7, 164, 166
authoritative discourse 55, 66–7
auto-criticism 56

Bakhtin, Mikhail 17, 55, 68, 168, 200 n.28, 201 n.30, 203 n.19
    authoritative discourse 66–7
    "Discourse in the Novel" 66, 68
    double-voicedness 67
Barthes, Roland 175
Black, Shameem 6
Booth, Wayne 91
    implied author 68, 72, 158, 199 n.10
    The Rhetoric of Fiction 199 n.10
Bowring, Richard 34, 39, 54–5, 74, 196 n.16
bundan (literary world) 15, 53, 56–9, 75, 112, 161, 169, 188, 199 n.10
bungei hyōron (literary criticism) 143. *See also* literary criticism
bunjin (men of letters) 33
Butler, Judith 8, 83–5, 173

Cather, Kirsten, "Noting Suicide with a Vague Sense of Anxiety" 141
Cavanaugh, Carole 151–2
coherence 9, 21, 48, 84–6, 97, 101, 134–5, 138, 141, 147, 149–52, 157, 167, 197 n.25
confessional literature 57, 59–64, 68, 193 n.3
confession (*zange*) 57
Confucian 20, 72
contact zones 4, 9
credibility 73, 76, 79, 202 n.3
critical orthodoxy 2–4, 15, 20, 34, 40, 106–7, 134–41, 169, 180, n. 22

The Dancing Girl (Maihime), (Ōgai) 1, 16–17, 36, 40, 51, 54–9, 61, 65, 67, 72, 86, 197–8 n.31, 197 n.25, 206 n.17
    Aizawa (fictional character) 41, 48, 198 n.31
    Elise (fictional character) 41, 43
    Hill on 42–4
    Ōta Toyotarō (fictional character) 41–9, 58, 62, 197 n.25, 198 n.31, 198 n.41, 199 n.42
    reflexive narration in 41–50
    Yōda on 46–9
De Man, Paul 131
    ostensible pathos 128–30
    reversed mirror-image 208 n.26
    on Rousseau's *Julie* 131, 208–9 n.27
Derrida, Jacques 127–8, 175
    "Cogito and the History of Madness" 128
    on textuality 127
desire(s) 5, 11–14, 17, 37, 46–7, 54, 57, 59, 77–8, 81–2, 84, 87, 89, 93, 115–16, 137, 143, 162, 200 n.28, 201 n.30, 203 n.19
    authorial 37, 42, 60, 67, 206 n.17
    diegetic 204 n.22
    metaphysical 78–9, 84, 203 n.19, 204 n.22
    mimetic 78–9, 204 n.22
    narrative 79
    object-oriented desire 78–9
    sexual 60–4, 67
dialogism 55, 66
    monologic 66–9
didactic fiction 25–6, 33, 36–41
diegesis 24, 84, 86, 101, 106, 116, 131, 156, 167, 170, 175, 187, 197 n.24, 204 n.22
Duara, Prasenjit 5, 42

Edo-period (1603–1868) 24, 194 n.8
emotions/emotional 2, 5, 27–8, 60, 85, 88, 94, 96, 98–9, 103, 105, 107, 109, 111, 113, 117–26, 128–31, 140, 142–3, 145–6, 158, 179, 189, 208 n.26
empathy 6, 25, 31, 72, 96, 167, 173, 190, 194 n.12, 204 n.27
epistemology 143, 149–50, 152, 154, 174, 190, 210 n.6

ethics 3, 5–8, 14, 17–18, 26–7, 37, 39, 41, 51, 55, 58, 68–9, 71–2, 87–8, 90, 94, 96–7, 107–10, 127–8, 134, 138–41, 145, 173, 178–80
  affective 94, 106–12
  articulating perplexity 88, 107
  ethical criticism 4, 6, 8, 18–19, 89, 91–2, 106, 111, 113, 170, 172, 179, 187–9, 201 n.2, 205 n.32, 207 n.24
  ethical identity 18, 93, 96–7, 103–4, 109, 111, 113
  ethical impulses 7, 18, 138
  ethical inquiry 8, 30, 82, 88, 98, 115, 131, 170
  ethical orientations 83, 107, 111, 177
  ethical reasoning 99, 103, 107
  ethical transformation 97, 110, 150, 175
  ethical transpositioning 174–80, 184, 190–1
  Harpham on 7, 26
  kinetic 177
  literary 5, 7–8, 19, 92, 98, 116, 168
  lyrical 98, 110, 115–17
  narrative 10, 22, 55, 72, 115–17
  philosophical thinking about 94
  real-world 66, 91, 95, 114, 168
  unreal ethics of mimetics 113–15
ethos 1–3, 16–17, 20–1, 50, 66–9, 71–2, 86, 91–3, 98–9, 108, 110, 113–16, 118, 129–30, 133, 144, 150, 158, 176, 180
  narative 72, 116, 131
Europe/European 22–5, 30, 37–8, 44, 53, 71, 91, 196 n.23

fantasy/fantasy world 63, 75, 98, 122–6, 128, 130, 169–73, 176, 178, 181–3, 185–91
feelings 9, 20, 25–8, 31, 45, 94, 104, 107–11, 113–15, 118, 126, 128–9, 145–6, 153, 155, 160–1, 163, 165, 168
A Fool's Life (Aru ahō no isshō), (Akutagawa) 18, 132, 134–6, 141, 149–56, 161, 163–7, 210 n.12, 211 n.17, 211 n.25
  affect, transmission of 159–63

figure of Icarus 155, 157–9, 212 n.31
formal experimentation 6, 9, 36, 53, 73, 201 n.2
formal innovation 14–15, 93
fractal realism 170, 174–81, 184, 188–90
frame 2, 5, 10, 12, 14, 29, 31, 43, 47, 49–50, 54, 58, 61, 65, 67, 78, 84, 88, 117, 120, 126, 130, 197 n.24, 203 n.13, 208 n.26. *See also* narrative framing
Frentiu, Rodica 34–5
Fukuda Renzon 138
  "Akutagawa Ryūnosuke" 137
Futabatei Shimei 16, 24
  Floating Clouds (Ukigumo) 23

Gallagher, Catharine 113, 194 n.14
genbun'itchi movement 23, 49, 194 n.7
Gerow, Aaron, *Visions of Japanese Modernity* 4
gesaku (frivolous writings) 94, 192 n.1, 203 n.13
Gibson, Andrew 205 n.32
Girard, René 17, 35, 203–4 n.19
  Deceit, Desire, and the Novel 78
"Green Onions" (Negi), (Akutagawa) 18, 112, 117, 131–2, 208 n.26
  Ali Baba (fictional character) 119
  artistic ecstasy (geijutsu-teki kangeki) 118, 122
  double-consciousness 121–2
  literary sensibilities and real-world relationships 117–26
  O-Kimi (fictional character) 117–26, 128–9
  O-Matsu (fictional character) 122
  real life and fictional reality 127–30
  sentimentalism (santeimantaaru na) 118, 120–1, 128, 131
  Tanaka (fictional character) 118–19, 122–5

Hale, Dorothy 173, 205 n.32
Harpham, Geoffrey 7, 26, 106–7
  Shadows of Ethics 88
Hasegawa Izumi 35, 54
hegemonic 66, 127, 171
heteroglossia 66, 68, 172
Hill, Christopher 42–3, 47–8

"Mori Ōgai's Resentful Narrator:
    Trauma and the National Subject
    in 'The Dancing Girl'" 42–4
Hokubō Sanji 36
  "The Responsibility of the Novelist"
    (Shōsetsuka no sekinin) 30–1
  "A Theory of the Novel Based on
    Medical Approaches" 196–7 n.23
honesty 72

identification 6, 85, 90–1, 97–8, 103,
    107–8, 111, 127–8, 155, 167,
    173, 205 n.32
Ikeuchi Kenji 74
Ima wa mukashi (Now it is then) 75
Imperial Literature (Teikoku bungaku) 57
implied author 68, 72, 158, 199 n.10
implosion 170–1
interpretation 4, 13–14, 24, 28, 31, 34, 37,
    40, 55, 57, 61, 66, 84, 96, 114,
    127–8, 143, 151
introspective reflection 27
irony 14, 19, 56, 58, 60, 67–8, 98, 118,
    120–1, 125, 128, 130, 132,
    136–7, 158, 207 n.10, 208 n.26
Isogai Hideo, *Mori Ōgai: The Meiji
    Twenties (Mori Ōgai-Meiji
    nijūnendai wo chūshin ni)* 33–4

Jacob, Frank 3
  "Between East and West: Mori Ōgai
    and the Beginnings of Modern
    Japanese Literature" 35
Jameson, Fredric 180
judgment 5, 9, 17, 19, 24, 26, 28, 37,
    45, 75, 77, 91, 93, 95, 98, 105,
    110–11, 113, 115–16, 131,
    136–7, 139, 145–6, 163, 167

Kabe Yoshitaka 34–5, 46
Kamei Hideo 6, 17
  non-person narrator 24
  Transformations of Sensibility (Kansei
    no henkaku) 23
Kant, Immanuel 37
kanzenchōaku 25–6
Karatani Kōjin 54, 169
Keene, Donald 3, 134

kinetic ethics 177
Knapp, James A., "Between Thing and
    Theory" 183
Kobayashi Hideo 30, 168
  "The Face of the Author" 212 n.32
  "Multiple Designs" 212 n.32
Komori Yōichi 169
Kume Masao 151, 211 n.25
Kyōka Izumi 14
  The Holy Man of Mt. Kōya 10, 12–13
kyō no kanjō (feelings of the present) 144–5

Lejeune, Philippe, *On Autobiography*
    197 n.25
Lippit, Seiji, *Topographies of Japanese
    Modernism* 135
literary affect 93, 99, 107–11, 117, 163,
    168, 207 n.24
  Altieri on 109, 115, 127
  novel theory of 141–7
literary conventions 21, 77, 87, 90
literary criticism 22, 24, 28–9, 32, 34, 38, 53,
    68, 72, 143, 147, 194 n.8, 198 n.31
literary ethics 5, 7–8, 19, 92, 98, 116, 129,
    168
literary experience 107, 110, 115–16, 122,
    152, 155
literary language 23, 50, 66, 68, 128, 131,
    168, 194 n.7, 212 n.32
literary representation 8, 16, 55, 57, 62,
    75, 91, 118, 129–31, 137, 155,
    166, 168, 196 n.19, 205 n.32,
    208 n.10
literary self-representation 55, 153
literary sensibilities 75, 95, 117–26
literary value 4–5, 24, 37, 95, 143, 146
literary violence 57–8
literary writing 23, 40, 51, 58, 131, 194 n.7
lyrical ethics 98, 110, 115–17
lyricism (*jojō*) 15, 110, 116, 144

Maeda Ai 86
Meiji period (1868–1912) 1, 21–5, 29–30,
    35, 42, 59, 133, 192 n.1, 193 n.2,
    194 n.8
  ethics, aesthetics, and self-
    consciousness in 22–32
  Meiji Restoration 22–3

metafiction 5–7, 18, 71, 91, 115, 117, 134, 144, 149, 152–3, 156, 166–8, 172, 179, 190
metaliterary 20–1, 59, 112, 119, 131, 139, 149, 153, 155, 163, 165, 167, 207 n.10
mimesis 3, 5–6, 25–6, 35, 71, 76, 78–9, 86, 126, 131, 134–5, 142–3, 149, 157, 168, 172–3, 179, 187, 189, 211 n.25
  unreal ethics of 113–15
mind-reading 204 n.26
Miyamoto Kenji 136–9, 151, 158
  "The Literature of Defeat" (Haiboku no bungaku) 135
Miyoshi Masao 2, 54, 74, 169
monogatari (storytelling) 2, 74, 76, 192 n.1. *See also* storytelling
monologic dialogism 66–9
morality/moralism 7, 13, 26, 37, 39, 57, 94–6, 108, 146–7, 174, 206 n.5
Mori Ōgai 6, 8, 15–17, 30, 32–6, 61, 67–8, 71, 85, 94, 96, 106, 111, 114, 168, 173–4, 179, 196–7 nn.22–4, 199 n.10, 200 n.28, 202 n.3
  vs. Akutagawa 15–16, 19–22, 93–6, 106, 111, 114, 126, 143
  authorial selfhood 55–9
  and Bowring 54–5
  bunmei kaika (enlightenment) 22
  The Dancing Girl (*see The Dancing Girl* (Maihime))
  dialectic vision of 36–41
  ethical aesthetics of 87–92
  Foam on the Waves (Utakata no ki) 72
  fukoku kyōhei (national strengthening) 22
  historical writing of 68
  vs. Murakami 173–4, 179
  "On the Novel" (Shōsetsuron) 37–8
  self-remaking of 53–5
  stereoscopic narration of 6, 16–17, 36, 40, 50, 68, 86, 89, 93, 197 n.23, 198 n.31, 202 n.3
  "The Tower of Silence" (Chinmoku no tō) 39, 206 n.5
  Vita Sexualis (*see Vita Sexualis*)

"Who Is Ōgai Gyoshi" (Ōgai Gyoshi to wa dare zo) 17, 51, 55–9, 62
The Wild Goose (*see The Wild Goose* (Gan))
Youth (Seinen) 39, 87
Murakami Fuminobu 34, 46
  Ideology and Narrative in Modern Japanese Literature 33
Murakami Haruki 6, 18, 167
  vs. Akutagawa 174, 179
  alterity and oscillation (new ethical theories) 173–4
  Colorless Tsukuru Tazaki and His Years of Pilgrimage 175
  fantasy of realism 170–3, 188–91
  criticism and
  fractal realism and ethical transpositioning 174–81, 184, 188–91
  Hard-Boiled Wonderland and the End of the World 177–91, 213 n.26
  immanent ethics of 169–70
  1Q84 171–2, 175–7, 179
  vs. Ōgai 173–4, 179
  reading models 180–5
  reading modes 186–8
  soft landing (*sofuto-randingu*) 178, 184, 191, 213 n.18
  world systems 175–8, 180, 184, 191

nani mono ka (something) 19, 97–8, 112, 150, 154, 160–1
narcissism/narcissistic narratives 6, 17, 60, 179
narrative acts 5, 40–1, 44, 64, 67, 80, 84, 94, 125, 157, 163, 167, 171–2
narrative desire 79
narrative ethics 10, 22, 55, 72, 115–17
narrative ethos 72, 116, 131, 146
narrative framing 2, 12, 51, 67–8, 78, 88, 125, 130, 197 n.24, 208 n.26
narrative manipulation 72–3, 83–4, 87–8, 90, 106, 204 n.22
narrative reflexivity 40, 55, 101, 201 n.2
narrative representation 9, 36, 73, 90, 105, 117, 199 n.10
narrative violence 84

new ethical theories 90, 173–4
Nishinodō Koji 31–2
 "On Criticism" (Hihyōron) 30, 32
 "A Theory of the Novel Based on Medical Approaches" 196 n.23
Nō drama 23
novel criticism 5, 29–30, 32, 38–9, 51, 87, 198 n.31
novel representation 1–2, 6–8, 15, 21, 25, 27–8, 30, 67, 72, 77, 90, 113, 141, 150, 158, 166, 168, 170, 172, 179, 197 n.23
novel value 3, 5, 16–17, 21, 27, 29, 141, 144–5, 196 n.23
Nussbaum, Martha 8, 173

objectivity 20, 31–2, 38, 45, 53, 57, 62, 197 n.23, 202 n.3
object-oriented desire 78–9
Ōgai Gyoshi. *See* Mori Ōgai
Olney, James, *Metaphors of Self* 197 n.25
omniscience 74, 77, 82, 84–5, 87
O'Neill, D. Cuong 35
ontology/ontological 116, 127, 131, 170, 174–6, 184
oscillation (between immersion and reflection) 17, 22, 31, 38, 60, 86–8, 96, 102, 108, 111, 114, 131, 137, 169–70, 173–5, 182–3, 187–9, 197 n.23, 205 n.32
ostensible pathos 128–30
otherness 4, 9, 107–8, 149–50, 152, 159–63, 165–8, 174, 184, 189
others 5, 36, 84, 97, 118, 128, 131, 145, 150, 154, 160–1, 164–8, 170–1, 173–4, 178–9, 184, 205 n.32

Palumbo-Liu, David 6
 The Deliverance of Others 4
parody 20, 59–60, 65, 68, 73, 90, 178, 186, 201 n.30
pathos 1, 16–17, 20–1, 50, 71, 91–3, 99–100, 108, 114–16, 118, 121, 125, 128–30, 150, 158, 197 n.23
Pence, Jeffrey, "Between Thing and Theory" 183
perspective(s) 2, 7–9, 14, 16–17, 20–4, 28, 30–2, 37–41, 44–5, 47, 49–51, 53–4, 56, 63, 65, 67–8, 71–81, 84–8, 92, 99, 101, 106–8, 110–11, 114, 167, 171, 177–8, 192 n.2, 193 n.16, 198 n.31, 199 n.10, 201 n.2, 202 n.3, 207 n.10
Phelan, James 116–17
poetic spirit (*shiteki seishin*) 19, 93, 131, 141–7, 159, 163, 168
poetic sublime (*shiteki sōgon*) 144
point-of-view (narrative) 41–2, 45–7, 59, 64, 67–8, 72–4, 77, 84–8, 107, 117, 153, 164, 203 n.15
prose fiction 1, 3, 5, 9, 16–17, 20, 23–6, 40, 71–2, 76, 87, 146, 192 nn.1–2

reader response 66, 180–1
realism/realist/reality 1–2, 5, 7, 14–15, 27–8, 41, 49, 51, 60, 65, 67, 73, 75–7, 79, 84, 86, 91–3, 95, 100–1, 106, 113, 115, 119–21, 124–6, 129–30, 136–8, 149, 156–7, 170–6, 179–81, 186–7, 189
reflexive narration/reflexivity 3, 5–6, 9–10, 12, 14, 16, 22, 24, 41–50, 53, 58, 65, 72, 86, 94, 101, 106, 108, 110, 114–15, 118, 121, 125, 127, 129, 141, 146, 149–50, 153, 159, 173, 179
 narrative 40, 55, 101, 201 n.2
 reflexive consciousness 111, 115, 214 n.29
rekishi shōsetsu (historical novels) 72, 74, 93–4
romanticism 95, 144
Rousseau, Jean-Jacques 128, 131, 193 n.3
 Confessions 154
 Julie 131, 208–9 n.27
Rubin, Jay 152, 207 n.7

Sakaki Atsuko 78
Sako Jun'ichiro, *Ethical Explorations in Modern Japanese Literature* (Kindai nihon bungaku no rinriteki tankyū) 104, 139
Sekiguchi Yasuyoshi, *Akutagawa Ryūnosuke* 140
self-absorption 15, 64, 151, 168, 212 n.32

self-authorization 36, 43, 46, 48, 55–6, 64–5
self-consciousness 3, 7, 9, 13–18, 20–2, 27–9, 31–2, 35–7, 41–2, 44–5, 48–50, 54–5, 61, 67–9, 71–3, 86–7, 90, 92–3, 96, 98–100, 106, 108, 110–12, 114–15, 118–20, 122, 125–6, 128–31, 133, 138, 147, 150, 153, 156, 158, 160, 162, 165–8, 173–4, 178–9, 188–90, 206 n.17, 212 n.32
selfhood 94, 98, 103, 133, 139, 153, 155–6, 159, 163, 171, 184
self-image 96, 103, 110, 115–16, 162
self-justification 44–5, 49, 104
self-other relations 15, 139, 141, 152, 213 n.26
self-overcoming 17, 36–41, 56
self-reading 5, 55, 61
self-reflection 57, 59–65, 94, 104, 107, 138, 146, 153, 155, 160, 174, 194 n.12
self-reflexive/-reflexivity 5, 8, 22, 112, 212 n.31
self-representation 20, 48, 55, 57–8, 79, 132, 136, 144, 153–5, 167
self-serving 5, 45, 72, 90, 97, 117, 204 n.27, 205 n.32
self-theorization 3–5, 8, 32, 36, 68, 108, 202 n.2
self-vindication (jikobengo) 62–3
semiotic domains 175–6, 178, 190
sensations 19, 60, 108–10, 124
setsuwa (spoken tale) 99, 101, 194 n.8
Shiga Naoya 145–7
 "The Paper Door" (Shōji) 14
 "The Shop Boy's God" (Kozō no Kamisama) 14
Shimazaki Tōson, *New Life* (Shinsei) 154
Shiokawa Tetsuya 72
shishōsetsu (I-novels) 59, 67, 74, 112, 193 n.3, 203 n.15
shizenshugi (naturalist) 2, 54
shōsetsu (novels) 1, 3–6, 8, 10, 12–17, 19, 21–2, 24, 32, 35–6, 39–41, 43–4, 48, 50–1, 53–4, 58–60, 63–5, 67–9, 71–2, 74–5, 77–8, 82, 84, 86, 88–91, 93–4, 96–100, 104, 106, 109–11, 113, 115–18, 125–7, 130–1, 133, 135, 140–7, 149–52, 158–9, 162–5, 167–8, 192 n.1, 193 n.2, 197 n.23, 202 n.2, 210 n.6
shōsetsu Youth (Seinen) 34
Sipos, George T., on modernist temptations 134
Snyder, Stephen 54, 75, 77
social reality 21–2, 27–8, 95, 125, 135
solipsism 17, 51, 63, 97, 123, 125, 135–6, 138, 162, 167–8, 170–1, 174, 184
Soseki Natsume 61
 Kokoro 161–3, 168, 211 n.12
 Sensei (fictional character) 160–4, 168
Spandri, Elena, *"Contact Zones": Rewriting Genre Across the East-West Border* 4
storytelling 2, 13, 40, 74, 77, 79, 81, 109–10, 114, 149, 161
Strecher, Mathew 171–2
 internal narratives 171
subjectivity 15, 31, 37–8, 41, 57, 73, 94, 96, 98, 127, 131, 135, 150–1, 162, 168, 170–1, 174, 184, 188, 197 n.23
symbolism 89–90, 121, 156–7, 211 n.17
sympathy 19, 85, 90–1, 103–7, 109, 114–15, 120–2, 128, 137

Taishō period (1912–26) 133, 136, 139, 151
Tanizaki Junichirō 141, 144–5, 164
Tanizawa Eiichi 25, 194 n.8
 The Concept of Modern Japanese Literary History (Kindai Nihon bungakushi no kōsō) 24
Tansman, Alan 5
 The Aesthetics of Japanese Fascism 15
telos 2, 43, 64, 102, 149, 166, 179, 197 n.25
Terada, Rei 117, 128
 Feeling in Theory 127
Tokō Kōji 171
translation 3, 53, 71, 82, 128, 147, 151, 153, 178, 192 n.1, 195 n.18, 196 n.16, 199 n.42, 201 n.1, 207 n.7

Tsubouchi Shōyō 1, 16, 26–32, 35–7, 192 n.1, 194 n.14
  "The Essence of the Novel" (Shōsetsu shinzui) 24–5, 28, 30, 194 n.12, 195 n.15
  The Temperament of Today's Students (Tōsei shosei katagi) 23–4
Twine, Nanette 195 n.18

Uchida Roan, "How to Become a Literati" (Bungakusha to naru hō) 33
Ueda Makoto 20, 139
  Modern Japanese Writers and the Nature of Literature 139
uncertainty 27, 47–8, 101, 107, 114, 138

Vermeule, Blakey 88, 173, 194 n.14
  Why Do We Care about Literary Characters? 113
Villon, Francois 154
Vincent, J. Keith 49, 78
  Two-Timing Modernity: Homosocial Narrative in Modern Japanese Fiction 35, 77
Vita Sexualis (Ōgai) 17, 51, 55, 57–65, 67–9, 72, 79
  Kanai (fictional character) 59–65, 67, 200 n.28, 201 n.30
  and self-reflection 59–65 (*see also* self-reflection)
Vogler, Candace 114–15, 117, 126, 130–1, 171
  "The Moral of the Story" 113

Washburn, Dennis 6, 20, 74, 77, 87
  The Dilemma of the Modern 73
The Wild Goose (Gan), (Ogai) 17, 35, 57, 64, 68, 71–81, 93, 126, 201 n.2, 202 n.3, 202 n.13, 203–4 n.19
  aesthetic effects in 87–92
  metaphysical desire 78–9, 84, 203 n.19, 204 n.22
  Okada (fictional character) 73, 75–82, 85, 89–90, 203 n.14, 204 n.22
  Otama (fictional character) 73–4, 77–80, 82–3, 85, 87, 89–90, 203 n.14, 204 n.26
  Otsune (fictional character) 81
  Suezo (fictional character) 73–4
  as reader 81–7
  triangular desire/relationships 78, 84, 89, 203 n.19
  Washburn's view on 74
Wollheim, Richard 189, 213 n.28
world systems 175–8, 180, 184, 188–91, 214 n.29

Yamada, Marc, "Murakami's Post-AUM Metafiction" 172
Yanagida Izumi 194 n.8
  Ideas of Literature in Early Meiji (Meiji shoki no bungaku shisō) 23
Yōda Tomiko, "First-Person Voice and Citizen-Subject: The Modernity of Ōgai's *The Dancing Girl*" 46–9, 198 n.34
Yokomitsu Riichi 168
  Shanhai 212 n.32
Yoshida Seiichi 28, 138–9
  "Akutagawa Ryūnosuke's Life and Art" (Akutagawa Ryūnosuke no shōgai to geijutsu) 138
"Yuki-onna" (snow woman) 11–13

Zola, Emile 37–8, 196 n.23
zuihitsu 146, 193 n.3